Women and the City

Bristol 1373-2000

Redcliffe Press/The Regional History Centre,
University of the West of England, Bristol

Women and the City
Bristol 1373-2000

Redcliffe Press/The Regional History Centre,
University of the West of England, Bristol

Editor Madge Dresser

First published in 2016 by Redcliffe Press Ltd.,
81g Pembroke Road, Bristol BS8 3EA

www.redcliffepress.co.uk
info@redcliffepress.co.uk

 RedcliffePress

 @RedcliffePress

ISBN 978-1-908326-31-7

British Library Cataloguing-in-Publication Data
A catalogue record for this book is available from the British Library

Design and typesetting by Stephen Morris www.stephen-morris.co.uk
Garamond 12/12
Printed and bound by Hobbs The Printers, Totton

Contents

Acknowledgments

This book, the third in the Regional History Centre series on Bristol, owes its existence to the original vision of John Sansom and to the professionalism and care of Clara Hudson, Stephen Morris and Angela Sansom all of Redcliffe Press. It has been a privilege to work with my co-authors, whose erudition and patience have been exemplary, and with Steve Poole whose energy and enthusiasm has been constant. The staff at the Bristol Central Reference Library, Bristol's Museum Archives and Galleries and the University of Bristol's Special Collections have been unfailingly helpful and professional throughout this book's progress. Particular thanks in this regard are due to Dawn Dyer of the Bristol Central Reference Library for both her expertise and unstinting support. Special thanks are also owed to both Julia Carver, Curator, Modern and Contemporary Art at Bristol Museums and Art Gallery, and to Julian Warren of the Bristol Record Office for kindly granting us permission to use a range of images from their respective collections. Thanks also go to Hannah Lowery and Michael Richardson of the University of Bristol's Library's Special Collections and to Deborah Withers for allowing us to reproduce material from the Feminist Archive. A private collector was good enough to give us leave to publish the wonderful painting on the front cover, and we extend our thanks too to the Estate of Phyllis Ginger for granting us copyright clearance to reproduce the image on the rear cover.

Other individuals and institutions were similarly generous in granting us permission to publish images in their possession. These include the Arnolfini, Lord and Lady Bathurst, Erynne Baynes, Duncan Greenman, Julio Etchart, Sherrie Eugene-Hart, Zehra Haq, the Bristol Aero Collection Trust, Bristol Cathedral, the *Bristol Post*, the Churches Conservation Trust, The Dean and Chapter of Westminster, Knowle West Media Centre, the National Portrait Gallery, the Parliamentary Art Collection, St. James Priory, Bristol, St. Mary Redcliffe Church, Bristol, St. Stephen's Church, Bristol, Specsavers, and Constance Ware. We also used images from The National Archives, the University of Bristol's Theatre Collection and FotoLab. Helen McConnell Simpson assisted me in organising all the visual material with efficiency and dispatch.

So many people contributed their knowledge, time and material to the book it is impossible to do justice to them all. Most are acknowledged above and in the endnotes but I would also like to thank: Victoria Arrowsmith-Brown, the late and lamented Anton Bantock, Roger Ball, Jonathan Barry, Elizabeth Bird, Jenny Body, Jane Bradley, Sarah Braun, Janet Brewer, Shirley Brown, Eugene Byrne, Pam Beddard, Gail Boyle, Diane Bunyan, Jamie Carstairs, Elaine Chalus, Stella Clarke, Martin Crossley Evans, Sara Davies, Allie Dillon, Rod Dowling, Jane Duffus, Carol Dyhouse, Julio Etchard, Grace Evans, Penny Evans, William Evans, Karen Garvey, Penny Gane, Sue Giles, Julie Gottlieb, Clara Greed, Francis Greenacre, Nicola Harwin, Carolyn Hassan, Sheila Hannon, Jonathan Harlow, Ruth Hecht, Catherine Ingrassia, Sharon Irish, Biddy Hayward, Anne Hix, Kim Hix, Shirley Hodgson, Ann Kay, Andrew Kelly, Ursula King, Knowle West Media Centre, Gill Loats, Holly McGrane, Margaret McGregor, Jeremy McIlwaine, Ellen Malos, Jayne Mills, Elise Moore-Searson, David Parker, Lucy Paterson, Sue Paterson, John Penny, Dawn Primarolo, Claire Radford, Nick Rogers, Harriet Screen, Shirley Shire, Deborah Simonton, Jenny Smith, Mary Smith, John Stevens, Richard Stone, Mari Takayanagi, Rosie Tomlinson, Melanie Unwin, Elizabeth Kowaleski Wallace, Kathleen Wilson and the Library of the Religious Society of Friends (London) for their encouragement and advice. A month's fellowship in 2013 at UCLA's Clark Library enabled me the time to develop my thoughts on women in Georgian Bristol, and benefit from the insights of members of the Seventeenth- and Eighteenth-Centuries Studies Seminar held there. I would like to record my appreciation of the support provided by my History colleagues at the University of the West of England.

I am especially grateful to June Hannam for going through the entire manuscript with her characteristic rigour and incisiveness and to Peter Fleming, Moira Martin, Marie Mulvey-Roberts, Glyn Stone, Helen Taylor and Christine Williams for their perceptive comments on particular chapter drafts. Any errors or omissions are entirely my own responsibility.

Madge Dresser

ABBREVIATIONS

BBHA Bristol Branch of the Historical Association pamphlet
BEP Bristol Evening Post
BJ Bristol Journal
BMAG Bristol Museums & Art Galleries (part of the Bristol Museum, Galleries and Archives service of Bristol City Council)
BMGA Bristol Museum, Galleries and Archives Service (under the aegis of 'Bristol Culture' of Bristol City Council)
BME Black and Minority Ethnic
BRL Bristol Central Reference Library
BRO Bristol Record Office
BL British Library
BM Bristol Mercury
BTM Bristol Times and Mirror
EAW Electrical Association of Women
ECCO Eighteenth Century Collections Online
EFF Election Fighting Fund
FFBJ *Felix Farley's Bristol Journal*
GCTPA Garden City and Town Planning Association
HMSO Her Majesty's Stationery Office
HTV Harlech Television (later Independent Television (ITV)TV West and Wales)
ILP Independent Labour Party
KWADS Knowle West Against Drugs
LNA Ladies National Association
NAPSS National Association for the Promotion of Social Science
NCW National Council of Women
NFWW National Federation of Women Workers
NSWS National Society of Women's Suffrage
NUWSS National Union of Women's Suffrage Societies
NUWW National Union of Women Workers
ODNB Oxford Dictionary of National Biography
PRO Public Record Office (now The National Archives)
TNA The National Archives
UBLSC University of Bristol Library, Special Collections
UCLA University of California at Los Angeles
WAAF Women's Auxiliary Air Force
WCG Women's Co-operative Guild
WDP Western Daily Press
WEA Workers' Educational Association
WIL Women's International League
WLL Women's Labour League
WLA Women's Liberal Association
WLM Women's Liberation Movement
WSPU Women's Social and Political Union
WVS Women's Voluntary Service

Broad Quay Bristol by an unknown painter of the British School.
(BMAG K514). *Bristol Museums, Galleries & Archives*

Introduction

This painting of Bristol's Broad Quay (now the city centre) in around 1760 (opposite) shows the bustling quayside of a city no longer medieval but not yet fully modern. Most of the many figures portrayed in this colourful depiction are men: there are merchants, dockers, a school teacher, a haulier as well as a young black servant whose presence has only recently been noted. But women also feature in the scene. One carries a pail on her head, another sits in front of a shop, a basket of produce at her side, others variously dressed, stroll by. Their public presence is taken for granted, unremarked and unremarkable. Yet the very fact they are portrayed at all raises the question about the role women played in the life of the city.

How, if at all, did women help to shape the city's economy, its politics and its increasingly diversified cultural life? Did their domestic role as mothers, wives and daughters preclude their making any meaningful contribution to civil society? Did they have more or less room to determine their lives as the rise of more individualistic values began by the eighteenth century to challenge the city's traditional corporate civic culture? What mark have women made on Bristol either collectively or as individuals by the Millennium's end?

Women and the City offers the first sustained and substantive consideration of such questions. It looks beyond the conventional readings of Bristol's past to consider what sort of impact women did have on Bristol and how they variously negotiated the restrictions under which they laboured. It charts women's changing access to education, to money and to the business and political networks needed in order to participate fully in public life. It argues that despite the very real limitations imposed upon them, women's activities were generally more wide ranging and had a greater impact on the city than has been previously assumed. In so doing, it challenges established demarcations between women's traditional domestic activities and public life, between the personal and the political, between charity and the market place.[1] It documents individual women, some well-known in their day but now forgotten, who made or attempted to make a significant contribution to the wider society in which they lived. A main aim of this book is to begin to reclaim their stories, from the 'enormous condescension' of oblivion and to place them in their wider historical context.

This book has been informed by the approaches taken, and the questions raised, in studies of women's and gender history that have proliferated in recent years. These have questioned the distinctions so often made between the public and the private, and between the personal and the political, and have pointed to the complex interrelationship between them.[2] It has been argued that the very meaning of politics has to be re-defined if we are to incorporate women's activity. As Kathryn Gleadle notes, the home itself can be seen as a 'political space' since it could be the site of 'salons, informal discussion groups...and ideologically motivated consumer choices'.[3] Attention has also been drawn to the ways in which women understood their own position and to what motivated them. Thus they might embrace the notion of their difference from men as a way to justify their participation in social and moral reform campaigns.

Questions have also been raised about the focus on women as a social group. It has been shown that other variables such as class, ethnicity, marital status and geographical location complicate any easy assumptions about the commonality of female experience. Women's goals were not always the same, and they made different choices about how best to achieve them. Sometimes, for example, they acted together as women in single-sex organisations, whereas at others they joined with men in mixed-sex campaigns.[4]

Any generalisations about women's activities tend to obscure regional differences in their experiences. Most women who took part in public activities did so at a local level. The work that they did, the social backgrounds that they came from and the organisations that they joined, were all affected by local social, political and economic structures and by particular civic cultures.[5] This case study of a provincial city, Bristol, will draw out the specific and complex ways in which women helped to shape the society in which they lived. It will contribute to the growing number of studies that seek to look beyond London in order to uncover the rich and varied experiences of women in different periods of history.[6]

Invisible women? Revisiting the surviving evidence

It is surprising how little has been written by academic historians of Bristol about Bristol women. Until recently, references to all but a few very prominent women such as Hannah More, Mary Robinson and Mary Carpenter[7] were scanty at best as Ernest Board's 1930 painting *Some Who Have Made Bristol Famous* neatly exemplifies.

Some Who Have Made Bristol Famous by Ernest Board, 1930.
(BMAG K917). *Bristol Museums, Galleries & Archives*

This began to change as social and cultural historians started to consider women's public role in the city. Helen Meller's *Leisure and the Changing City 1870-1914* published in 1976, led the way by including some discussion of women involved in the development of Bristol's cultural institutions, but it would be another decade before Jonathan Barry's work on the cultural history of early modern Bristol, Elizabeth Baigent's examination of the city's social geography in 1775 and Ellen Malos's article on radical activists and women's suffrage in the nineteenth and twentieth centuries, shed further light on women's participation in urban life.[8] Generally speaking, women's experience was neglected or mentioned only in passing in more mainstream academic studies of Bristol's economy during the 1980s and in a general history of

Bristol written by two established local historians in 1996.[9]

Since then texts looking at specific aspects of Bristol's history have made more explicit reference to women, or have developed a gendered analysis. Mary Fissell's book on the eighteenth-century Bristol poor vividly addressed the gendered nature of poor law policy and treated women as actively engaged in the way that policy was implemented.[10] Martin Gorsky's study of nineteenth-century Bristol philanthropy included a consideration of women's voluntary activity, while Moira Martin's examination of Victorian Poor Law policy in Bristol highlighted gender issues.[11]

The lives of individual Bristol women have been written about by literary historians, critics and biographers. Mary Waldron's study of the life and times of the eighteenth-century 'milkmaid poetess' Ann Yearsley took class and gender into account, while Marie Mulvey-Roberts's new collection on *Literary Bristol* provides some gender-sensitive studies of Bristol authors since the late eighteenth century.[12] Publications intended for a more popular audience, including *100+ Women of Bristol* and *Go Home and Do the Washing!*, have also identified a wide range of 'pioneering women' in the city's past.[13]

Other studies have focused on women's experiences as a social group. These include June Hannam's reconsideration of the Bristol women's movement, Madge Dresser's studies of religious women in eighteenth-century Bristol and Peter Fleming's pioneering publication on *Women in Late Medieval Bristol*.[14] Recent texts by Lucienne Boyce and Jill Liddington have further enhanced our understanding of the Bristol suffragettes.[15]

Studies of Bristol intended for the general reader, for example recent histories of the city during the First World War, are now more likely to feature women as significant historical actors.[16]

Building on this previous work, *Women and the City* aims not only to restore forgotten individuals back into the historical record but to set them in their economic and political context with gender in mind. It queries both how public life has been defined and why women have so long been seen to be at its margins. Although the focus of the book is on women as a group we have been mindful throughout of the differences, be it of class, religion, marital status and ethnicity which distinguish their respective experiences. It documents not only the achievements of exceptional women but also those who have acted collectively to promote the interests either of their own sex or of society in general.

Researching this book has not been an easy task. Covering over 600 years of such an under-researched topic is wildly ambitious, not the least because the availability of surviving evidence varies widely over time as does the very notion of what constitutes 'public' life. Establishing women's participation in the economic, political and cultural activity of Bristol is also dogged by problems of evidence. Robust statistical data is rarely available until the nineteenth century and even thereafter seldom categorises gender differences in a consistent and comparable manner. Even qualitative evidence is limited, skewed by the fact that educated men with property and some degree of leisure are by far the best documented in the historical record. The existing records are fragmentary, widely dispersed and often need to be 'read against the grain' in order to unearth information about both women's activities and their wider significance.

But taking the 'long view' has its rewards for we found some surprising continuities as well as changes in women's ability both to determine their lives and to make their presence felt.[17] The 'story' we have so far pieced together shows an increasing number of women becoming more visibly engaged in the public arena but challenges any simple narrative of unalloyed progress.

The book is comprised of four main chapters interspersed with short contributions on an eclectic range of themes. The first chapter by Peter Fleming covers the late medieval and early modern period from 1373 when Bristol became the first English town to enjoy county status, to 1660 when the monarchy was restored and colonial expansion began to revive the city's fortunes. Madge Dresser's subsequent chapter on the long eighteenth century charts the new opportunities afforded women during Bristol's so-called 'Golden Age,' predicated on the rise of Atlantic slavery, and continues into the early nineteenth century when rising class divisions and gendered notions of 'respectability' began to reshape the nature of women's participation in public life. The public role of women in Victorian and Edwardian Bristol is then examined by June Hannam and Moira Martin with a view to establishing their contributions as workers, philanthropists and political campaigners.

Writing the final chapter proved a particular challenge. For though the twentieth century (1914-2000) spans the period when women gained the vote and legislation progressively removed many of the other barriers formerly barring women from public life, few historians of the city have as yet established a narrative for this period, especially for the years after 1945. But we felt it important to attempt to begin the task in order to facilitate and encourage further research. Chapter Four is a collaborative effort with June Hannam focusing on the city up to 1945 and Madge Dresser taking up the story from then up to the millennium.

Aside from the four chapters, *Women and the City* also features nine, double-page 'drop-in' contributions to the story. Some of these are written by the principal authors and some by guest contributors including both established and new scholars.

Unavoidably, this book has been selective in its focus. Whatever its short-comings, we hope it provides new insights into Bristol's past and will inspire others to undertake further research into women's role in urban life.

Women in Bristol 1373-1660

Peter Fleming

Introduction: Later Medieval and Early-Modern Bristol

This chapter begins at the end of the 1300s and ends with the Restoration of the Stuart monarchy with Charles II in 1660. In 1373 Bristol was granted county status by the king, Edward III, roughly a generation after the demographic catastrophe of the 1340s when the Black Death ravaged England – carrying off between one third and one half of the population in a few months. Bristol was particularly badly affected. Subsequent epidemics prevented any meaningful recovery of numbers until the Tudor period, so that England's population stagnated for over a century.

By the 1370s, the consequences of this disaster had become apparent in a qualified rebalancing of power: wages were higher, rents and food prices were lower. Consequently, the century or so following the 1370s has been described, with some justification, as the 'Golden Age of Labour', and, more controversially, as a 'Golden Age for Women' with, supposedly, greater demand for labour resulting in more opportunities for ordinary women to break out of the restraints of what were considered appropriate female activities.[1] While attractive and superficially sensible, given the undeniable existence of new equations between capital and labour, this view has not always borne up to detailed scrutiny.[2] While the details of these arguments may remain contentious, it is plausible to assert that the end of the fourteenth century marks the beginning of the transition in England from 'medieval' to 'modern', that is, from a basically 'feudal' economy to a 'capitalist' one. Also, the end of the fourteenth century sees the emergence of primary sources that allow us, for the first time, to be able to get close to relatively ordinary people and, more particularly, to women as individuals. This is especially true of women in towns. From the 1380s we have the wills of the 'middling sort', including the wills of women, in useable quantities, as well as other new categories of records, such as the proceedings of the Court of Chancery, a tribunal that specialised in commercial cases and cases involving the property aspects of marriage. [*Fig. 1.1*]

The end date has been chosen because the Restoration was surely also a turning point in English – and Bristol – history. Bristol endured particularly dreadful experiences in the Civil Wars (1642-51) between King and Parliament, when it was twice taken by siege. The first time, by Royalists led by Prince Rupert, ended with the surrender of the city in July 1643, and the second, by the Parliamentarian New Model Army in September 1645, saw the city stormed. Bristolians suffered greatly during the course of these assaults and subsequent occupations. The suffering was compounded by an outbreak of plague in 1644 to 1645.[3] The Restoration promised a brighter future. For about thirty years before the Restoration Bristolians were already beginning to take advantage of England's colonial expansion in the Caribbean, and such activities naturally affected the city's female population. While this chapter ends with Bristol on the brink of playing its central role in the first British Empire, throughout the later medieval period Bristol's position as England's major west-country port had also determined its history.

Medieval Bristol's significance arose in large part from its position at the centre of English colonialism: it provided the most convenient bridgehead for English military and commercial expansion into southern Wales and Ireland, and with the addition of the rich vineyards of Gascony to the English crown in 1154, Bristol soon became England's paramount provincial port for the importation of Gascon wine. From the second half of the fourteenth century Bristol's cloth industry provided it with a highly-valued export commodity with which to balance its wine imports. While Bristol's weaving industry gradually lost out to rural clothiers, the town continued to be a centre for cloth finishing (fulling, that is, breaking up, or 'felting', the individual fibres), and dyeing. England's loss of the Hundred Years War with France in 1453 brought an end to significant English territorial interests beyond Britain and Ireland until the period of trans-Atlantic expansion beginning in Elizabethan times. The loss of England's French possessions dealt a serious blow to Bristol's economy, and the town's economic depression lasted for about a generation. By the end of the fifteenth century its French trade was recovering, supplemented by increased trade with Spain, but from the beginning of the sixteenth century it is clear that Bristol's first 'golden age' was over. The Reformation period, beginning in the 1530s, brought about a major dislocation of Bristol's internal economy, transferring considerable wealth, particularly landed property, from ecclesiastical to lay proprietors, and severely damaging some aspects of its culture, as well, of course, as disrupting the religious lives of its inhabitants. The roots of Bristol's second 'golden age', based on the trans-Atlantic economy, can be discerned in the first half of the

1.1 Probate Copy of the Testament of Johanna (Joan) Geffereys, widow, of Bristol, 1494. The vast bulk of female wills were made by widows, since the wives of living husbands could only make a will with his permission, and few did so. This one is written in English, but most, before the middle of the fifteenth century, were written in Latin. A large number of Bristol testators, like this one, had their wills proved by the Prerogative Court of Canterbury, held at Lambeth (now South London) rather than, or in addition to, the diocesan consistory courts held within either Worcester or Bath and Wells or, after the creation of the diocese in 1542, Bristol. There was considerable social cachet in having one's will proved centrally, rather than locally.
TNA 11/10/171.

seventeenth century, but the city's tumultuous experiences during the Civil Wars bring the period covered in this chapter to an end amid crisis and uncertainty. However, despite the problems of the period from the Reformation to the Restoration of the Stuarts, Bristol was alone among cities in Southern England in being able to maintain its commercial and social independence from London: while ambitious Bristol men might seek their fortunes in London, their home town never became simply a glorified 'outport' for the metropolis, existing largely to provide the capital with another port through which commodities could be exported and imported.[4] So, throughout this period, it is clear that Bristol was an important place; less clear is an answer to the question of how we can know about the lives of – probably – over half of its population. What sources are available from which we can learn about female Bristolians?

Researching the History of Later Medieval and Early-Modern Women
Bristol is no exception to the general rule that finding sources from which to reconstruct the lives of non-noble lay women in the pre-modern period is difficult, but far from impossible. There is a, perhaps, surprising quantity and variety of Bristol sources from which to construct a fairly detailed picture of some aspects of women's lives, with the usual caveats that in treating of around half the population we are in danger of assuming an unhelpful essentialism, that, in other words, women's gender gives them a commonality of interest that transcends socio-economic or political power, or religious outlook, in a way that we do not assume for men: a trap into which this chapter, despite its author's best intentions, doubtless falls on more than one occasion.

This chapter surely also fails to negotiate successfully the equally dangerous trap of over-emphasising the lives of members of small and unrepresentative elites, since it is they who have left us with the most evidence of their lives. Insofar as these conceptual and methodological traps allow, the themes of the book will be addressed, in terms of women's economic roles and their capacity to influence political, social and cultural life within a place that was near the heart of England's commercial and imperial ambitions.[5] We shall begin with women's economic position.

The Evidence of the Early Tudor Subsidies
Taxation records promise to give an overview of demography, wealth, and social structure for both women and men, but Bristol is not well served by these: detailed returns for the late fourteenth-century poll tax do not survive

for the town, and so the earliest usable tax returns come near the middle of our period, with the Tudor subsidies of the 1520s. The most complete return for Bristol comes from 1524. The valuation was, broadly speaking, divided between property and wages. Property was defined as land or goods, and in the cases discussed here this was always goods rather than land, because we are discussing town-dwellers, most of whom owned little, if any, landed property. In Bristol the subsidy was levied on individuals worth at least twenty shillings ($£1$) in terms of annual property value or income from wages. There were 1081 property-holders (individuals assessed on land or goods) listed in the return, and 225 individuals assessed on wages. Most of the wage-earners were described as servants. The property-holders would have been heads of households, and therefore behind most of them would have been an unknown number of dependents. There were far more employees than the 225 assessed, but these others earned less than $£1$ *per annum* and were therefore not recorded. In total, the taxed population of Bristol, including the dependents of heads of household, probably amounted to about half of the town's entire population (of around 8,000), which in turn means that approximately half were too poor to be taxed.[6]

No women were assessed on wages, which means that none earned an annual wage of $£1$ or more. Female domestic servants were fairly common, but the 'superior' servants, receiving annual wages of $£1$ or more, were apparently all male. Forty-three living women were named as taxed on property. With one exception, all of these 43 were described as widows. The exception, Katherine Dee, assessed on $£2$ of property, may have been a propertied woman who had not married up to that point, but may also have been a widow whose status was accidentally omitted by a careless scribe. Therefore, and not surprisingly, perhaps, the only female householders to be taxed were widows, with one possible exception, an obvious reflection of the fact that single females from the lay propertied classes tended either to be young and destined to be married, or had survived at least one husband, and so were widows.

The average assessed property holding of these 43 women was just under $£17$, considerably more than the average for all Bristol assessed property-holders of $£11$ 2s. For the most part this is evidently a group of widows who were financially fairly comfortably off, but there was considerable variation. For example, among the 31 widows assessed in Trinity Ward (one of five wards into which Bristol was divided), at one extreme we find Joan Broke in Redcliffe Street, whose goods were assessed at $£40$, her near neighbours Cecily Bedford, assessed at $£80$, and, wealthiest of all, Joan Ap Rhys, widow of a Bristol-Welsh-man living on Welsh Back, with goods valued at £200; at the other extreme, six out of these 31 widows in Trinity had goods valued at only the £1 minimum, while another ten were valued at £2 in goods, meaning that half of the widows in this ward were living in relatively humble households.

Only two of the 43 assessed women are listed as having servants assessed for taxation, in both cases a male servant assessed on the minimum, £1 *per annum* in wages. This does not mean that the widows necessarily lived without servants – they probably all had some kind of servant – only that with two exceptions their servants were paid less than £1 per year, and were probably hired for periods of a year or six months at a time. As a whole this group of 43 women constituted a tiny minority of the town's property-holding taxpayers, and its members controlled a small share of Bristol's total wealth. Early-Tudor Bristol's property-holding society was overwhelmingly male, but some of the small number of female property-holders (exclusively, or almost all, widows) were wealthy and, presumably, could use that wealth to influence the lives of their fellow Bristolians. In addition, as we shall see, women, whether wives, widows, or even, perhaps, apprentices and servants, could also make an impact on this male-dominated society.[7]

Widows and Married Women

To some extent, the evidence provided by the Tudor Subsidy can stand for what we know about women in later medieval and early modern Bristol more generally: because women, apart from widows, were under the legal shadow of men, whether as fathers, guardians, husbands or employers, and hence tended not to appear in the documents that recorded public life, we can know relatively little about them. Widows, or at least those widows who enjoyed a certain level of property, operated much more independently, and so we are likely to know more about them. Hence, they tend to figure disproportionately prominently in our historical accounts, and the present chapter cannot be an exception.[8]

However, some married women with living husbands did leave evidence of their activities. Married women occasionally made wills. Their right, or need, to do so was severely constrained, since on marriage any landed property women owned – their real estate – continued in their possession but was controlled by their husband, while most of their moveable property passed completely into his ownership. Nonetheless, there are some Bristol examples, such as the will of 1489 made by Joan Twynyho, daughter of the Bristol merchant Thomas Rowley and his wife Margaret, in which she was careful to state that she had made the will by the licence of her husband, Roger Twynyho, a Somerset esquire, and to him she bequeathed all the Bristol messuages – houses and associated land – and other property left to her by her parents' wills.[9] Another example is provided by Joyce Deyos, a widow at the time of writing her will in 1599, who subsequently married her last husband, Thomas Prinne, between making her will and her death in 1601; Thomas added a codicil to the document, giving permission for it to be enacted.[10]

Women as Independent Traders

There was the option, available to some married women, of trading independently of their husbands, as *femme sole,* able to conduct business and contract debts in their own right, even though their husbands were still living. The financial records of Bristol's governing body, the Mayor's audits, are only extant from the 1530s, but in a sample ten years from 1532 there are occasional references to women paying to be registered as *femme sole.*[11] Even before the 1530s there are references to women trading as 'sole', but it is not clear if this meant that they were genuinely single – widows, or unmarried – or married women who had registered as *femme sole.* For example, in the 1430s the Bristol merchant Robert Sturmy and his wife Ellen claimed before the Chancery Court that she, 'being sole', had been bound in an obligation of £100 to abide by an arbitration between herself and William Reygate of Ireland, and while this could have been an agreement made by Ellen before her marriage, she may equally have been operating as a *femme sole* while being married to Sturmy. The Exchequer customs accounts give us further evidence. In the 33 years between 1461 and 1494 six Bristol women are described in these accounts as trading as *femme sole.* It would seem that some, at least, of these women had husbands who were living, indicating that the women had registered to trade independently of them.[12]

Another option available to women who wished to trade independently, at least until the 1470s, was to pay a fee to be officially recognised as a portwoman (on similar terms to a portman), which meant that they could operate as a small-scale retailer. The status of portwoman allowed them to act legitimately as retailers without incurring the costs of entering the 'freedom', that is, of becoming burgesses – members of a small elite of full citizens who were able to trade freely and to have a say in the town's governance. In 1366 a town ordinance established that those 'strangers' – that is, non-burgesses, not necessarily non-Bristolians – who could not afford the full £10 fee that would allow them to become burgesses by redemption (that is, by paying for the privilege), could pay a lesser fee for a smaller bundle of rights as portman or portwoman. What they were buying was the status of portman or woman. The 'port' element in this name has nothing to do with Bristol's port function, but derives from an earlier meaning of the word, relating simply to trade, not necessarily of the water-borne variety.

The designation of portman and portwoman is found fairly frequently in the Bristol records, whereas the equivalent phrase for burgesses is 'burgesses and their wives'. This indicates that both portmen and portwomen could enjoy the status and freedom given by being a legitimate lesser retailer. This is distinct from the burgesses, where women could pass on the freedom through marriage, and could trade as burgess widows or *femme sole*, but usually could only do so as dependents, or former dependents, of male burgesses, and could not share their political rights. While the existence of female burgesses was countenanced in fourteenth-century Bristol, there is no mention of actual examples before the mid-1500s.[13] The fifteenth century saw a steady decline in the status of portmen and portwomen, accompanied by increasing constraints on their activities. From 1454-5 portmen and women were allowed only to sell bread and ale, while in 1470-1 even this concession was withdrawn, effectively putting an end to this 'bargain basement' alternative to the freedom as enjoyed by burgesses.

The 1454-5 ruling is noteworthy as evidence of the significance of portwomen, since the association of women with selling bread and ale was well established by then. For example, an ordinance of 1344 concerning brewing which mentioned only male brewers (in Latin, *braciatores*), had to be re-issued to include their female equivalents (*braciatrices*). The same ordinance required bakers to pass their bread on to female hucksters, who would sell it at retail.[14]

Women in the Textile Industry
The virtual abolition of the rank of portwomen by 1471 followed an attempt to abolish female labour in the weaving industry a decade earlier. An ordinance of the Weavers' Guild, issued by the masters of the guild in 1461, made illegal the employment of weavers' wives, daughters and maidservants in their craft. This came at a time when Bristol was suffering an economic downturn, and was evidently intended to protect male employment within a shrinking industry. However, two years later a group of weavers petitioned the mayor that their masters' attempt to prevent the employment of their wives made it virtually impossible for them to carry on, and as a result this

restriction was lifted.[15] Their petition demonstrates the importance of female employment to Bristol's fifteenth-century crafts, of which there are many other indications. For example, female dyers are specifically mentioned in an ordinance of the mid-1440s, and burgesses' wives and daughters were specifically excluded from a general ban on non-guild members practising wire-drawing and card-making in 1469/70 (wire-drawing was a stage in the production of cards, or wire combs, used to 'card' the wool before it was spun into thread).[16]

Female Servants

The greatest single category of employment for young people of both sexes was domestic service. Urban households tended to employ a greater proportion of female servants than was the case in the countryside, where household servants were predominantly male. However, even in towns female servants were in the minority. That said, female servants, usually young and unmarried, figure frequently as beneficiaries in the wills of Bristol testators. For example, the wills of two burgesses, William More, in 1411, and William Warminster in 1414, each mentioned two female servants, and William Cropenel's will of 1417 left bequests to the maid servants of three other male Bristolians, while by her will of 1574 Jane Compane left clothes to her three maidservants.[17] Female servants were usually left fairly modest bequests, but some testators rewarded particular maidservants much more generously.[18] Bequests of money to help fund the marriages of maidservants were made in the wills of Henry Lokkein 1415, John Benley in 1416, James Cokkes in 1423, and Thomas Baker in 1492.[19] In 1436 Edward Rede, parchment maker and burgess, left to his servant Alice Edward a life interest in three shops along with a bullock.[20] In his will of 1474 the merchant William Hoton left bequests to five named female servants, while a sixth, Elizabeth Cromwell, was to receive £8 and a quantity of cloth, and an additional 50s if her brother George Cromwell had died by the time of William's burial.[21] Even more generous was Agnes Spelly, by whose will of 1404 her maid, Isabelle Ken, was to receive Agnes's bed with its accoutrements and the sum of £15, which was raised to £20 in a codicil.[22] Topping all of these was John Bathe, who in his will of 1421 left one of his female servants, Katherine Lewys, a number of bequests, including £10 in money, silver cutlery and kitchenware, a gown, his best bed, and his cottage in Bath.[23] William Clifford, in his will of 1498, also left a house to his female servant, but she was to have this for only 15 months after her marriage.[24] In addition, female servants might on occasion be charged with the responsibilities of acting as their employer's executor, as was the case with Alice Maisy, appointed as executor by her mistress, Margaret Joons, in 1597.[25]

Not all female servants were young and unmarried: in his will of 1492 the grocer Thomas Baker left bequests to his servant Alice Bernard and to her daughter Joan Bernard when she reached the age of 16.[26] Sometimes female servants appear to have been related to their masters: in 1404 Thomas Knapp, former mayor of Bristol, left £50 to Anys Knapp, his servant, towards her marriage, while in her nuncupative will of 1602 Joan Bonner left all of her goods to her servant, who was also her niece, and whom she made her sole executor.[27]

Most servants were probably English or Welsh, but a few came from much further afield. Among the clauses in the 1486 will of Alice, widow of Nicholas Wisby, butcher, was, 'Item, I leave Margaret Yseland a gown of brown colour' and a silver spoon.[28] Alice's servant had probably come to England as an Icelandic youth, kidnapped or purchased by English merchants to work as virtual slaves in the houses and workshops of Bristol and the east coast ports; while Margaret Yseland may not have arrived in Bristol willingly, she was at least thought worthy of the gift of a gown and a silver spoon by her mistress.[29]

We usually assume that most domestic servants, whether medieval or modern, were temporary staff hired for a period of a year or less, and as such had little opportunity – or little desire – to form close relationships with their employers. While this was probably the case for *most* household servants in later medieval Bristol, the evidence from wills demonstrates that this was not *always* so. Nor does it seem that female servants were mainly remembered by female testators; in fact, the gender ratio between master/mistress will-makers and male/female servants seems roughly even. As we have seen, the two servants taxed as members of widows' households in 1524 were both male.

Women and the 'Freedom'

The most crucial distinction within Bristol society, as in any other large town or city, was between those who were included in the freedom, as burgesses, and those who were excluded. Only the former enjoyed the full panoply of commercial and political rights, and only they were regarded as citizens. The rest, even if they were Bristol-born, might be regarded as 'strangers'. The evidence for female burgesses is slight, but not non-existent in this period. The burgess books, recording entries to the freedom, begin in 1557, and they refer to a handful of female burgesses over the following century.[30]

While rarely appearing as burgesses themselves, women still played a central part in two of the four ways by which men could become Bristol burgesses. Men could enter the freedom if they were the sons of a Bristol burgess, or if they married the daughter or widow of a Bristol burgess. Hence, in both cases marriage was crucial. The other two ways were redemption, by which an outsider might be allowed to purchase the freedom, provided he was deemed suitable, and apprenticeship, whereby an apprentice could enter the freedom if he successfully completed his apprenticeship to a Bristol master and mistress and, once again, could satisfy the civic authorities of his suitability. The roles of women as conduits for the transmission of burgess status as wives and mothers are dealt with later. However, women could also employ apprentices, and be apprenticed themselves.

Women and Apprenticeship

Apprenticeship was almost as common a feature of the urban environment as domestic service.[31] The institution of apprenticeship provided training for young people, typically from the ages of 14 to 21, leading, in some – by no means all – cases to entry into the freedom, as burgesses. Bristol registers of apprenticeship indentures are extant from 1532. Taking the first decade as a sample, the great majority of Bristol indentures name both the husband and wife as master and mistress, and the general assumption was that the wife would play her part in the training of the apprentice.

Widows were expected to continue the training of their apprentices after their husband's death. Sometimes this was only until apprentices could be found new masters, but some widows carried on trading, and training apprentices, for years. While they may be largely invisible in the historical record, it seems certain that wives assisted in their husbands' business activities, implying the informal acquisition of skills before and/or during their marriages. In addition to couples, the Bristol Apprentice Book reveals thirteen women between 1532 and 1542 who took on apprentices alone, not as one half of a married couple. At least one, Alice Saxby in 1534, was described as a single woman rather than a widow.[32]

There are also *female* apprentices among the Bristol indentures. From 1532 to 1541 there were 56 female apprenticeships, out of a total number of nearly 1500 (around 4%); from 1542 to 1552, 50 out of around 1800 apprentices (around 3%) were female.[33] In the eleven years between 1617 and 1628, 100 female apprentices were registered. From 1640 to 1658, 56 female apprenticeships have been found in the register.[34] While a tiny minority of apprentices (never more than 4% of the total number of registered apprenticeships), female apprentices were a feature of Bristol life throughout the period.

Most, but not all, of these female apprentices were trained by a mistress, rather than by a master, in relatively low-status, 'female' occupations. In the decade from 1532, for example, only two girls were apprenticed to single male masters, one a mercer, the other a pin-maker. The rest were apprenticed either to single women or to a wife. Of these 54 girls apprenticed to mistresses, one was apprenticed as a seamstress, one as a mercer, and one as a tailor, all three to widow-mistresses, indicating in the case of the tailor and mercer that the woman was carrying on her husband's trade. Another three were apprenticed as knitters to women whose husbands were still alive. The remaining 48 were divided fairly evenly between those set to learn the trade of shepster, or needlewoman – an activity associated with women and of less prestige than tailor – and those committed to training in housewifery. For the most part, then, these girls were apprenticed to low-status crafts. A very few were evidently expected to pursue 'male' crafts, but what we may be seeing here is the tail end of a declining trend towards full female participation in more lucrative male-dominated crafts. In the following decade, from 1542 to 1552, of the 50 female apprentices registered, seven were apprenticed as needlewomen, 17 as housewives, while in the remaining 26 cases no occupation was given; so, none of the more prestigious 'male' crafts are mentioned as being taken up by female apprentices. By the seventeenth century female apprenticeships in relatively high status 'male' crafts have virtually disappeared, and over 30% of female apprenticeships were in service, with around half of the remainder being in a combination of domestic service and knitting and/or spinning.

The long-term diminution in the status of female apprentices over the course of the sixteenth and seventeenth centuries is indicated in other ways. In the twenty years from 1532 nearly half were the daughters of craftsmen, with gentry and yeomen, merchants and traders, and husbandmen making up most of the rest of the groups of parents, these three categories being represented in roughly equal proportions, and a little over half of all female apprentices were non-Bristolians. By the first half of the 1600s, however, about a quarter of female apprenticeships were arranged as part of the provision of parish poor relief, and the overall number of gentry and yeoman daughters had shrunk to around ten per cent. Fewer came from outside Bristol, and more were orphaned – that is, their fathers, but not necessarily their mothers, were dead – the proportion of fatherless daughters rising from less than a fifth in the 1530s to nearly two-thirds. The probable reasons for this are complex, and we should hesitate before assuming that this is clear evidence of the end of any kind of later medieval 'golden age' for women, but there is no doubt that the sons of the gentry were increasingly taking up Bristol apprenticeships, making their acquisition for the children of lesser parents, be they male or female, more difficult.

Female apprentices were occasionally remembered in their masters' and mistresses' wills. This was the case with the testators Edith Mulward in 1388, Alice Wodeford in 1407, John Goodson in 1419, and Joan Wilshire in 1505.[35] Among the apprentices named in the 1409 will of Walter Seymour, burgess, were Juliana and John Littilton: one of Walter Seymour's servants was Agnes, John Littilton's sister; it would seem, therefore, that Walter Seymour was master to three Littilton siblings.[36] In 1421 Margaret Lowys, the apprentice of John Bathe, was left by her appreciative master 40s, a piece of silver weighing 5oz, and a silk girdle with silver letters spelling 'Jesus have mercy on me'.[37] Another female apprentice, Alice Reed, was the subject of a dispute that ended up in the Chancery Court: Margaret Sopemaker and Edward Rede, the latter presumably Alice Reed's relative, could not agree over which of them should have her as their apprentice, and so 'certain friends ... laboured between them to set them at rest', and the two parties bound themselves in £20 each to abide by an arbitrated settlement. When this proved unsuccessful, the case was taken to Chancery. As with most Chancery cases from this period, the outcome is unknown.[38]

Female Merchants

Overseas trade with an area that stretched from Iceland to Andalucía gave Bristol its special character as a port. Exchequer customs accounts reveal that a small number of women were involved in this trade. In the 33 years after 1461 around 50 female merchants appear in the accounts. The most famous of these is Alice Chestre. The death of her husband Henry Chestre in 1470 allowed, or forced, Alice to step into the historical record. She was a property-owner in her own right, [*Fig.1.2*] and in 1472 she made a contract with a carpenter to build her a new four-storey house on High Street. The following year Alice appears in the customs accounts for the first time, and she continues to appear until her death in 1485. In these voyages she traded alone, often shipping goods in her own vessels. She traded cloth, wine, iron and other commodities with Ireland, Spain, Portugal and Flanders. During her fifteen years of widowhood Alice was engaged in various charitable activities, particularly in relation to her parish church of All Saints, using the rental income

1.2 Alice Chestre was notable as a widow who was also very active as a businesswoman in her own right after the death of her husband, Henry Chestre, a prominent Bristol merchant, in 1470. This document is an indenture binding Stephen Morgan to build a 'newe house' of good 'timbre and boards' on the High Street of Bristol for Alice Chestre.
BRO P.AS/D/HS/C/9 *Bristol Museums, Galleries & Archives*

from some of her property to fund these activities, [*Fig. 1.3*] but her most notable gift was to pay £41 for a new crane on the Back, 'for the saving of merchants' goods of the town and of strangers'.[39]

Alice Chestre is exceptional in the scale of her trading activities and in her wealth, but as a widow carrying on her late husband's business she is typical. However, most such women appear only briefly in the customs accounts, and were evidently simply honouring their recently deceased husband's commitments. Such, probably, were Joan and Margaret Rowley. Joan had been the wife of William Rowley, a Bristol merchant who by the time he made his will in 1478 was living in Bordeaux, and she was the sister-in-law of the Joan who made her will in 1489 as the wife of Roger Twynyho. For a year after her husband's death Joan Rowley imported sugar, oil and wax from Lisbon and woad – a much-used dyestuff – and wine from Spain into Bristol, but then stopped. Margaret, mother of both William Rowley and Joan Twynyho, née Rowley, was widowed within months of her son's death in 1478, and contin-

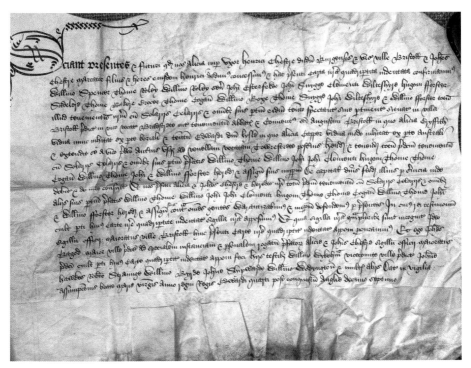

1.3 This document of 1477 shows Alice Chestre acting with her stepson, John Chestre, another merchant, to appoint a group of prominent men as trustees to ensure that the rent from a property in Broadmead that they hold is used to pay for religious services.
BRO P.AS/D/BS/B/13. *Bristol Museums, Galleries & Archives*

ued her husband's business until 1481, shipping madder, tar, wainscot and hops from Flanders to Bristol in a Spanish vessel, and importing wine and woad from Bordeaux, madder – another dyestuff – from Flanders and oil from Seville.[40] [*Fig. 1.4*]

Female Executors

For most of Bristol's propertied widows, honouring a recently-deceased husband's commercial commitments was but a small part of their involvement with his estate. Most husband-testators appointed their wives as their executors, very often as the sole executor. One particularly dramatic deathbed scene involving the appointment of an executor is described in the 1599 nuncupative will of Agnes Mason, and reveals that she had been appointed by her deceased husband as his executor, but that she had forgotten this in her final illness:

1.4 The brass of Margaret and Thomas Rowley, in the Church of St John the Baptist, Broad Street, Bristol. The Rowleys were members of a prominent Bristol merchant family. The brass states that Thomas died on 23 January 1478 (by modern reckoning, 1479) but leaves Margaret's dates blank, perhaps indicating that she was still alive when the brass was made. In his will of January 1478 Thomas appointed Margaret as the administrator of their son William's will, which had been made the previous November. William had been resident in Bordeaux. Like Alice Chestre, Margaret carried on trading after her husband's death: in February 1480 she shipped carrying madder, tar, wainscot and hops from Flanders to Bristol. *Photograph Norm Stewart*

Being willed to make her will she answered they say I have nothing then she being told that her husband made her full executrix and that all was hers to dispose at her will saying who shall be your executor she the aforesaid Agnes Mason straight away put her hand forth and took her cousin Ann Clovyll by the hand and said Ann and therewith all held her fast...[41]

Widows were sometimes appointed without a male supervisor or overseer. In some instances however, the male overseers were explicitly instructed to guide the inexperienced executrix: this was the case with both male and female testators. By her will of 1599 Margaret Langton appointed her granddaughter as her sole executor, but also desired her two male overseers 'to be as fathers to my executor, and to see that she be ruled for her own good'.[42] Such occasional instances apart, the frequency with which widows were appointed as sole executors strongly suggests that wives were expected to assist their husbands in the management of their affairs, and so to familiarise themselves with the conduct of his business, since an executor should have a detailed and informed appreciation of the deceased's estate, as well as some knowledge of property law.

The responsibilities shouldered by many Bristol widow-executors would have been considerable, since they had to see that the provisions of the will were fully implemented, including their late husband's desires for burial and commemoration, charitable provisions, and the satisfaction of his debts. This process could take many years. William Lewis, a Bristol burgess, appointed his wife, Agnes, and another Agnes Lewis as his executors. William's widow died, leaving the other Agnes with the task of recovering a debt which she claimed William had contracted with the Abbot of Evesham in 1466: at least 52 years later she was still petitioning Chancery for satisfaction.[43]

In some cases widows refused to act as their deceased husband's executor because they realised that if they did so they would become liable for debts that could not easily be paid. However, this was a dangerous tactic, since using any part of her husband's estate made her its administrator, a position carrying similar liabilities as executor. In the 1520s this is what Agnes, widow of the Bristol merchant John Vaughn, discovered to her cost when her admission that she had used some of her husband's estate to meet his funeral costs meant that his creditors could prosecute her as the administrator of his will.[44]

Women and Inheritance

Equally difficult could be the process by which widows claimed what was legally theirs. On marriage, women surrendered ownership and control of most classes of whatever moveable goods they brought to the partnership. They also lost control, but not ownership, of landed property, or real estate, to their husband, but on his death control reverted to his widow. A Bristol widow could also benefit from a share of her husband's moveable goods and real estate. Traditionally, she was entitled to *legitim*, a share of her husband's moveables (one-third if there were surviving children, otherwise a half), dower in one third of her husband's real estate, identified at the time of the marriage, and freebench, the right to occupy her husband's principal dwelling until her own death or remarriage. By the Tudor period, however, these arrangements had been supplemented by the jointure, a legal device whereby a certain proportion of the husband's property was held by a group of trustees for the couple in joint survivorship, so that if the husband should predecease the wife the trustees would automatically continue to hold it, but in her name alone and to her use. Often, male testators would include provisions in their wills preventing their widows from claiming both dower or freebench alongside jointure. For example, in his will of 1601 David John Lloyde, a miller, granted his wife the life occupancy of his tenement and garden (that is, her freebench), together with a weekly pension of 2s 6d, on condition that she did not claim any dower. That such a provision was sometimes a legal formality, rather than an indication of tension between husband and wife, is indicated by the will of a Bristol gentleman, Patrick White, made in 1600, in which he provided £600 for a lifetime annuity for his 'well-beloved' wife, whom he trusted to do anything necessary to bar her own claims to dower.[45]

The problems that could be presented by the presence of local customs coexistent with different, common-law ones, applicable nationally, is indicated by a dispute that occurred between 1527 and 1538. This involved Anne Norton, the widow of Andrew Norton, a Bristol gentleman with holdings in Gloucestershire, his son Richard, and after Richard's death (by 1531), Richard's widow Margaret and her second husband George Gilbert. The case centred on contending claims to the George Inn, which stood on High Street, close to Bristol Bridge. After Andrew Norton's death his widow Anne claimed that the property should be her common-law dower, as representing one third part of the value of the estate Andrew held during their marriage, but her claim was denied by, first, Richard, Andrew's son, and then by Margaret, Richard's widow and executor, later joined by her second husband George. Richard, Margaret and George all claimed that Bristol custom negated Anne's claim to this property by dower, since by its terms only property allocated immediately prior to the wedding could be so assigned, and that in Anne's case this did not include the George Inn. For some reason a jointure agreement does not seem to have been made between Anne and Andrew Norton.[46]

Occasionally, husbands declared their trust in their wives' abilities and the contribution they had made to the family's prosperity. Such was the case with

1.5 The tomb of Joan Young and husband at Bristol Cathedral. Joan Young (d.1603), daughter of John Wadham, a Somerset esquire, sister of the co-founder of Wadham College Oxford, and her second husband, Sir John Young (d.1606), are shown here. Sir John had the 'Great House' built for him on the site of the Carmelite Friary in Bristol (now Colston Hall), and he was able to do this through his marriage to Joan in 1563, by which he acquired the extensive Dorset and Somerset estates inherited by Joan from her first husband, Sir Giles Strangways.
Courtesy Bristol Cathedral

John Ley, who in 1598 stated in his nuncupative will:

> That which he had was gotten between his wife Joan and him and that the children which he had were hers as well as his and what debts were owed she knew better than he and therefore he did give her all which he and she had and willed her to pay all his debts and use her discretion therein.[47]

Another fulsome deathbed declaration of a husband's debt to his wife was made by Harry May in 1573, in whose nuncupative will he said:

> I know I shall now die and not recover and there is but one way with me. And therefore touching my worldly goods, so it is that I brought little or nothing to my wife Katheryn, and therefore I will not take or give any thing from her, but do refer all to her discretion and make her my executrix…[48]

A similar sentiment was expressed by Richard Williams in 1593, who gave all his goods to his wife for her to use according to her discretion, adding 'and all little enough for her'; while in his nuncupative will of 1601 a joiner, David Williams, declared that, 'I am a poor man and all the goods and chattels that I have I give and bequeath to Dorothy my wife and would so do if I had ten times as much'.[49] Such declarations of trust and indebtedness towards wives

Women *and* Funerary Commemoration c.1373-1660 Peter Fleming

One of the few ways in which images of women of this period survive is by way of funerary brasses and effigies. Of course, such memorialisation was an option open only to the rich. At the top of the range was the alabaster effigy on a stone tomb chest: in the late fourteenth century. This could cost over £17, a prohibitively expensive option for all but the wealthiest merchant, and for this reason likely to be the most impressive.[1] Two surviving examples of this form are the tombs of William and Joan Canynges and of Philip Mede and Isabel, both in St Mary Redcliffe Church.

William Canynges, five times mayor of Bristol, was one of the wealthiest men in the later medieval town, having made his fortune from ship-owning and international commerce. He had married Joan, daughter of John and Joan Mylton, by 1436. Joan died in September 1467, and William did not remarry.[2] ▶

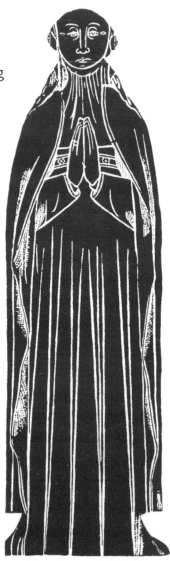

Brass rubbing of an unknown lady (c.1460), taken from Temple Church, Bristol. Temple Church was badly bombed in the Second World War and all of its original brasses were lost. Image from C.T. Davis, *The Monumental Brasses of Gloucestershire (1899)*

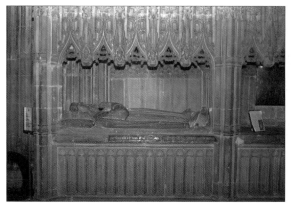

The Mede Tomb, St Mary Redcliffe Church. This was constructed on the orders of Philip Mede (d.1475), and the western aperture contains his effigy, together with his wife Isabel's.
Courtesy St Mary Redcliffe, Bristol

Effigy of Joan Mylton (d.1467), wife of William Canynges (d.1474), from their tomb in St Mary Redcliffe Church. This tomb seems to have been constructed before 1474, since after Joan's death William took holy orders and became Dean of Westbury-on-Trym College, and as such was depicted in another monument, originally placed in Westbury-on-Trym Church. He probably commissioned the monument to himself and to his wife before taking orders. So, this is likely to have been a rare instance of an attempt to portray a medieval woman's actual likeness.
Photograph by Lobsterthermidor, Wikipedia

William Canynges paid 6s. 8d. to the church wardens of St Mary Redcliffe for the site of his wife's grave in October 1467, less than a month after her death.[3]

The Mede tombs take the form of a double tomb chest under an elaborate canopy. In the western alcove are the effigies of Philip Mede (d.1475), three times mayor of Bristol, and his wife Isabel, the daughter of John and Joan Sharp of Bristol.

The next bay is designed to contain matching effigies, but instead has a brass plate set in the rear panel above the surface of the tomb chest, depicting Philip and Isabel's son Richard (d.1491), and his two wives Elizabeth, granddaughter of John and Joan Sharp, and secondly Anne, daughter of Thomas Pauncefoot of Gloucestershire. Brasses were considerably cheaper than stone effigies: by 1500, depending on the size and complexity, brasses usually cost between £2 and £10.[4]

Robert Kitchin, alderman of Bristol, died in 1595, and in his will he asked to be buried next to his first wife Joan, in St Stephen's Church.[5] The brass plaque commemorating the couple may still be seen on the church wall, and it carries a verse crediting them both for charitable works and bounty. ∎

Brass plaque commemorating Alderman Robert Kitchin and his wife.
Courtesy St Stephen's Church, Bristol

seem to appear relatively more often in nuncupative wills, which made up a tiny proportion of the total number of recorded wills, suggesting that in the more formal, written, documents this evidence for the nature of the marital relationship was often hidden by the more sober details of arrangements concerning the disposal of property.

Relationships between Women and Men

There is a temptation for historians to dwell on relationships that fail, on disputes and on conflict, simply because it is such things that tend to generate the most documentation. This is certainly the case in the medieval and early modern periods, when much of our evidence comes through legal processes. Other sources, that could tell us more about the unexceptional, such as personal letters and diaries, are much scarcer before the latter half of the seventeenth century. Hence, we are left only with fragments from which to get a sense of the day-to-day relationships of women in later medieval and early modern Bristol. Women were denied direct access to civic decision-making, and, probably, were increasingly sequestered into the 'private sphere' of the household, and so what influence they could exert on the 'public sphere' largely resulted from their ability to persuade their menfolk – be they fathers, brothers, male guardians, masters or husbands – of their points of view. Thus, the nature of relationships between men and women is a crucial factor to be considered in any discussion of women's role in shaping the development of the city. Since, by definition, such influence would have been exerted in private, and so was not recorded, we are left only with the evidence of female-male relationships, not of the possible influence that women might have exerted through them.

From the seventeenth century come records of depositions made by witnesses in local disputes. These are still documents produced through the processes of law, but they can reveal aspects of everyday life previously hidden from the historian. For example, we are told how, in 1645, a young, unmarried woman, Mary Brookebanke, was repeatedly importuned by a sailor, John Barrow, his efforts coming to a head in an encounter in the Lamb Tavern in Tucker Street. Also present at this meeting was a glover, William Prowt, a close friend of Barrow. Barrow asked Prowt for his opinion of Mary, and he replied that, 'he liked her very well and that she might be a good wife to him'; Barrow,

> thereupon asked the said Mary Brookebanke whether she would have him
> or not and said he would be resolved of it before she went out of the

room, and thereupon the said Mary Brookebanke being fearful of his constancy having been deluded by one young man before, told him so much there, and asked whether he would be constant to her, and marry her, and said that if he would, then she would have him. And there upon the said Barrow took her by the hand and vowed, that he would have nobody but her, and would be married to her very shortly…[50]

More prosaically, perhaps, he also promised that as his wife she would receive an annual income of £16. A week later Barrow arranged for the banns to be read.[51] Mary's caution was the fruit of a bitter experience doubtless mirrored by other instances of young women duped by unscrupulous suitors, but her experience was recorded, as a chance remark in a legal testimony.

Depositions also give some indication of the physical violence that some women suffered in seventeenth-century Bristol. In 1644 a 30-year-old spinster, Elizabeth Edgly, deposed that she had been sitting in her mistress's doorway one May evening when she saw a man, whom she afterwards learnt was called Simon Plomer, walking by on the other side of the street with Katherine Shipman, a maid living in the house of Ann James, a neighbour. The deponent recalled that after an exchange of words between the two,

the said Plomer struck the said Katherine Shipman on the head with his fist, and presently again gave her another in the neck with his fist and with it struck her down, who giving a great cry (and after rising again, being amazed with the blow) she reeled against the bulk [the wooden stall in front of a shop], but as soon as she came to herself ran home to the said Ann James as fast as she could…[52]

The extent of domestic violence against Bristol women in this period can never be known, but it would be wrong to characterise relations between men and women as being universally cold and exploitative. We have already seen evidence of male testators expressing their gratitude toward their wives in their final dying breaths. There are further indications that relations between wives and their husbands could be cordial, even warm. For example, by her will of 1596 Agnes Baylie granted the goods due to her from her first husband to her second, Francis Baylye, and appointed him as her sole executor, describing him as loving and dear to her.[53] Other female testators state explicitly that they were carrying out their late husbands' wishes, such as Juliana Gosnell, who in 1597 bequeathed all of her goods to her grand-daughter, 'for that it was her husband's mind it should be so': it is impossible at this distance to fathom what this comment implies about Juliana's relationship either with her deceased husband or with her grand-daughter.[54]

Husbands were certainly capable of enforcing their wishes on their female kin, even from beyond the grave. For example, in his will of 1593 Francis Dennys, gentleman, made the unmarried Mary Dennys his sole executor (with a cousin and another man as overseers) and legatee, provided that she followed the advice of two other men when it came to choosing a husband; in 1597 Maurice Hill declared in his will that his legacy of £100 to his under-age daughter was only to be paid 'if she match by the consent of her friends …', while the same year Edward Nicholls included a similar condition in his will, stating that his daughter was to receive £20 when she reached 21 provided she married 'by her mother's discretion', and, also in 1597, Thomas Rogers left all of his property, including two houses, to his wife Welsyon, but on condition that should she choose to remarry her new husband must be approved by his male overseers, or else she would forfeit the properties:

> …but and if my wife do chance hereafter to marry with any man that
> William Cox and James Bellman, being my overseers shall like well of
> him that then the two houses which she have shall remain to the use
> of my son Edward and to bring him up to school…[55]

The exercise of male control over women evident in these documents could be manifested in many other ways. One of the most chilling, perhaps, is the policing of female discourse through accusations of scolding, punishable by being ducked in the Frome in the ducking stool. This device was repaired in 1557, and rebuilt in 1621, after which it was used with some regularity, being employed to punish a woman from Redcliffe on two separate occasions that same year, while in 1624 two women were ducked together, and the chamber-lain's accounts for 1625 record the purchase of ropes and *aqua vitae* (the latter presumably to bring the woman back to consciousness after her punishment) for the purpose of ducking.[56] Ducking was abandoned under the Republic (only to be resumed with the Restoration), but this did not mean that women's freedom was no longer constrained by the threat of public humiliation: in 1654 a butcher's wife was set in the stocks for three hours for having uttered profanities in a fit of passion, while her husband was also tried for having allegedly attempted to rescue her.[57]

Women and Overseas Expansion

Bristol's later role in England's Atlantic empire was presaged in the second quarter of the seventeenth century when it became a significant participant in the trade with Barbados, which was settled by the English from the 1620s.[58] Barbados presented great opportunities for Bristolians, but the great distances involved threatened to destabilise family life for some. This appears to have been the case for Elizabeth and John Sherman, who were among the first English people to settle in Barbados, moving there from Bristol at the end of the 1620s and acquiring a plantation. The couple's six-year-old daughter, Elizabeth, was left behind in Bristol, in the care of a nurse. By 1642 the Shermans had died, and Elizabeth, now of age, appeared before the mayor to claim her inheritance. A similar instance of children being left in another's care while their parents pursued their fortune in Barbados is presented by the case of Mary and Thomas Williams, the children of the Bristol merchant Thomas Williams, who left them in the care of their grandfather while he settled in Barbados; in 1650, their father having died. Mary and Thomas, aged 15 and 14 respectively, appeared before the mayor to state their wish that their grandfather be appointed as their guardian in order to recover their Barbadian inheritance.[59]

Ireland was the location of other English colonies with which the port of Bristol was closely connected. In November 1641 the indigenous Catholic Irish revolted against the Protestant English settlers, with the result that over the course of the following year approximately 400 refugees appeared in Bristol. Some of the women among them appear in the historical record, allowing us a glimpse of their plight. Such was the widow Elizabeth Gayney, forced to leave her house in Waterford and flee to Bristol, having entrusted her property to her brother-in-law, Edward Abbott, an English tobacco pipe-maker who had been allowed to remain in Ireland, allegedly because his trade was one that the Irish rebels valued but could not themselves practise. Another was Elizabeth Nethercott, a poor orphan who after her arrival in Bristol was bound apprentice in the craft of button-making.[60] After the revolt was suppressed Bristol's normal commercial and social links with Ireland were resumed. Ireland promised fortune for some, but, as with the Barbadian colony, this could sometimes come at the price of disrupting family life. In 1651 the mayor was informed that the previous year Richard Graves had taken his four children to Ireland, leaving his pregnant wife behind; she died giving birth to a daughter, Jane, and meanwhile Richard and all four of their other children had died in Ireland, leaving the infant Jane as heir to the family property.[61]

Women and Political and Religious Protest

The participation of women in political and religious protest is a particular area where we are hampered by the sources, since, after all, as far as the male elite were concerned, this was not an area with which women should meddle, and it was the male elite on whose behalf our written sources were produced. The overall story is one of isolated instances of female participation through most of our period, with the appearance, right at its end, of a more coherent picture of concerted female involvement centred on emergent 'puritan' and nonconformist religious movements.

In the spring of 1400 a royal commission investigating Bristol merchants' evasion of the duty on cloth provoked an attempt by a gang of Bristolians to murder the customs collector. Remarkably, the gang seems to have been largely composed of the wives of Bristol burgesses. Their scheme was foiled by the mayor, who broke up the gathering, assisted by other 'good men' of the town. The male ringleaders were imprisoned and ejected from the freedom of Bristol, but there is no record of actions taken against the women.[62]

This protest does not seem to have had any religious dimension, but by the early fifteenth century a movement of religious heretics, the Lollards, had appeared, inspired by the teachings of the fourteenth-century Oxford academic John Wycliff. The Lollards' beliefs had enough in common with the Protestants of the sixteenth century to lead some historians to believe that early English Protestantism may have owed something to surviving Lollardy. Bristol was notorious as a centre for Lollardy, which in the fifteenth and early sixteenth centuries tended to be found among urban artisan house-holds and be associated with the textile industry, so Bristol's association with the heresy is unsurprising. Among other things, Lollardy is notable for allow-ing women a far greater voice than was the case in mainstream Catholic Christianity, and there are examples of women helping to organise Lollard cells and of female preachers. One notable Bristol female Lollard was Christina More. She and her husband, William, a Bristol burgess, kept a prominent Lollard household, including a Lollard chaplain. After William's death in 1412 Christina took over as a Lollard leader. In 1414 there was an uprising against the government of Henry V, which was portrayed by the authorities as a 'Lollard Rebellion', and Bristol contributed the single largest contingent. Among them were Christina's chaplain and a household servant, whom she supported in this doomed endeavour. We know this because she was prosecuted for this offence: luckily for her, her punishment was no worse than being made to do penance. Others were hanged or burnt alive.[63]

A story of, if not political or religious dissent, then at least of what appears to be female assertiveness in the face of male obduracy, relates to the Hospital of St Bartholomew, founded by Sir John de la Warre of Brislington in the thirteenth century. Originally, both men and women made up the religious community that cared for the inmates. However, in the 1330s the sisters expelled the brothers and master and elected a prioress. The bishop of Worcester (in which diocese the hospital was located) forced the women to allow the men to return in 1386. In 1412 the women tried again to expel the men, but failed. In 1445 Bristol's mayor and common council, working with the de la Warre family, refounded the hospital as the Fraternity of St Clement, to care for poor sailors. This seems to have put an end to any tussles between the sisters and brothers – perhaps because the sisters were evicted.[64] [*Fig. 1.6*]

By the early seventeenth century groups of religious radicals, or 'separatists', had emerged to challenge what they saw as the established Anglican Church's lack of rigour and true commitment to the Bible.[65] Bristol was an early centre of such agitation: the first Quakers, for example, appeared in the city as early as spring 1654, and women were prominent among these radicals. Of these Bristol radical women the best documented is Dorothy, wife of two separatist husbands, a grocer, Anthony Kelly, and Matthew Hazzard, vicar of St Ewen's church. From the 1620s she and her first husband Anthony were at the centre of a group of separatists among whom women figured prominently. They were allowed to preach, much to the violent ridicule of Bristol's more conservative male majority among its political-religious elite. After Anthony's death, and before her second marriage, Dorothy made a point of keeping her grocer's shop open on Christmas Day, since she and her followers did not approve of celebrating feast days. Her marriage to Matthew Hazzard around 1640 allowed her to use the St Ewen's parsonage as a refuge for other radical women awaiting passage to New England or who wished to escape churching, the process of purification of women 40 days after childbirth that most of the city's Anglican clergy insisted upon. In 1640 Dorothy was also a signatory to the foundation of the Broadmead Baptist Church, the first dissenting church in Bristol. There was a total of five involved and meetings were held at her house in Broad Street. Like most of her fellow separatists, Dorothy actively supported Parliament during the Civil Wars, and during the Royalist Prince Rupert's assault in July 1643 she, along with another radical Bristol woman, Joan Batten, led a group of 200 women and children in defence of the Frome Gate, later declaring that they had been prepared to put themselves and their children in front of enemy bullets. Dorothy gave

1.6 This 1820 watercolour, executed by 'Saunders of Bath', shows the City School in Christmas Street, which incorporated some of the remains of the medieval St Bartholomew's Hospital. (BMAG M2584). *(Braikenridge Collection) Bristol Museums, Galleries & Archives*

evidence against the Parliamentarian commander of Bristol, Colonel Nathaniel Fiennes, at his subsequent trial for dereliction of duty. She had left all of her goods in the castle for safe-keeping before the siege, having been assured that Fiennes would defend it to the upmost, and their loss added to her anger at what she saw as his cowardice. [*Colour plate 4*] Dorothy and Matthew Hazzard fled Bristol after the Royalist takeover but returned in 1645 when the city changed hands again. She remained there, as a stalwart of the Baptist community centred upon Broadmead, until her death in 1674.

Conclusion

Telling the story of women in later medieval and early modern Bristol is inevitably hampered by imperfect, fragmentary evidence. The paucity of primary sources is matched by that of the poor, who constituted about one half of the city's total population, but whereas the male elite were saved from obscurity as their actions and thoughts were increasingly commonly recorded

1.7 *Jacob Naylors einzug in Bristol.* In November 1656 the radical Quaker James Naylor entered Bristol in what seemed to be a conscious imitation of Christ's entry into Jerusalem, as commemorated by Christians on Palm Sunday. For this perceived blasphemy he was prosecuted in London and severely punished. This depiction of James Naylor's entry into Bristol in 1656, is taken from Benedikt Figken's translation into German of Richard Blome's *Fanatick History* of 1660, published in 1701 as *Historia Fanaticorum, odereinevollkommene relation und wissenschaft von denen Schwarmern, alsalten Anabaptisten und neuen Quackern, Frankfurt.* Blome was an opponent of Quakerism, and so portrayed Naylor in a very unflattering light, and, as this translation suggests, his interpretation was both widely disseminated and highly influential. The women who accompanied Naylor, depicted here as shouting 'Heilig!' (Holy), were not, as far as we can tell, Bristolians.
University of Bristol Library, Special Collections

– as one approaches both the later seventeenth century and the higher reaches of the socio-economic hierarchy – their female counterparts are much less evident in the historical record. That said, it is possible to offer some tentative conclusions. In many ways, Bristol was similar to other English towns and cities, in that its female population was denied access to the levers of economic and political power that their male counterparts – at least among the elite – took for granted. Women were able to pursue occupations as traders and manufacturers, sometimes independently of men, but as the later middle ages gave way to the early modern period it seems that their access to the more high-status occupations was increasingly restricted. Most did not benefit from the formal training offered by a craft apprenticeship, but wives were still expected to acquire many of the skills practised by their husbands, and as widows, generally, were entrusted with the family business. While the evidence for female political or radical religious thought and activity is sparse in most instances, there were pockets of radicalism, beginning with Lollardy and ending with mid-seventeenth-century separatism, and Bristol seems to have been particularly prominent as a centre of such agitation. The willingness with which Bristol women were prepared to engage with such movements, often at very considerable personal risk, suggests that their apparent absence from long stretches of Bristol's history of political and religious radicalism was not a matter of choice on their part, but is the result of their being discouraged or prevented from participating, and of being imperfectly recorded even if they did manage to break through male prejudice. [*Fig. 1.7*]

Bristol Women in the Long Eighteenth Century c. 1660-1835

Madge Dresser

Introduction

This chapter covers the era that begins with the Restoration of the monarchy in 1660 and ends with riot and reform. During this 'long eighteenth century,' Bristol, enriched by the rise of the Atlantic slave economy, was transfigured by its new Georgian squares and crescents and by a rising, if embryonic, middle class. [*Fig. 2.1*] By the 1750s, manufacturing industries grew and evangelical religion and enlightenment ideas became increasingly influential. Class divisions polarised as the city swelled from less than 20,000 at the beginning of our period to nearly 120,000 by its close.[1] After the Bristol Riot of 1831 highlighted the widespread discontent with the existing political system, the Reform Acts of 1832 and 1835 opened up Parliament and local government to middle-class men but explicitly excluded women from political power.

So what part did Bristol women play in the city's development at this time? Recent scholarly work has claimed that women in various European, American and British cities, played an indispensable, though often under-recognised, role servicing the needs of urban life, with women from the middling ranks playing an especially dynamic role in this respect.[2] To paraphrase Deborah Simonton, such women

> left bequests…managed household economies, bought luxury goods and fostered cultural production. They were also – and significantly – active in urban commerce and their status as traders was widely recognised.[3]

But as time has passed, the economic and social contributions of women were often rendered invisible. This has been particularly the case for married women, whose identity, as we have seen, was usually subsumed under that of their husband. The intention here is to reassess Bristol women's involvement in economic affairs and to reflect upon their engagement in the city's cultural

2.1 A female servant and young male slave are depicted with their genteel master and mistress. *The South East Prospect of the City of Bristol* by Samuel and Nathaniel Buck, 1734. (BMAG LEAA21.9). *Bristol Museums, Galleries & Archives*

and political life.

To this end the chapter begins with a brief overview of Bristol and then looks to see what we can learn about women's employment in the period. It asks how far women's occupations were gender specific and goes on to consider women's contribution to what might be called the 'knowledge economy' – the rise of print and theatrical culture, literature and the arts and educational provision. It then looks anew at women's involvement in charitable work, social reform and politics, asking to what extent their participation can be divorced from mainstream developments in the city's public affairs.

A social and economic overview of Bristol

The expanding Atlantic economy in particular afforded new opportunities for women as well as men in Britain's port cities.[4] Bristol was no exception, though its particular civic and social structure, its involvement in the slave and plantation trades and its history as a centre for Protestant Nonconformity shaped these opportunities for women in distinctive ways.

Throughout this period, Bristol was an entrepôt for regional, European and colonial trade. But Bristol's 'golden age' unequivocally rested in large measure on the labour of enslaved Africans and the products they were forced to produce.[5] This commercial wealth spawned new members of Bristol's wealthy merchant elite and soon attracted visiting gentry who flocked to its Hotwells spa.

Bristol was an industrial city as well as a port. Its manufacturing enterprises were closely allied to the particular nature of its foreign trade: sugar was

2.2 Unaccompanied ladies walking in Queen Square. *North Prospect Queen Square*, Benjamin Cole after William Halfpenny, 1732. (BMAG M1616). *Bristol Museums, Galleries & Archives*

refined, tobacco processed and cloth woven.[6] The manufacture of soap, brass and metal-ware, pottery and glass were important, as was brewing and distilling. These and lesser-known trades such as the production of hats and clay tobacco pipes combined to form the backbone of the city's manufacturing sector.

Retailing and services grew as the city prospered, and women played a 'disproportionately great role' in their expansion.[7] Given that women had never been bound up in the traditional guild and craft structure to the same extent as men had, the growth of the tertiary sector meant that their employment patterns were to become 'ever more divergent' from that of men.[8]

By the mid-eighteenth century Bristol was deposed from its status as Britain's second city by both Birmingham and Liverpool, but still remained an important international port and regional capital. Its diverse commercial and industrial base ensured it continued to play a vital role in what Peter Clark has called 'the wider modernizing process affecting English society'.[9]

By the 1760s, Bristol was said to have caught 'the London itch' for consumer goods. New networks of elegant squares and crescents, assembly rooms, theatres, libraries and shops – the spatial and cultural expressions of new economic realities – made the cityscape more genteel and in some respects more 'female-friendly', even as it signalled the evolution of a more socially polarised society.[10] [*Fig. 2.2*] By the 1770s, the middle classes were noticeably expanding and more reform-minded professionals and manufacturers began to challenge the city's governing elite and the older civic institutions that underwrote them.

But the city's merchant princes showed remarkable staying power, managing to forge some alliances with those more progressive new professionals and manufacturers who, as the gulf between prosperity and poverty increased, 'had become increasingly uneasy about the threat the poor posed to the social order'.[11] The aftermath of the French Revolution marked a watershed in how the middling classes related to the lower orders and these emerging class divisions had a gendered dimension.

Bristol's high concentration of Nonconformist Protestants also had an effect on gender relations. On the one hand, Dissenting Protestants (Quakers, Baptists, Unitarians et al) along with such newer groups as the Methodists and Low Church Evangelicals, believed in spiritual equality and emphasised the importance of Christians of both sexes acting in concert with their consciences. Such religious individualism provided a counterpoint to traditional patriarchal values. But in other respects this 'new wave Puritanism', with its concomitant emphasis on domesticity, sexual restraint and propriety, increasingly helped to limit the range of activities open to 'respectable' women. In any case, women within the emerging 'middle classes' were still limited in their access to education, commercial activity and wealth.

Despite the city's wide range of industries, which by the turn of the nineteenth century grew to include the cotton, the boot and shoe and the garment industries, the lives of the vast majority of Bristol's inhabitants, both male and female, were often hard and precarious. Baigent estimates that perhaps 65 per cent of the population in 1775 were actually or potentially poor, and this proportion expanded at times of economic crises.[12] These 'poor' included an increasing proportion of immigrants to the city, most but not all of whom were from the West Country and Wales, seeking work as domestic servants, sailors and factory, shop and home workers. The Irish came through the port, too, often as short-term agricultural workers, and some settled in the city's most crowded courts and dwellings. The consensus is that women worked primarily in the dress, boot and hat manufacturing industries and in the expanding service sector in food or drink provision and laundering as well as general domestic service.[13] As insecure as the lot of the middling ranks could be (and most of them led rather austere lives by modern standards), it was this majority of the city's population that suffered most from recurring economic downturns and an increasingly inadequate urban infrastructure. Women were over-represented amongst the city's labouring poor, and amongst the 'paupers' i.e. those dependent on poor relief. Even middling women, if they became detached from familial financial support structures, could all too easily face impoverishment and even destitution. Studies of other commercial towns in the early modern era point to the existence of women workers living outside the family household: widows, single women, deserted wives, the wives of impressed men – some residing on their own, others banding together in what Olwen Hufton has termed 'spinster clusters', and who variously turned their hands to whatever labour

2.3 The women in the foreground are exercising the traditional right of airing their washing on Brandon Hill. They may be domestic servants, as may the young women flirting with youths.
The North West Prospect of the City of Bristol by Samuel and Nathaniel Buck, 1734. (BMAG M5288). *Bristol Museums, Galleries & Archives*

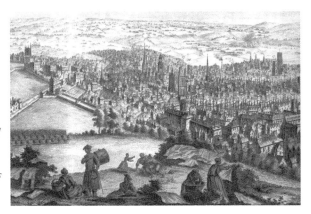

might enable them to survive without having recourse to poor relief. It is known, for example, that the women living communally in Bristol's Moravian single sisters' house worked at embroidery (tambour work) and found it a struggle to earn a living. We do not know how many more lived together in less formalised arrangements.[14]

That being said, although Bristol women were over-represented amongst the poor, nearly a fifth of the city's 4,500 rate-paying households were headed by widows and, contrary to expectations, the bulk of these households were 'neither very rich nor very poor', with a third of such households being relatively well off.[15] Bristol's proportion of female property holders included some wealthy women, and their role in the city's economic life as investors and patrons and the extent to which their presence distinguishes Bristol from other cities awaits further study.[16]

Women's employment[17]

Though few visual representations of Bristol servants survive, we know from tax records that domestic work was probably the largest single employer of women at the end of the 1600s and that even relatively modestly well-off families employed such servants within their household.[18] [*Fig. 2.3*] It isn't until the first occupational census of 1851 that the importance of female domestic service as an employer of women is reliably confirmed.[19]

Surviving records yield even less information about other ways women of the 'labouring poor' earned a living. A late-eighteenth-century portrayal of Bristol's quarry area is one of the only surviving pieces of evidence to show that women worked as stone carriers.[20] [*Fig. 2.4*] Advertisements and visual sources sometimes capture the presence of female musicians and fairground performers,[21] but even though it is widely assumed that spinning was a

2.4 Female quarry workers in *View of the River Avon from the Stone Quarries* (detail).
Braikenridge Collection, Vol. XXIX. BRL

2.5 Trade card showing a woman employee in earthenware workshop,
not dated but c. late-eighteenth or early-nineteenth century.
(BMAG T7384). *Bristol Museums, Galleries & Archives*

commonplace activity for many, if not most, of Bristol's women, especially
early on in our period, there are surprisingly few documents confirming this.[22]
The evidence is similarly fragmentary in other trades. Only passing mentions
in diaries and letters, and business and court records, corroborate the fact
that women in this era were employed in such manufacturing trades as copper
wire and nail making, pottery manufacture, stay making, and as coal hauliers.[23]

[*Fig. 2.5*] Reclaiming the working lives of most ordinary women in Bristol thus awaits more specialised research. Consequently, this chapter will mainly investigate the lives of women from the 'middling ranks', who have left more of a trace in the historical records.

But who are these 'middling women'? This imprecise and porous category was commonly employed before notions of 'middle class' and 'working class' came into fashion after the 1830s. It denotes a diverse group of people positioned between 'the labouring poor' and the gentry and aristocracy. Those who qualify as 'middling women' or 'women of the middling sort' do so not only on the grounds of their occupation but also because of their social and family connections and their independence from parish support. Constituting as much as a third of the population, 'middling women' will be deemed here to range from illiterate but independent artisans and traders (often of quite limited means) on the one hand to very wealthy and educated women whose income might in part be derived from annuities and rents on the other.[24]

Traditional civil restrictions on women's participation in economic life:
burgesses and apprenticeships
Though civic society was highly patriarchal, there was some 'room for manoeuvre' for a significant number of enterprising women to make their mark on civic life, in particular for those with the right family connections and access to capital. This was especially true for widows and, to a lesser extent, spinsters, but even married women were not always in practice as constrained by the law of coverture (which consigned their property to their husbands) as is commonly believed.[25]

Only freemen or burgesses enjoyed the rights to trade, to vote for members of the Corporation and to take on apprentices. Women were not explicitly banned under these ordinances, but if they were married their identity was subsumed under that of their husband. If they were widowed, they were customarily able to take on apprentices. If they were spinsters, they were in theory eligible to become burgesses so long as they fulfilled the conditions for burgess status.[26] In practice, only two spinster women were admitted as burgesses in their own right over our period: the milliner Cicell Carue in 1700 and the saddler Mary Herring in 1768.[27] But these were exceptional cases and it is notable that although they had the right to trade, the right to vote did not apparently go with their status as it did with male burgesses. [*Fig. 2.6*]

Apprenticeship, though it was to decline over this period, was still an important part of this traditional system. Most apprentices were formally

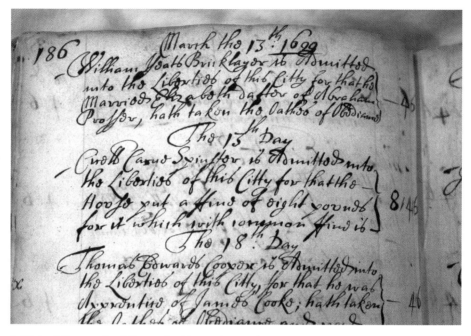

2.6 Bristol Corporation Minutes for 13 March 1699/1700 showing the name of Cicell Carue, spinster, as a burgess. BRO 043594. *Bristol Museums, Galleries & Archives*

indentured to a master and his wife, indicating that both were still seen as crucial to the success of a family business. The role wives played would have varied according to the internal politics of the individual family, but the fact that they (as well as widows and some spinsters) had a responsibility for apprentices meant that women made a contribution as managers and trainers to the local economy.

In a small and declining number of cases, male apprentices were assigned to widows of established craftsmen, some of whom had run their businesses long after their husbands had died. Thus, Mary Orchard, the widow of John Orchard, took on nine apprentices to help her run her pottery business making delftware in Temple Street for nearly a quarter of a century, from 1698 to 1720.[28] Honnor Batchelor (the widow of the pewterer John Batchelor, who had employed eleven apprentices over his working life) employed two apprentices in her own right after her husband's death, and was listed as the 'patron' when one of them became a freeman in 1728. Her pewter bears a stamp or touchstone with both her husband's initials and her maiden name, which was French.[29] But as apprenticeship and the guild system declined, the number of such independent women masters dwindled into insignificance.[30]

The Corporation also had the power to grant stipends for widows of deceased Corporation officials, but such paternalism could work to confirm women's inferior status. Mary White, the widow of the governor of Bristol's Bridewell prison, petitioned in 1749 to be kept on in her husband's office, on the grounds that she had long standing experience of the duties involved. She was temporarily granted the post and the profits that went with it, but she was soon ousted by a male candidate for the permanent appointment. Having been thus reduced to 'mean circumstances', she was eventually awarded a small widow's stipend.[31]

Women Defying Civic Restrictions on Trading
Up to the late eighteenth century, various council pronouncements banned the right of 'foreigners', men and women who did not have burgess status, to run a shop or other retail premises in the city and both sexes were prosecuted for defying this ordinance. Between 1738 and 1745, a quarter of the 24 people who were formally served with notice that they were contravening the city's regulations on trade were women. One, Mrs Elizabeth Hawkins, was prosecuted twice in 1740 and 1742.[32] These strictures seemed to have been increasingly defied as the economy expanded, with councillors in 1752 threatening to impose a £5 fine on anyone who contravened their rules.[33]

Some lower status trades, such as keeping an alehouse, did not require burgess status providing an annual licence was obtained from the Corporation. Thus some women became licensees of alehouses though others persisted in running breweries and alehouses illegally from their homes.[34] In 1690 one female Friend successfully requested a loan from the Quaker's Men's Meeting to 'enable her to build in her house, an oven and some other accommodations for Bakeing cakes and selling ale whereby she proposes to Rayse a Lively hood.'[35] Similarly, a number of seamen's wives were involved in running illegal shops providing lodgings, food and other goods whilst their husbands were at sea. Thus Susanna Dean, the wife of James Dean, was forced to shut down her business in 1697 and hers was one of a number of similar cases persisting into the second half of the eighteenth century.[36]

Middling women and the urban economy
The surviving evidence indicates that for much of the period the majority of middling Bristol women, like others in London and elsewhere in Britain, were confined to a cluster of occupations deemed to be extensions of the 'natural'

domestic role: the provision of food and drink, clothing, accommodation and the caring 'professions' of nursing and education.[37] This is confirmed by Bristol's first trade directory, *Sketchley's*, published in 1775.[38]

Sketchley's did not provide a comprehensive picture. Less than 8 per cent of the city's 55,000 inhabitants were listed, including 700 women, of whom only 288 were listed as working in specific trades. Nonetheless it does indicate that women were also to be found in a surprisingly wide array of traditionally 'masculine' occupations. Among these are Elizabeth Chew, an organ builder and harpsichord maker, Rebecca Cohoan, the (probably Jewish) 'trader in ship's ballast,' as well as a tin-plate worker, a cutler, a plumber and a painter and glazier.[39] The one female sexton also mentioned reminds us that women were very occasionally appointed as parish officials. In other sources we find Betty Skuse, a soap maker on Christmas Street in St Nicholas parish early in the eighteenth century. Her apparent Baptist connections underline the partic-ular correlation between the Dissenting community in the city and trade.[40] A number of women worked as smiths, including Margaret Braine a gunsmith who with two other female smiths supplied wares to the slave ship *Jason* in 1743.[41] [*Fig. 2.7*] In the early eighteenth century a few women also seem to have obtained licences to work as hauliers, overseeing the transport of heavy goods across the city and employing between one and five journeymen or apprentices to drive a like number of horses.[42] [*Fig. 2.8*]

Sketchley's Directory enables us to begin to map tradeswomen's presence in individual streets. The painting of Broad Quay c.1760 [*see page 8*] takes on a new dimension when we realise that 11 of the 90 trades people listed on Broad Quay were female and ranged from a corn chandler, a cheese monger and the proprietor of a 'sale' [sail?] shop to a slop (cheap clothes) seller and wool-card maker. No less than a third of the street's 16 pub and innkeepers were women.

Class and marital status
Although, traditionally, women of the gentry saw remunerative work as beneath them, this does not seem to have been true of some higher status women who lived in cities, especially in the early part of our period.[43] Dorothy Woodhouse is listed in tax records for 1696 as a vintner in Bristol High Street, a high-status trade with long antecedents in the city.[44] Alice Sloper (d.1719), the niece of Sir John Duddlestone, part of an eminent gentry family in Bristol, ran a millinery shop and collected rents on properties in Wine Street and Bedminster,[45] while Ann Bright, part of the Bright merchant dynasty, ran

2.7 List of suppliers for the slave ship *Jason* on its voyage from Bristol in August 1743 containing names of women as smiths (including a gunsmith), a chandler etc. Account book for the Becher family. BRO 45167/1. *Bristol Museums, Galleries & Archives*

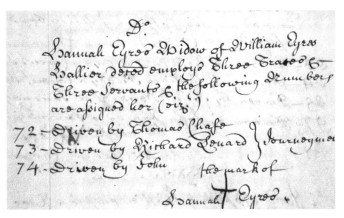

2.8 Detail from the *Halliers Register* for 11 October 1735 listing Hannah Ayres as a licensed haulier. She signed her name with an X indicating she was illiterate as so many women were in early-eighteenth-century England. BRO 05074 (1). *Bristol Museums, Galleries & Archives*

the family pewterer and braziers' firm under her own name for four years after her husband Allen's death, finally selling up in 1768.[46] The unnamed widow of Thomas Wall, a Presbyterian Whig bookseller and former goldsmith (d.1688), reportedly 'carried on...his trade [in Corn Street] with great reputation'.[47] Her descendant, Hannah Wall, who was probably her granddaughter, seems also to have carried on the business, being described in the press as a 'very eminent book seller' with 'a considerable fortune' who retired from her trade only shortly before her marriage in 1763 to a Gloucestershire landowner.[48] A Miss Spackman operated as a successful silversmith in Bristol's High Street until her marriage to 'an eminent watchmaker in London' in 1764. Significantly, both seem to have given up their trades upon marriage.

But this was not always the case for married women. Even if an enterprise were in their husband's name, some women could be found trading alongside their husbands, a point implicitly acknowledged by a misogynist Bristol broadside of the early eighteenth century which disapprovingly portrays a 'shrewish' wife refusing to serve in her husband's goldsmith shop, on the grounds that

Gentry Women
Lily Thornton

Rebecca Elbridge, Jane Whitchurch (senior) and Ann Smyth, are members of the landed elite who lived around the Bristol area in the eighteenth century. Considered here are some of the documents they left behind. These include letters, wills and account books. Much like instant messages and emails today, letters from the past reveal the intimate lives of people and analysed in conjunction with more impersonal sources, can provide a more rounded understanding of women's past lives. Such evidence shows that these women were involved in the lending of small loans, estate management, book keeping, event planning and social networking. Through such activities they were thus able to exert their influence beyond the immediate household and be active contributors to their estates, businesses and communities.

Rebecca Elbridge's family founded and ran the Spring Plantation in Jamaica. She inherited part of the plantation from her uncle John Elbridge and married Henry

Portrait of Elizabeth Smyth (1669-1715). (BMAG K1712). *Bristol Museums, Galleries & Archives*

'**Annuity to teach poor children**. In accordance with desire of his late wife Elizabeth, d'ter of Sir Samuel Astry and Dame Eliz. Astry, Sir John Smyth grants out of his third part of manor of Westerleigh an annuity of £20 to be paid to two men or women, each to teach 10 poor children born of parents living in Westerleigh who shall be members of Church of England to read English and learn the catechism, the children to continue at school until 12 yrs. or can read good English.'

Letter by Rebecca Woolnough (née Elbridge) about the Jamaican plantation

In her will Ann Smyth establishes an educational charity within the parish of Henbury and Ashton for the training of local girls.

Received August 14 1767 of Mr Gardiner Vicar Jn Pope & William Clark Church Wardens of the Parish of Henbury the Sum of five Pounds due ye 24 of June last being half a Years Annuity or Rent charge Issuing out of ye Lands called Redcliff Meads in the Parish of Bedminster in ye County of Somerset for teaching Girls of this Parish to Read, Knit & Sew pursuant to the Will of Mrs Ann Smith

Woolnough in 1737.[1] In 1761 her daughter and heir Elizabeth Woolnough married John Hugh Smyth of Ashton Court. The letter (*opposite bottom*) is one of a number written by Rebecca after she was widowed in 1746 and shows her actively engaged in the running of the Spring plantation. The extract transcribed below expresses her disquiet with William Swymmer, her agent in Jamaica. Complaining that she had not received adequately logged accounts she gave him an ultimatum:

Last March I expected an account of the Spring Plantation and a remittance of my moiety (half) for the year 1751 but to no purpose...I have waited with a great deal of patience till this time, and cannot bear it any longer, and must acquaint you that you use me very ill, in not sending me the account, or let me know the reasons for not so doing; you have had opportunities enough and you can't make any excuse for that, and now I do assure you that if in case I don't hear from you in a short time, be assured I will send a Power to some other gentlemen to act for me whom it is hop'd will be better stewards for me.[2]

Jane Whitchurch's correspondence includes references to her making small loans to family members, friends and neighbours who lived on, or near, her estates. A letter to her from her nephew concerns such a loan[3] and her response (transcribed below) is typically hard-headed:

My reasons for waining [wanting back] my money, was the trouble you gave me, in getting my interests...But as the affair is in Mr Windley's hands you must give him a letter that you will fully satisfy him and also a promise of paying me my interest punctually.[4]

Both Rebecca Elbridge and Jane Whitchurch demonstrate their astuteness and ruthlessness towards the managing of their estates and businesses. Jane is highly critical of poor business practices and is not afraid to say so. Such letters highlight the impact these women had on the wider community and more research is needed to document their interest and role in political networking.[5]

Ann Smyth's will and letters suggest she had a strong personal sense of duty towards the people who were in her community.[6] In her will she establishes an educational charity within the parish of Henbury and Ashton for the training of local girls.[7] Ann's charity lasted for over a hundred years and was carried on by her male descendants. ■

having brought a dowry to the marriage she should not be expected to demean herself by engaging in trade.

> Was I married Sir to be a Slave? Did I bring you a [marriage] portion, you prodigal Knave? To look after your Shop did I marry?[49]

It certainly became less fashionable for married women to work alongside their husbands as prosperity increased and notions of gentility gained wider currency. Nevertheless, the idea of a companionate marriage', based on shared values and mutual respect, particularly but not exclusively espoused by the Quakers and other religious Dissenters, may have empowered some wives to act as their husband's *de facto* business partners. Their participation, however, usually emerges into the public record only once they are widowed. Mary Sarjeant (1678-1718) who married Abraham Darby I of Coalbrook-dale-fame, was reportedly well informed about the techniques involved in the production of iron pots at her husband's foundry in Bristol.[50] Anna Fry, whose marriage to Joseph Fry, the chocolate manufacturer, was described as a 'truly happy' one, continued the business after his death as 'Anna Fry and Son'.[51] [*Fig. 2.9*] As we shall subsequently see, the Unitarian Sarah Guppy took an active if informal interest in her husband's metal work business.

Further down the middling ranks, court records confirm married women's active involvement in their husband's businesses. We know, for example, that in 1746 Mrs Jefferis, a baker's wife, was working in her husband's shop because it was she who was personally served with a city order for her husband's illegal trading. In 1765 Molly Moses, the wife of a Jewish silver-smith, testified to the magistrates that she was selling gold buckles in her husband's 'shop on the Key [Quay]' when an attempt was made to sell her stolen goods and there is similar testimony from other working wives and daughters in the Quarter session records.

Food and Drink Trades
By 1760, just under 62 (17 per cent) of the 371 licensed victuallers and alehouse keepers in Bristol's seven inner parishes were women, and victuallers constitute the largest single female occupational group listed in *Sketchley's Bristol Directory* of 1775. In port cities taverns and inns were an important place to meet and exchange goods and intelligence. Hester Richards, who kept The Superb at Bristol Back, wrote in 1744 to her absent sailor husband with news of privateers, prize monies and local news for his shipmates. Mary

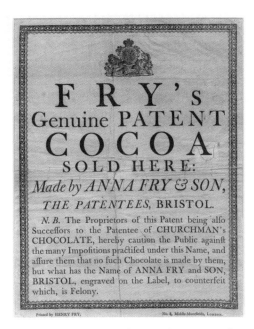

2.9 Advertisement for Anna Fry & Son's chocolate enterprise in Bristol. (BMAG TC2746).
Bristol Museums, Galleries & Archives

Williams's house at the Sign of the Cross in Stokes Croft was the venue for the distribution of prize monies for officers and sailors belonging to the *Fox* privateer in 1747.[52]

Women victuallers and tavern keepers worked in a wide range of premises. At the higher end of the market was Elinor Biggs, who kept the Lamb Inn, with 11 'chambers' for her guests, in Wine Street until her death in 1687 when her property was valued at £91.[53] Some like Elizabeth Morgan who ran the White Hart in 1718 were prosperous enough to take out fire insurance.[54] Others used their premises to enhance their financial prospects as in the case of Elizabeth Boon proprietor of the Plume and Feathers who would often invite the newly widowed and well-heeled Bristol merchant Thomas Deane 'to come thither [to her tavern], to eate and drink together', allegedly 'out of a design to draw him from being a Batchellor', before charging him for her hospitality when her matrimonial plans failed.[55] In rougher areas such as Marsh Street, where publicans were notorious for conniving with unscrupulous labour agents to ensnare sailors into serving aboard slave ships, five of the 17 victuallers listed there in *Sketchley's* 1775 directory were women.

Coffee House and Tea Room Proprietors

By contrast, coffee houses embodied a new politer type of public space, one that attracted businessmen, politicians and the literati, who came to read the newspapers, gossip and network. Female proprietors included Mary Ledbetter, who in the 1720s kept the Elephant Coffee House in All Saints Lane; Mrs Read (or Reed), who in 1742-3 famously had the poet Richard Savage imprisoned for an £8 debt owing to her (he referred to her thereafter as 'Madam Wolf-Bitch'); and Ann Barry (d.1748), who held the lease of the Exchange Coffee House in Corn Street, the city's most prestigious coffee establishment. In 1768, Mary Whealen and Sarah Perry were running the West India Coffee House and the American Coffee House (in Corn Street) respectively.[56] If coffee houses seem to have attracted a mainly male clientele, a 'ladies tea room' was advertised at Hotwells in 1759 and in 1768 Elizabeth Rees's 'Long Room' offered spa visitors of both sexes 'coffee, tea and chocolate' as well as meals.[57]

Purveyors of Colonial Produce
The colonial goods coming into Bristol were essential components in this new consumerism. Women's 'presence in a wide range of distributive businesses meant they were ideal intermediaries between the producers of new goods and services and the consumer'.[58] New opportunities opened for women in the retail sector as they sold produce linked to colonial trade, including teapots, sugar bowls and earthenware goods. Victuallers were particularly well placed to provide information and support services crucial to the development and expansion of the wider Atlantic economy.

There were already a small number of women acting as merchants in the late 1600s. Most such women were widows who continued to carry on their husbands' business, though the case of Elizabeth Swymmer, who took an active role in her family slave-trading business,[59] indicates some married women were also involved under their husbands' names in overseas trading.[60]

It was slave-produced goods rather than enslaved Africans in which most such traders were dealing. Female merchants traded in small amounts of colonial goods relative to that of their male counterparts. They never numbered above 3 per cent of those recorded in the seventeenth-century port books and their participation declined into insignificance by the mid-eighteenth century. Nonetheless, their presence confirms that the Atlantic trade opened new opportunities to those few women with capital, connections and a sense of enterprise. In 1660, for example, Cecily [aka Cicily] Hooke (widow of the Barbadian and Virginia merchant Humphrey Hooke) teamed up with a Mrs. Bridgeman of Amsterdam to share a consignment of 4 casks of muscovado sugar and 16 bags of cotton from Barbados which had been shipped into Bristol aboard the *Great John*.[61] Elizabeth Yeamans was the most prominent female trader listed in the Port Books of 1671-2 but though she was among the top 12 per cent of importers that year her imports were worth only £785 compared to the top Bristol merchants who were importing between £10,000 and £20,000 worth of goods that same year. Certainly, fewer than a dozen women were still importing sugar and other such goods into Bristol in 1728, a minority of whom were also involved as exporters too. Elizabeth Hollister for example, was listed that year as exporting 1300 glass bottles along with beer bottles and a consignment of 'worsted stuff' [woollens] to Boston aboard the *Cotham* and as importing millico and muscovado sugar into Bristol aboard the *Mary*, the *Katherine* and the *Matilda* of Jamaica.[62]

Tobacco

The overlap between small merchants, retailers and manufacturers involved in colonial produce is neatly illustrated in the tobacco trade. Surviving records show women employed in all its aspects. Elizabeth Alises was listed as one of 11 owners whose Bristol ship the *Alexander* was captured by Dutch privateers in 1666 with a cargo of over 500 hogsheads of Virginian Tobacco.[63] Bristol's Port Books show women importing small amounts of tobacco into Bristol from Virginia along with more established merchants from at least the 1660s. The Quaker, Martha Harford, for example, imported 173 hogsheads of tobacco into Bristol in 1698.[64]

Though most tobacco retailers were men, there were female tobacconists in Bristol too in this early period, such as the Baptist Priscilla Fry, widow of the Wine Street tailor John Fry. The inventory of her spacious premises (she lived over her shop) in 1706 were valued at over £300 and included both quantities of tobacco and also 'tobackopresis' [tobacco presses], 'tobacco wheals' and a 'tobackoingen' [tobacco engine], presumably for their processing. As well as tobacco and tobacco papers, her shop also sold 'barbadus' [Barbados sugar], 'chocke' [chocolate?] and a wide array of other consumables.[65] A marriage settlement of 1753 lists Mary Staines as a tobacconist, and fragmentary references to other such women in leases and advertisements later in the century suggest that women had a longstanding if under-documented involvement in the trade, some probably working with their husbands.[66]

The increasing trade in tobacco also engendered an industry in clay pipes, and the pipe makers' guild established in the mid-seventeenth century included women amongst its founders. Though guild rules stipulated that any further women admitted into the guild would have to be a relative of existing

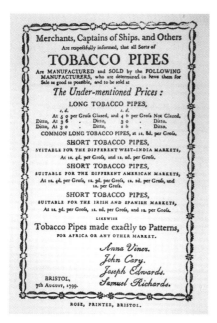

2.10 This 1799 trade announcement by Anna Viner and other manufacturers of clay pipes shows how widows were not always the passive inheritors of their husbands' enterprises as many historians have routinely assumed. *Tobacco Pipe Makers* book, 17 August 1799. BRO 40241. *Bristol Museums, Galleries & Archives*

members, tobacco pipe manufacture did provide an important source of female employment from the mid-seventeenth century. Some female pipe makers seemed to have a respectable living from this trade, such as Rebecca Arthurs, who in 1749 bequeathed her Lewins Mead home, premises and apprentices to her daughters Elizabeth and Margaret Jones.[67] In 1770, Anna Viner (1731-1805), the widow of pipe maker George Viner, publicly announced her move from her house in St Stephens parish to premises in Horse Street (now Host Street) off St Augustine's Back, and advertised herself as one who supplied 'captains and merchants with tobacco pipes for the Africa and American trades'.[68] She expanded her husband's business and acted as manufacturer, retailer and small merchant as she both made her pipes and exported them to Africa, New York, Canada and Barbados, sometimes utilising family connections to do so. [*Fig. 2.10*]

Women and the Slave trade

The fact that Viner shipped some of her pipes aboard slave ships is a reminder that Bristol's slave trade afforded some opportunities for women in the trades and crafts. Five out of the 28 suppliers for Cranfield Becher's slave ship, *Jason Galley* in 1743, were women, including the previously mentioned gunsmith Margaret Braine [*see page 54*]. Margaret Hayhurst, a ship's chandler, was amongst those who supplied James Rogers' slave ship the *Pearl* in 1785. Though women seemed mainly confined to supplying food to Rogers' and other such ships

2.11 Advertisement of sale of slave ship at Mrs Clement's Mud Dock in 1768. The Mud Dock, then located by the present day Prince's Bridge, was where ships were repaired and fitted before the floating harbour was built. Mrs Clement appears to be its proprietor. *FFBJ* 31 December 1768. BRL

by the end of the century,[69] it is worth noting too that in 1768, Catherine Stroud is reported as the co-owner of a Bristol slave ship. That same year the slave ship, the *Kitty*, was being sold by Elizabeth Clements, the female proprietress of Bristol's Mud Dock (one of the Quays for unloading cargo), albeit probably on behalf of male ship owners.[70] [*Fig. 2.11*]

Market Traders
Despite the rise of permanent shops from the late-seventeenth century, foodstuffs and other wares were still sold at markets, fairs or door to door. Sources as diverse as scurrilous poems and Corporation records leave us in no doubt that many of these traders and hawkers were female, and numerous pictures of Bristol street scenes show women with baskets on their heads full of agricultural produce or accompanying pack horses laden with goods.[71] [*Colour plate 5*]

Though such women might be more properly designated as 'the labouring poor', they constituted – as Sheryllynne Haggerty has noted – part of the wider trading community.[72] They were a diverse group and the more well-established and prosperous individuals amongst them could arguably be characterised as members of the middling ranks, especially at the beginning of our period. The respectable farmers' wives who brought their wares into the city from the adjoining counties, and who surface in the press only when they were robbed on their way back from market, indicate it was not just the poorest who had goods to sell.[73]

Eighteenth-century Prostitution in Bristol Marion Pluskota

Popular culture often associates prostitutes with port cities and eighteenth-century Bristol was no exception. Prostitutes' lodgings and places of sociability were spread all over the city during the long eighteenth century. The old centre, with its numerous taverns and its proximity to the docks, was the busiest place for prostitution, but even in the wealthiest parishes of the city, prostitutes could be seen in the streets and it is only later, in the nineteenth century, that residential segregation occurred and that prostitutes were pushed towards the rundown areas of Bristol.

Prostitution commonly occurred in 'disorderly houses' which in Bristol were often alehouses with upstairs rooms. These were not licensed as inns (sometimes not as alehouses either) and it is interesting to notice that prostitutes were often asked to be witness against the owner of such illegal houses. Complaints were made when the people meeting in such premises were too noisy and/or when the neighbours felt threatened, though little action was taken by the magistrates to prevent their reopening.

The attitude of the people of Bristol in the eighteenth century towards prostitutes was marked by episodes of moral panic, which made them target prostitutes and disorderly houses: at the end of the seventeenth century, the Society for the Reformation of Manners targeted lewd women; in 1749, 1751 and 1767 disorderly houses were ransacked whilst soldiers helped prostitutes escape the premises; at the beginning of the nineteenth century, some local reformers decided to open an institution to 'rescue' these women. Yet generally, women who sold their body seemed to have been well integrated in the city, with little evidence of criminal behaviour: only 13% of prostitutes appeared twice (as witness, plaintiff or defendant) in the quarter session archives between 1780 and 1805 in Bristol.

Magistrates during the quarter sessions and assizes did not condemn prostitutes more harshly than other female offenders; however members of the upper middle-class elite (led by women) felt more and more concerned for these women, who were characterized as 'some of the most depraved of the human race'. ■

Bristol Penitentiary. The opening of a female penitentiary or Magdalen hospital in Bristol on 24 June 1801 was part of a wider charitable initiative which aimed both to help and to control the young and poor women under their charge. Time in the reformatory establishment was spent praying, doing needle work or being trained for a future life in domestic service.

BRISTOL PENITENTIARY.
In Magdalen Lane, Established June 24th 1801.

'The Poor Prostitute'
Felix Farley's Bristol Journal, 10 August 1799

The romantic turn in literature also influenced Bristol poets: on 10 August 1799, *Felix Farley's Bristol Journal* published a poem entitled 'The Poor Prostitute', written by one of his readers (whose gender is unknown) under the name Scholasticus. The newspaper editor's willingness to publish Scholasticus' poem suggests that he thought his readership would be receptive to both its choice of subject and its approach. The poem stresses the wretchedness and sadness of a prostitute's life possibly with a view to promoting support for the opening of a refuge or penitentiary for such women. The stereotypes prevailing in the poem's depiction obscure the fact that prostitution could be understood as a rational economic choice for those facing poverty and that becoming a prostitute was not necessarily the result of being seduced and abandoned.

'The Poor Prostitute'

What tho' the prude thy sad request repay
What tho' the coldly virtuous turn away
And the proud Levite walk indignantly by
With harsh reproof instead of charity;

Poor hapless Outcast! Thou shall have my mite,
Why should I chide thy Crimes or mock your Grief?
Why from thy talk of sorrow turn my Sight
And deaf to Pity's voice, withhold Relief?
....

Oh! She was beauteous once and virtuous too
And not e'en Envy dared to stain her Name
Now bitter Tears her sallow cheeks bedew.
Disease and Famine prey upon her frame.

Fled are her virgin honours, virgin charms,
And all the triumphs of her youthful years.
Ah! Fled's the Youth that won'd her to his arms
And poured fond tales of love in her ears.

Think foul seducer, on her cruel fate!
And can't thou look for Mercy from Above?
Ah! No, some secret Curse does him await
Who violates the Rights of virtuous Love.

Scholasticus

An 'old bawd' leading a young woman into prostitution in Samuel Coleman's *St James's Fair*, 1824.
See also colour plate 8

The Welsh traders on Bristol Back (also known as Welsh Back) also illustrate this point. Women sailed in aboard their trows every Wednesday to sell their poultry, fish and dairy products. By the late-eighteenth century, Carl Estabrook reckons, 'as many as 30 women and never more than 4 men' had a public presence at the market there.[74] Though contrasted unflatteringly in 1712 with 'the politer ladies of Queen Square', these 'cackling Dames' with their 'medley stock' of 'feath'd Cacklers'[75] surely qualify for inclusion as members of the middling sort. They had goods of their own to sell and the initiative, organisational skills and social networks that enabled them to profit from regular voyages into the city. In 1767, Mrs Gethen, a 'Fowl Merchant' aged 60, died from 'the fever' whilst voyaging to Bristol to sell her flock. That her death was recorded in the diary of a Welsh schoolmaster in Bristol and that her body was reportedly taken back to her native Monmouthshire to be buried, indicate she was a woman of some social and material standing.[76] By the 1770s, Bristol Corporation kept a register of Welsh traders renting stalls at Welsh Back and 85 per cent of those listed between 1776 and 1778 were women.[77] [*Colour plate 7*] However, it does seem to be the case that the overall status of female market traders diminished by the end of our period as public space became more and more regulated and anxieties about female propriety and class disorder became more apparent.

Medicine

This reminds us that as new opportunities opened up, so others declined, in particular in metal work and medicine. In the early part of our period, women worked as medical practitioners since medical practice was not yet seen as an exclusively male activity.[78] The widow Margaret Page, *alias* Woolfe, in 1681 took on Sarah Saunders, the daughter of a Somerset yeoman from Brislington, contracting to 'teach inform and instruct her according to her best skill and knowledge in the art and business of Doctress and chirurgery which she the sayd Margt now useth.'[79] Mary Fissell estimates that from 1700 to 1750 about half of the surgeons and apothecaries who died in mid-careers were succeeded by their widows in what was then a shop-based career.[80]

Miss Plunket, the daughter of a doctor, is mentioned in a Bristol diary of 1762 as someone who practised surgery 'especially the excision of cancers'.[81] In 1764 the widow of Dr Speakman first advertised in the press that she 'cureth the French distemper' at her late husband's house 'next door to Mr. Whitefield's Tabernacle'.[82] As late as 1775 at least one woman ran a successful apothecary's shop and another, Mrs Clokowski, not only devised cosmetics and hair dyes but advertised herself as a dentist of sorts, cleaning and pulling teeth.[83]

At the same time that women were edged out of the medical profession as physicians and surgeons and the like, the demand for female nurses and midwives grew.[84] A few women achieved managerial status as matrons of hospitals. The socially ambiguous position of the matron is illustrated by the case of Mary Preece. In 1778 she had been elected by the board of 'ladies and gentlemen' in charge of the Bristol Infirmary to serve as head matron. Conscious of the honour and considerable responsibility this post conferred on her, she took her duties seriously. Robert Smith's (senior surgeon at the Royal Infirmary 1812-1843), vivid depiction clearly satirises what he sees as her social pretentions:[85]

> Mrs Preece was a friendly and motherly woman but considered it necessary to keep up a state of dignity in order to over awe the nurses and house-hold. She never appeared but in the full costume of a Lady of those days. Her hair was always toupeed and fully dressed She wore a large pair of mock pearl earrings and a necklace of what was called Machevells's Eyes a pair of white gloves and ruffles decorated her arms and a large patterned stiff brocade gown was stuck out by a hoop. When she visited the wards she was always followed by her servants and the moment she began to move 'Madam is coming' 'Madam is coming' was echoed through the House and all was speedily in order to receive her. She would not reply to the term 'Mistress.' –
> 'Mistress! Don't mistress me! Every wench is mistress now-please to remember that I am "Madam Preece".'[86]

Mrs Preece may have dressed like 'a Lady' but clearly Smith didn't consider her to be one, and if his account is to be believed, Mrs Preece herself was anxious about her status. In any case, his focus on her gentility serves to obscure her actual achievement as the long-serving manager of a major Bristol institution.

Middling women and the knowledge economy: print, teaching and the arts
Readers of *Sketchley's Bristol Directory* of 1775 might conclude that women played little part in Bristol's book and print trades. Of the city's 13 listed booksellers, only one was female and only one woman was cited as a printer. Yet, in fact, Bristol women were involved in the production and dissemination of a burgeoning print culture from the 1660s onwards, as publishers, printers

and booksellers, and most probably – as elsewhere in British and French cities – as hawkers, chapmen and broadside sellers and later as proprietors of circulating libraries.[87] I have documented the history of Bristol's female printers elsewhere, noting that a significant proportion of women in this trade had Dissenting backgrounds and, after 1740, Methodist ones.[88]

Newspaper Proprietors

Women were involved in newspaper publishing in Bristol as early as 1742, but it was in 1753 that Bristol's two main papers, *Felix Farley's Bristol Journal* [hereafter *FFBJ*] and *The Bristol Journal* [hereafter *BJ*], were separately bequeathed to two female relatives. Elizabeth Farley (*c.*1710-1779) took over her husband Felix's paper, *FFBJ*, on his death in 1753 a year after he had split from his brother Samuel Jr. Samuel set up the *BJ* as a rival paper and on his death (also in 1753) the paper was handed on to his niece, Sarah – daughter of another brother, Edward Farley.[89]

Whilst the rivalry and estrangement between these two brothers and their female successors has attracted historical notice,[90] little attention has been given to the wider networks and activities of either woman. But a search of newly available digitised databases reveals that both combined the running of their respective newspapers with other printing contracts. They employed agents to distribute their papers and established links with other newspapers in the region.[91] They also continued the longstanding practice of selling patent medicines and other products from their newspaper offices and in so doing supported some female enterprises.

Both women expressed their political values through their newspapers. A Wesleyan Methodist, Elizabeth Farley was even more wedded to the High Tory cause than her husband had been, and she used her paper to back a virulent campaign against the naturalisation of Jews in 1753 and also pursued an extravagantly worded campaign against alleged Whig corruption which brought her to national attention as the first newspaper proprietor to be (unsuccessfully) prosecuted for libel.[92]

Elizabeth Farley printed a wide range of material between 1755 and 1765, including poetry and at least 23 Methodist books, hymns and pamphlets, among which were sermons by John Wesley and hymns by his brother Charles, with whom she was personally acquainted.[93] She sold these through various booksellers, such as John Palmer, whose father was a leader of one of John Wesley's first bands in Bristol.[94]

Her rival and niece, the Quaker Sarah Farley, was brought up in Exeter, where her father Edward was a printer and where women were not uncommon in the printing trade. Though Edward appears to have bequeathed his Exeter newspaper to her brother, her uncle Samuel left the *Bristol Journal* to her on condition that she remain a Quaker and that, should she choose to get married, she do so within the Society of Friends. Farley ran the *Bristol Journal* from Small Street and later from Castle Green from 1753 until her sudden death in 1774, employing a Quaker foreman and clerk but also utilising the services of John Palmer's Methodist widow Elizabeth,[95] along with those of the Presbyterian printer and bookseller Thomas Cadell, to distribute her publications. In contrast to her aunt's paper, its politics were sufficiently Whiggish for her to become the preferred printer of the Corporation from 1760.[96] When the radical John Wilkes came to address his Bristol supporters in 1771, Sarah Farley showed herself to be, according to the Bristol chronicler John Latimer, 'sufficiently venturesome' to print the speeches of his Bristol supporters whilst ensuring that any direct mention of 'the demagogue's name or his own after-dinner oratory' was 'carefully suppressed'.[97]

Like many printers, including her uncle and grandparents, Sarah Farley sold medicinal remedies but also reportedly published a catalogue of medicines by a visiting Italian doctor and personally testified in favour of a patent remedy.[98] She seems to have been on friendly terms with other Bristol booksellers, through whom she sold her other publications. She ensured the books and papers she printed were distributed beyond Bristol, utilising Thomas Cadell's London contacts and liaising with other provincial newspapers such as the *Salisbury Journal*. She published editions of two of Hannah More's plays,[99] letters on the building of Bristol Bridge by the architect John Wood[100] and sermons by the Anglican divine and economic reformer Josiah Tucker.[101]

By the 1770s, Sarah Farley's circle included not only Quakers like Sarah Champion Fox and the industrialist William Cookworthy but Evangelicals like Hannah More and Thomas Skone, a young surgeon at Bristol's Infirmary who courted her unsuccessfully before leaving for the Caribbean. Sarah Champion Fox affords us a rare if somewhat eulogistic appraisal of Sarah Farley's public reputation, recording in her diary shortly after her friend's unexpected death that:

> She had been to us a near and very kind neighbour, and her benevolence and universal acquaintance rendered her removal a great loss and generally regretted. Men of distinguished abilities, of all ranks and descriptions, resorted to her house and were fond of her conversation. She succeeded

her father or her uncle in the printing business, and it was not by education, but by superior talents that she emerged from obscurity. The poor bewailed her death as the loss of a benefactor. She was a single woman, but was at this time *earnestly* solicited to become a wife by her neighbour [the merchant] Wm. Green, whose entreaties had hitherto been unavailing.[102]

Farley was clearly a woman of intellectual substance with an extensive network of accomplished people. The esteem in which she was widely held was further indicated by the fact that in 1777, three years after her death, her paper was renamed *Sarah Farley's Bristol Journal* by its male proprietors.

It seems odd, given the family and commercial rivalry between Elizabeth and Sarah Farley that Sarah bequeathed the newspaper to Elizabeth's daughter Hester. Certainly, her foreman, Samuel Bonner, and her ex-Clerk, Thomas Middleton, both Quakers, refused to work with Hester, preferring to go on to found another longstanding Bristol paper, *Bonner and Middleton's Bristol Journal*.[103] But it seems unlikely that their action was prompted by religious differences, for although Hester was a friend of Susannah Wesley, Charles Wesley's daughter, she became the wife of Thomas Rutter, a local Quaker brush manufacturer and preacher who had been a visitor to her Aunt Sarah's home.[104]

Hester Farley briefly ran the paper whilst her mother was still running *Felix Farley's Bristol Journal*, but soon sold it in 1775 to the Routh Brothers, George and William – the men who renamed the paper after Sarah.[105] It seems that Sarah Routh, the widow of William, then took over the business in 1800 and continued until selling it in 1806. A surviving invoice she issued in 1805 proudly proclaims her as the 'printer of *Sarah Farley's Bristol Journal*'.[106]

Schoolmistresses and School Proprietors
Female school teachers worked in Bristol since at least the late medieval period. Margery Manymoney was employed as a schoolmistress in the All Saints parish church school in Corn Street as early as 1467.[107] Women continued to play a role both as teachers and educational promoters in the centuries that followed. The first post-medieval parish school in Bristol (reportedly the second in the nation) was funded by a bequest from Mary Gray of Temple parish in 1699, and women played a significant part in the provision of both private and charitable schools throughout the period.[108] Jonathan Barry lists 26 female teachers recorded in the city before 1700 and 76 between 1700 and 1775, but there were also others running informal dame schools, such as the 'old woman' who taught reading to the Bristol pipe maker and poet John

Frederick Bryant.[109] Women's role as schoolmistresses and teachers is on the one hand traditionally feminine but could also be innovative, depending on the individual involved. There was a world of difference between Joan Dixon, the ill-educated, elderly schoolmistress at The Red Maids' School dismissed from her post in 1723 for not keeping up with the 'new regime', and some of the more dynamic and cultivated women such as Selina Mills, who ran one of the city's leading female schools later in the century.[110]

Girls' boarding schools began to proliferate by the 1740s as the expansion of Bristol's cultural life and the increasing gentility of its upper middling ranks provided ever more avenues for female employment in such professions as teaching and personal services. The widow of the Rev. Mr Becher was running a boarding school in the exclusive area of College Green in 1743 and one Mrs Bickers advertised hers that same year.[111] The curriculum of such genteel schools, so far as they had one, seems in most cases to have been geared to teaching 'young ladies' of a certain class the accomplishments needed to secure a husband. There was some anxiety that this might preclude the more utilitarian skills such as needlework and housewifery that women needed to be useful in the home, and it is telling that such skills were certainly taught in the charity schools where the Dissenting women had a strong presence – such as the Ladies Charity School set up in 1755 for the express purpose of 'teaching [poorer] girls to read and spin'.[112]

Anne Barbara Rosco, an embroiderer who reportedly came to Bristol from London, first opened a boarding school on St Michael's Hill in 1749 for 'little masters as well as misses' with her husband, a well-known retired comedian at Jacob's Well theatre in the city. Widowed in 1762, she then set up a companion school for young ladies with her daughters and a French teacher. The students there certainly did a good deal of embroidery, but the ethos of the school seems to have been more imaginatively progressive than was perhaps conventionally the case. One of her daughters, an established actress who had performed in Drury Lane, gave up her own career to help her mother. By the late 1760s, Mrs Rosco was staging public reading events to celebrate the achievements of her star pupils and was lauded in verse for championing the cultivation of the female intellect. At least one of her pupils went on to open her own day school in the less genteel environs of Stokes Croft.[113]

The spinster sisters of Hannah More opened their school in 1758, first near College Green, for 'daughters of the affluent'. This school was apparently underwritten by a female patron, Ann Lovell Gwatkin, the cultivated Cornish wife of a Bristol soap manufacturer who had inherited money from her father.[114] By 1762, the school had prospered sufficiently to take on 60 pupils and had to relocate to larger premises in Park Street. It continued to flourish and numbered Mary Darby (later Mary Robinson (1756/8?-1800) amongst its pupils.

By 1775, schools had proliferated to such an extent that half of the 47 schoolteachers or proprietors of schools listed in *Sketchley's* were women. Women ran half of the existing 10 boarding schools for girls. The precise number of schools is difficult to establish as it is unclear if some of those listing themselves as schoolmistresses or masters ran an establishment of their own. A noticeable divide emerges between those schools situated in high-prestige areas such as Clifton Hill and those 'schools for children' run in the back courts of poorer central parishes.

By the end of the century, the school established by the More sisters was being run by their protégée, Selina Mills, the Anglican daughter of Robert Mills – a Quaker bookseller and publisher in Bristol. Running a school in a competitive environment could be testing. Then, as now, a reputation for propriety was crucial for a school's survival, and Mills's school came under threat in the 1790s when one of her pupils, a 14-year-old 'sun kissed' West Indian heiress, eloped with the adventurer Richard Vining Perry to Gretna Green. Though Mills's school survived, the trial that followed proved an ordeal for Mills, personally as well as professionally.[115]

Despite such pressures, boarding schools proliferated.[116] By 1829, the Unitarian social reformer Mary Carpenter had returned to Bristol to help her mother to run her boarding school.[117] A year later, in 1830, Emma Martin (1812-1851), a dedicated Baptist, founded a short-lived ladies' Baptist academy in the city. By 1835, she had become the editor of *The Bristol Literary Magazine* and shortly thereafter was a free-thinking socialist campaigner.[118]

More progressive and child-centred methods of teaching, advocated by Sarah Guppy and others, were also beginning to be adopted by more innovative educators in Bristol. For example, Mr and Mrs Evans's school for young ladies in St James's Square offered a 'polite and liberal education conducted in the spirit of [the Swiss educational reformer Johann Heinrich] Pestalozzi's methods.'[119]

With a little capital, a woman running her own school could make a respectable living,[120] although female schoolteachers, who along with govern - esses proliferated by the end of our period, were poorly paid. Both local employers and aspiring governesses seemed to assume that 'a high salary [was] not so much an object as domestic comfort and kind treatment'.[121] Nonetheless, it is clear that women school proprietors and their female employees made a significant contribution to the spread of literacy and expanded the cultural horizons of those whom they taught.

Actors and Artists

The contribution women made to the expansion of the city's knowledge economy was not confined to publishers and teachers. Itinerant women actors, performers and artists also enlivened and broadened the city's cultural life as they sought to make a living from their craft. Home-grown talents included the Bristol-born actresses Jane Hippisley (1719-1791) and her sister Elizabeth Hippisley (1742-1789), the daughters of the impresario and actor John Hippisley, who ran a theatre at Jacob's Well. Both sisters worked in London, Bath and Bristol during their careers and Jane, who performed at the opening of Bristol's King Street Theatre in 1766, was much acclaimed in the press – despite the rumours that she had a son (Samuel Cautherley, born *c.*1747) by the celebrated actor-manager David Garrick.[122] [*Fig. 2.12*] Jane, who later married to become Mrs Green, died in 1791. But intriguingly the memorial that her artist son John Green had designed for her in the hopes she would be buried at St Paul's Cathedral was not approved and in the end his mother was buried in St Andrew's Church, Clifton. The epitaph he composed pointedly celebrates her respectability:

> as a comedian she was…deservedly admired in public, while in private life her virtues gained her distinguished esteem.[123]

The itinerant artist, Sarah Harrington, was also a tutor, writer and inventor and an advocate of women's education. She worked in Bristol for some months in 1775 before going on that same year to patent her invention (the pantograph). This device, which reduced reflections from a camera obscura down to miniature size, enabled her to offer accurate and relatively cheap 'likenesses' of her clients. Harrington went on to establish herself as one of the leading miniaturist silhouettists in the country, and she and her Bristol business partner and fellow artist Sarah Collins exemplified a commercial acumen not usually associated with women artists in this era.[124] More typical perhaps was a Miss Milton who in 1783 operating from Mrs Quinn's Clare Street fruit shop, advertised herself as a portrait painter offering customers 'striking likenesses' for a fee of 1-3 Guineas.[125]

Catherine Andras (1775-1860) whose life-sized wax effigy of Nelson now

2.12 1803 etching by an unknown artist of Jane Green née Hippisley (1719-1791) playing Mrs Cadwallader in Simon Foote's 1757 play *The Author*. Green toured London, Bath and Bristol as a noted comedienne. (NPG D2803). ©*National Portrait Gallery, London 2015*

2.13 Model of Nelson now at Westminster Abbey. The model was made by the Bristol-born Catherine Andras who was appointed 'modeller in wax' to Queen Charlotte in 1802.
Courtesy Dean and Chapter of Westminster

stands in Westminster Abbey, [*Fig. 2.13*] was born in Bristol to Moravian parents. She worked there as a toy modeller in wax in her widowed mother's toy and perfume shop in Clare Street before patrons got her to London where she exhibited her miniature wax models at the Royal Academy from 1799. She was appointed 'modeller in Wax' to Queen Charlotte in 1802, the same year Madame Tussaud first arrived in England with her own wax models. Forgotten in her native city, Andras's likenesses of political and royal figures can now be seen at the British Museum, the Royal Collections and the Victoria and Albert Museum.[126]

An important member of the Bristol school of painters which flourished in the first two decades of the nineteenth century was Rolinda Sharples (1793-

1838). Her mother, the artist Ellen Sharples (1769-1849), was born to a wealthy Quaker family and was the third wife of the painter James Sharples (1751/2-1811), from whom she learned her craft, since before becoming her husband, he was her drawing teacher. All three of their children worked as artists, but it was their daughter Rolinda whose career was to become the most notable. [*Colour plate 9*] After an extended sojourn in America, the Sharples family returned to England and on the death of her husband in 1811, Ellen and her daughter settled in Clifton. Their respective careers, which span America and Britain, are documented elsewhere.[127] Significantly, Ellen began as an amateur but was driven to accept paid commissions in order to safeguard her family's financial security. Noted for her deft copies of her husband's portraits of George Washington and other notables, she also did some original work and, like her daughter, exhibited at London's Royal Academy.[128]

Though Ellen presents herself in her diary as retiring from artistic activity in 1811 to devote herself to her daughter's career, she actually supported herself for almost 40 years as a miniaturist, and she took commissions for her needlework and other painting. Ellen Sharples was careful to cultivate a respectable reputation and to network with other artists. Associated with the Bristol Society of Artists, whose members included the men who comprised the Bristol School of Painters, Ellen's contribution to the city's cultural infrastructure has been overshadowed by her male counterparts. Significantly her legacy of over £6,000 and the gift of family paintings establish her as the main patron of the Bristol Academy for the Promotion of Fine Arts, later Bristol's Royal West of England Academy.[129]

Rolinda Sharples's contribution to the city is of a different order. Her vivid paintings were of Bristol and her witty depiction of real people at real places and events, such as St James's Fair, and the Clifton Racecourse, show her to have been a keen social observer engaged with the economic and political issues of the day. She documented such high-profile events as a credit crisis in the city in 1826 (*The Stoppage at the Bank*) and the aftermath of the 1831 Bristol Riot (*The Trial of Colonel Brereton*) painted in 1834. Exhibited both locally and nationally, her paintings helped to shape the city's image of itself.[130]

Women writers

One of the earliest books printed in Bristol (in 1714) was written by Lady Frances Norton to her cousin Elizabeth Freke and entitled *A Miscellany of Poems Compos'd and Work'd with a Needle on the Back and Seats etc. of Several Chairs and Stools*. Lady Norton first stitched her verses into the chairs and stools she embroidered at her husband's estate at Leigh Court in Abbot's Leigh near Bristol. Her pious admonition that stitching was more suited to women than writing – 'Needles best Pens for Ladies are'[131] – reminds us that writing, especially for the public, was still seen by many to be an unsuitable occupation for women. Those women who did venture to publish usually did so under the mantle of religious testimony and had the patronage which enabled them to get in print.

Quaker women such as Dorcas Dole had published in the 1680s on behalf of the Society of Friends. But though Hannah More and Mary Robinson were beginning to make their mark as writers later in the eighteenth century, few Bristol women found their way into print except in religious testimonials. Progressive publishers such as the Methodist editor of the *Bristol Chronicle*, William Pine, had begun to invite contributions from 'the learned, the witty, the curious and the candid from both sexes' as early as 1760,[132] but attitudes about the propriety of women participating in the public arena, and in particular increasing anxieties about sexual reputation as proto-Victorian notions of 'respectability' become more hegemonic, meant that most women writers were more likely to write anonymously or under a male pseudonym. In 1799, the female editor of the diary of the Methodist philanthropist Elizabeth Johnson, did not put her name to the volume which William Pine published.[133]

Few men and a good deal fewer women in the city had access either to the education or the patronage enjoyed by such literary luminaries as Hannah More (1745-1833) and more infamously Mary Robinson (1757-1800), whose notoriety as the mistress of the Prince of Wales and other gallants obscured the fact that she wrote seriously both about women's education and other social issues and was often published in the Bristol press. A famous if short-lived exception was Ann Yearsley (bap. 1753-1806), or Lactilla the 'milkmaid poetess'. Yearsley, whose poem 'On the Inhumanity of the Slave Trade' was published the same year as Hannah More's on 'Slavery', was a more complex and accomplished figure than the rustic milkmaid she was later characterised to be [*colour plate 12*]. The self-educated wife of a Clifton smallholder, she had been rendered destitute and literally starving when the family property was enclosed by the Merchant Venturers. More learned of her plight and became her patron. [*Fig. 2.14*] She utilised her extensive social contacts to raise subscriptions in order to get Yearsley published. But the relationship ended in the utmost acrimony. For, having raised the monies to publish Yearsley's work, More was gravely affronted by Yearsley's subsequent wish to share control of her earnings with her Trustees – namely More and the aristocratic

2.14 *Miss More Presenting the Bristol Milkwoman to Mrs. Montague* [sic]. This engraving illustrates Yearsley's dependence on the patronage of Hannah More who in turn deferred to her social superior Elizabeth Montagu. All three women were writers but the differences in rank and wealth variously determined their public reputations.
UBLSC

Miſs More *presenting the* BriſtolMilkwoman *to* Mʳˢ Montague.

bluestocking Elizabeth Montagu. Yearsley was partly motivated by a wish to protect her children's inheritance, but she also wanted to establish for herself a more dignified and less servile public identity.[134] Before their split, More complacently boasts to a friend about her success in raising monies for the publication of 'Mrs. Yearsley's Manuscripts':

> I continue to get fresh subscriptions every day, quite unsolicited. You will be glad to hear that I have near eight hundred names. Mrs. Montagu has given twenty Guineas, Lord Stormont 5, Duke of Northumberland 5 – In short I have met with so much kindness and liberality on this occasion that it is in danger of making me in love with the world.[135]

More, who was about to move to more commodious premises in Wrington, outside of Bristol, then betrays her defensively superior attitude toward Yearsley by disingenuously characterising herself as being as poor as her protégée:

> I know you wou'd not forgive me if I did not say a word of Cowslip Green. I have signed and sealed; and I hear they are building at a ruinous Rate. I wish I may not be tempted to convert some of Lactilla's Guineas into Shrubs, and to embellish my little lawn with her bank bills. Don't you think the temptation is perilous, when one poor bard is broker to another?[136]

Yearsley continued as a published author after her banishment from More's favour, and a play she wrote was staged in both Bristol and Bath in 1789. But though she initially enjoyed the esteem of more radical circles, the lack of patronage began to take its toll. Her poetic repudiation of a powerful Bristol mayor, whose henchman had beaten up her son for trespass and whose intimidating behaviour subsequently caused Yearsley herself to miscarry, was itself a political challenge. In 1793, friends helped install her in her circulating library in Hotwells, which she ran with moderate success, stocking radical books for her readers.[137] In 1795, her literary reputation was sufficiently intact to attract a well-known firm of progressive London publishers, who published her novel *The Royal Captive*. But her star was waning and in 1796 ill health and family tragedy precipitated her move to Melksham, where she died. Feted in her heyday, she was briefly part of the radical literary network that involved Southey and Cottle, and a 1787 engraving of 'the Bristol milk woman and poetess' shows a self-possessed woman with a dignified expression. Her tombstone in St Andrew's Churchyard in Clifton proclaimed her as 'The Bristol poetess'. Yet in the political backlash that followed the French Revolution, when Yearsley's old friends retrospectively distanced themselves from her in their memoirs, her talent was called into question and her very image recast and denigrated.[138]

By the end of the century and into the end of our period, however, despite the growing anti-radicalism and emphasis on female propriety, there were increasing avenues for women to be published if they could get the patronage. Though subscription was still a major way of achieving the finance needed and though one still needed social networks to obtain subscribers, the ranks of the professional and middling classes were expanding and with them the numbers of would-be subscribers. Anne Powell's poems on Clifton and Hotwells, which describes her 'native city' in 1821, numbers the Quaker teacher Sarah Hoare of Frenchay among her subscribers, and Hoare herself published some poems on botanical themes in the same period.[139]

However, for those without capital, the road to publication was still a real struggle. The story of Mary Bryan, a widowed printer who aspired to become a published author, is a case in point. Though intellectually cultivated, she lacked the money and patronage to be part of Bristol's literary circles and ultimately had to leave her city to achieve a more established literary career.

Mary Bryan's husband, a locally prominent printer (whose mother had previously run the family business), did not approve of his wife publishing works under her own name. However when he died prematurely, leaving the family in debt, Mary, who had six children and faced financial ruin had no choice but to take on the business and to try and supplement her income through her own publications.[140] Assisted by the practical support of her ageing parents, she solicited the financial assistance of family friends and sought the patronage of literary figures, including Sir Walter Scott, with whom she had a long-term correspondence. In 1815, she self-published a collection of sonnets under the name of the family firm, justifying her temerity in going 'public' on the grounds of economic necessity. Significantly, she dedicated her verses to the writer Charlotte Smith, who, like her, had a difficult life and also wrote to provide for her children.[141] Despite financial anxieties and ill health she continued to run the printing business until 1826, and also published *A Sketch of the Life of the Late Richard Reynolds of Bristol*, honouring that nationally prominent Quaker ironmaster and philanthropist.[142] Bryan secretly remarried to a surgeon at the Bristol Infirmary who was disinherited for making an imprudent marriage. They were forced to move to Suffolk where he found a new post and it was here that Mary, despite losing her sight, made a career as the published novelist, Mrs Bryan Bedingfield. Her difficulties in making a living as an author and printer attest to the particular limitations individual women whatever their determination and talent still faced in the public arena.[143]

Women, charity and 'social entrepreneurs'

Edward Colston and Richard Reynolds are to this day remembered as icons of Bristol's charitable largesse,[144] but how did charitable provision change over this period? What role did women play in the funding and running of the city's charitable institutions and how might a gendered analysis illuminate our understanding of these questions? Aside from individual bequests, Bristol's traditional charitable institutions were financed by endowments and variously administered by the parish, the Corporation or trustees acting on behalf of an individual trust. The almshouses, hospitals, schools and doles so financed were the means by which individuals could work for their spiritual redemption and by which they and the communal associations could ensure the continuing stability of a hierarchical civic society.

Though women, especially widows, played a significant role in charitable giving, mainly through individual bequests and as fundraisers, it was men who played the dominant role in the provision and administration of Bristol's established endowed charities, even of those funded by women. Of the 23 charities reportedly endowed between 1666 and 1789, plus those reported by

John Cranidge in 1818, eight (just over a third) were funded by women and this is probably an underestimate.[145] For example, neither an almshouse in Milk Street, established in 1722 by the will of Elizabeth Blanchard, nor Mrs Mary Webb's charity, which set up a school in Fishponds near Bristol in 1729, were included in this list.[146] Some women's legacies to charities were, as time went on, absorbed under the names of other charities and thus forgotten as in the case of a charity founded in 1799 by Mary Beck which was subsequently absorbed into the Charities Relief in Need Fund. Women's contribution to charities was not always fully acknowledged. The founding of Bristol's first charity for the blind is usually credited to Richard Reynolds and the sugar refiner, Alderman John Merlott, yet it seems to have been Merlott's surviving sister Elizabeth who, in 1810, bequeathed the largest amount to it.[147] And while Mary Ann Peloquin's 1779 bequest of £19,400 was one of the largest of that century, her reputation in succeeding years was dwarfed by those of Edward Colston and Richard Reynolds.[148]

By the eighteenth century, the endowed charities had been joined by a new type of philanthropic organisation, known as voluntary or subscription societies. These were more varied and responsive to the economic and political concerns of a modernising city.[149] Some of these, such as the Colston Societies, restricted their membership to 'Gentlemen', but the Bristol Infirmary, established in 1738, numbered women amongst its founding subscribers.[150] So, too, did The Bristol Library Society, which replaced the more elitist King Street library in 1773 and included at least a dozen women subscribers, though as late as 1791 'ladies' were not formally admitted to the new library.[151] By the late 1770s, these newer types of voluntary society proliferated drawing new players into charitable provision. Elizabeth Braine was the first Secretary and Treasurer of the Bristol Dispensary for the Relief of the Sick Poor and by the end of our period, four of its nine largest subscribers were women.[152] Clearly, voluntary societies afforded a more flexible outlet for the energies of women from the middling ranks at a time when ideas about female propriety and domesticity rendered them too genteel for paid employment.

But although this period sees the expansion of a specifically female form of voluntary activity, the leadership of most such organisations continued to be male dominated. Their division of labour often reflected that existing in Nonconformist chapels, with women's committees organising day-to-day activities such as visiting the needy, but with men having the final say in overall management. The degree of female autonomy and reformist intent varied from society to society, but women-headed organisations were smaller and poorly resourced.[153] Some, like the Bristol Auxiliary Bible Society, were focused on evangelising the poor as a way towards social improvement. Others were involved in issues which were seen as extensions of female domestic concerns, like the Female Misericordia and the Bristol and St Phillips Dorcas Societies, which specialised in supporting 'lying-in' women (that is, those giving birth). These societies would not cater for single mothers, restricting their largesse to married women with local connections, unlike the more inclusive Lying-in Society.[154] By 1801, we see the rise in Bristol, as elsewhere, of 'magdalens' or asylums for 'fallen women'; headed by men but staffed by women visitors and matrons.[155] [*See pages 64 to 65*].

The many 'single-issue' charities which arose in the period such as the Bristol Samaritan Society, the Strangers' Friends Society and the Asylum for Poor Orphan Girls, co-existed with charitable bequests for homeless women such as the £200 willed by Mrs Mary Gresley of St Thomas parish, the profits of which were 'to be used to hire as many rooms as possible to accommodate poor industrious women of parish not receiving alms, each to have a room for rest of [their] life...'[156] It is harder to categorise the wide-ranging charitable work of Elizabeth Johnson (1721-1798) who worked under the Wesleys in a variety of evangelising and philanthropic endeavours including working with the blind and assisting two young Africans who had been kidnapped by slave traders. The daughter of a West India merchant, she did not come into the family inheritance until her sixties on account of her Methodist and anti-slavery beliefs but was memorialised in print as a woman 'well known in the city of Bristol for more than half a century for her piety and benevolence.'[157]

The turn of the nineteenth century also sees the rise of mutual aid or 'friendly societies', into which working people paid subscriptions in order to fund their funerals or draw sick or unemployment relief in times of need. Female friendly societies were established in the city as early as 1795, with the founding of a club in the parish of St Mary Redcliffe whose members saw 'no reason why women…who are exposed to equal if not greater Sufferings [than men in terms of sickness and misfortunes] should not unite'.[158] By 1803, there were no fewer than 15 such registered societies for women, comprising some 939 members. This meant that 20 per cent of all registered friendly societies in Bristol that year were female, exceeding the national average of 5 per cent. These apparently female-led organisations (where husbands and children were explicitly barred from membership) were thought to have attracted women working in the city's manufacturing and service industries.[159]

The period between 1790 and 1830, then, saw the emergence both of mutual aid societies amongst the lower orders which were more resistant to forms of external control and an array of new subscription charities led by different factions within the middling ranks. The paternalism (or in some cases the maternalism) and condescension that such charities often exhibited toward those they were trying to help are grating to our more modern sensibilities. Nonetheless, some of the new charities had an explicitly reformist agenda and were pioneering in their day. One example is the Bristol Adult School Society established in 1813 which founded some 18 single-sex schools catering for over 500 men and women in Bristol by 1814. Thomas Pole is rightly associated with the rise of the adult school movement both nationally and locally, but it is a Bristol woman whom he credits for both founding Bristol's first school 'for those of her own sex', and for being a 'zealous campaigner in the cause of educating the adult poor'. Yet, by her own request, she remains anonymous in Pole's published account of the movement. Such were the prevailing notions of female modesty.[160]

Women from Dissenting, especially Quaker and Unitarian, backgrounds predominate in the most progressive of these new types of subscription associations. When we piece together the various activities of the individual women so engaged, we can see both how important social, religious and family networks were and how certain such women played a significant role in reformist activity. Today we use the term 'social entrepreneurship'[161] to denote those ethically informed campaigning organisations that are financially self-sustaining. Some of the women discussed below are better understood as social entrepreneurs rather than as traditional 'lady bountifuls'.

One such forgotten campaigner was Susannah Morgan, a wealthy spinster in Clifton who in 1815 published an excoriating and well-informed pamphlet on the state of Bristol's gaols. It is telling that she felt she had to do so anonymously (though it was soon publicly attributed to her). She also wrote to the local press under her own name urging the adoption of Bentham's Panopticon[162] plan for prison construction, which was advocated in her pamphlet.[163] In 1812, Morgan had also published the rather coyly titled *Hints towards the Formation of a Society for Promoting a Spirit of Independence among the Poor*. This led directly to the establishment of The Prudent Men's Society 'for the purpose of encouraging thrift among the poor'. Although the Society was headed by the philanthropists Richard Reynolds and T. Sanders, Morgan was was also a founding member of The Society for Promoting a Spirit of Independence among the Poor which seems to have become The Prudent Men's Society. The Society initially had separate men's and women's management committees and

Morgan was the secretary of the latter. The committees soon merged and by 1820, 14 of its 32 members were female.[164] Morgan also served for many years on the management committee of the Savings Bank, an allied institution which afforded banking to working men and which by 1830 numbered five women amongst its 25 managers.[165]

Under the aegis of the Savings Bank, Morgan and other women tried to set up a fundraising event in aid of 'Distressed Manufacturers'[166] and it seems likely that she was behind an Association for the employment of prisoners.[167] By 1820, Morgan was a shareholder in the Bristol Institution for the Advancement of Science and, soon after, a major sponsor of Thomas Manchee's report on Bristol Charities.[168]

Sarah Maria Guppy (1770-1852), whose talents as an inventor are again beginning to be recognised,[169] was also engaged in social enterprises. Luminaries such as Thomas Telford and Isambard Kingdom Brunel acknowledged her ideas about bridge and railway construction and she is credited with a diverse and widely reported range of patented inventions, some of which were under her own name and some under those of her first and second husbands. Her ideas include more domestically oriented ones such as a machine that brewed coffee or tea whilst boiling an egg, a cooker hood and a bed which doubled as a storage facility and exercise machine. If the last attracted ridicule by a supercilious male reviewer, most of the press at the time seemed mainly respectful of her achievements.[170]

Surviving documents also establish Sarah Guppy as a social reformer, writer, philanthropist and businesswoman whose interests went well beyond Bristol and Clifton, where she spent her adult life. When married to her first husband Samuel she was a member of Bristol's Lewins Mead Unitarian congregation, who, like the Quakers, had a somewhat less traditionalist view of a women's potential and her inventions suggest she took an active interest in his brass and metalworks business. She was an early investor and promoter of the Clifton Suspension Bridge and a substantial shareholder in the Great Western Railway. She took an active interest in environmental issues, including animal welfare and conservation, and in the education of children. Her proposals for the recruitment of servants and the provision of housing for women of middling and genteel status are an uneasy amalgam of conventional middle-class values and innovative social vision. She lobbied politicians and businessmen to effect various social reforms and her forthright individualism shines through in the few letters and public statements left to us. Like Morgan, she attempted to effect reform at a time when even women of

Changes *in* Women's Occupations *in* Bristol *from* 1775 *to* 1830 Victoria Barnes

Trade directories in the nineteenth and eighteenth centuries included the names, occupations and addresses of the city's notable inhabitants. An analysis of two local directories, *Sketchley's Directory* of 1775 and *Pigot's Directory* of 1830, identifies changes in the patterns of women's employment and opportunities.

Women's names featured in the directories but were in the minority. Though most of those named were clearly male, the gender of some was not always clear. Despite this, it is evident from those whose female identity was clearly indicated that the number of women's occupations listed in the *Directories* increased between 1775 and 1830.

In 1775, just 250 women were noted

By 1830, almost 1,000 were identified as females

In 1775, women had 115 unique occupations

By 1830, this number had risen to 163

The increase in the number of women listed in *Pigot* suggests that the range of opportunities available to women had expanded by 1830.

Yet the fact remains that women were still concentrated within particular industries. Few genuinely new occupational areas existed for women.

Changes in occupations

In 1775, around one fifth of women found employment as victuallers. Victuallers owned or managed inns, taverns and other establishments serving food and drink. By 1830 trends had shifted and the majority of women were employed in the making of clothing.

Clothing was not an area open to female proprietorship. In 1830, men constituted more than 90% of those who *manufactured* clothing.

By 1830 accommodation and inn-keeping by women had declined proportionately, but even so, almost half of the innkeepers listed were women.

Teaching proved consistently to be a feminine occupation.

The most noticeable change between 1775 and 1830 is the growth of 'other trades'. This encompassed professions: bankers, lawyers and state officials, but also largely middle-class women – such as 'Mrs', 'Misses' or 'Lady' – who had no stated occupation.

In 1830, although almost 200 people were listed as being employed in 'nursing and medicine', just one individual was identified as female. ▶

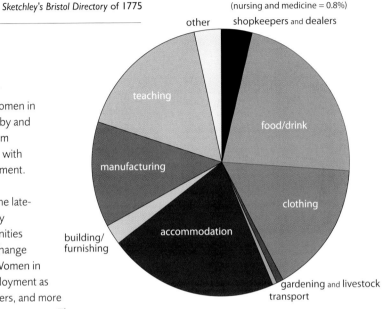

Sketchley's Bristol Directory of 1775

(nursing and medicine = 0.8%)

Labels on pie chart: other, shopkeepers and dealers, teaching, food/drink, manufacturing, clothing, building/furnishing, accommodation, gardening and livestock, transport

The service sector employed most women in Bristol; they were by and large excluded from sectors associated with industrial development.

Although across the late-eighteenth century women's opportunities expanded, such change proved modest. Women in Bristol found employment as innkeepers, teachers, and more generally in the service sector. The overwhelming number of Bristol women listed were recognised for their middle-class status rather than occupation – in stark contrast to the manufacturing cities and towns of the north west. ■

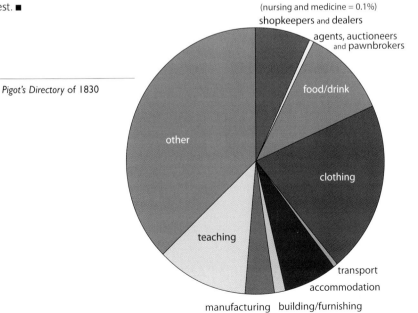

Pigot's Directory of 1830

(nursing and medicine = 0.1%)

Labels on pie chart: shopkeepers and dealers, agents, auctioneers and pawnbrokers, food/drink, other, clothing, teaching, transport, accommodation, manufacturing, building/furnishing

property were excluded from official policy making. She managed both to affirm and challenge conventional notions of bourgeois female propriety. Her second marriage at 67, to a man 30 years her junior, ultimately undermined both her fortune and her subsequent reputation. Overall, her extraordinary life exemplified the difficulties that women of exceptional energy and intelligence had in being taken seriously.[171]

Women and politics

Though women were excluded from formal political power, there were a number of ways in which they participated publicly in politics in this period. The political atmosphere during election time was rumbustious, ribald and often violent. Ordinary women cheered, booed and followed Parliamentary candidates as they processed through the city. They and their more genteel counterparts wore cockades and ribbons to support favoured politicians. The more affluent hosted political candidates at their homes, as Hannah More and her sisters did for Edmund Burke during the election of 1774.[172]

However, public political engagement could leave women open to charges of impiety, immodesty and corruption. As discussed in the previous chapter, daughters and widows of Bristol freemen could convey free status and its attendant voting power on any 'foreigners' who married them. This unusual privilege gave them some standing and influence, especially during elections, though it was increasingly charged by (male) reformers that certain women abused this by taking bribes and conferring voting rights by making marriages of convenience.[173]

As we shall see, some poorer women participated in the riots that erupted in the city throughout the period. A few resisted the impressment of their menfolk through writing letters or even through direct confrontation with the press gangs themselves.[174]

In this era, much of women's political involvement was often mediated through their religious commitments. Dorcas Dole, a radical Quaker, in the 1680s published some accounts of her suffering at the hands of Bristol's civic authorities after she, along with other Friends, was imprisoned for refusing to pay church tithes.[175] Susanna Moore, the widow of the Baptist printer Richard Moore, came to the notice of the authorities for selling seditious literature having received 50 copies of the *Fire of London* by her fellow Baptist the radical London bookseller Elizabeth Calvert.[176]

Later in the period, the evangelical movement, though professedly apolitical, engaged many women in political issues by way of its focus on moral reform. As we have seen, disquiet about the cruelty of the slave trade produced protest poetry in the late 1780s from the Evangelical Hannah More (1745-1833) as well as by her more political and religiously radical former protégée Ann Yearsley. Many Bristol women petitioned about the Queen Caroline affair in 1820 which inspired a popular poetic address by Elizabeth Cranidge, the daughter of a radical Bristol schoolmaster.[177] The campaign against the continued enslavement of Africans in British colonies after the ending of the British slave trade, rallied many Baptist and Methodist women and resulted in the formation in 1829 of the non-denominational Bristol and Clifton Ladies' Anti-Slavery Society. And the gender neutral description of a huge anti-Catholic Emancipation Rally in Queen Square in 1829 suggests women as well as men attended it. Missionary zeal inspired an interest in the campaigns against Sati in India and Mary Carpenter (1807-1877) was amongst those Unitarian men and women who hosted Ram Mohun Roy, the Hindu reformer, in Bristol, which led to her later work in India and her interest in international political issues.[178] [*Colour plate 10*]

Women and Riot

Riotous behaviour was a recurring feature of Bristol's political life throughout this period. Protests against high food prices and tolls mobilised women as well as men. By 1753, the Kingswood rioters, protesting against tolls imposed on them for bringing coal into Bristol, included women and children, the women reportedly carrying stones in their aprons for their men to hurl at the authorities.[179]

Women were certainly found among the crowds present during the so-called Bristol Bridge riots of 1793, when protesters against continuing bridge tolls were indiscriminately fired upon by the Herefordshire militia. Three of the eleven people shot dead were women, and five of the fifty-two wounded. Sarah Wilcox was looking for her husband and had just crossed the bridge when she was shot, the ball passing through her hip and out through her groin; she was made lame and could never work again.[180]

And such abuses by the civic authorities were publicly deplored in verse by Bristol resident Jane Cave Winscom [*Fig. 2.15*] in her poem, 'Thoughts Occasioned by the Proceedings on Bristol-Bridge, and the Melancholy Consequences, on the Awful Night of Monday Last, Being the 30th of September.' Published anonymously, 'by a Lady,' within a week of the event, a revised version under her own name along with another poem which also dealt with both the riot and the wider political issues they raised around civic order and individual rights were published the following year in a compendium of her work. Ann Yearsley, too, versified about the riot, her 'Bristol Elegy' 'offering a feminized, pacifist response to the ill-considered masculine policy' which caused so much suffering to the families of those killed and injured.[181] Though Cave and Yearsley took an explicitly political stance, both were careful not to condone mob violence. Their repudiation of violent social protest was not universally shared by other Bristol women: three years after the riot, feelings still ran high and women were recorded pelting the Herefordshire militia with stones and cursing them as they marched through the city.[182]

Women also seem to have been amongst the rioters seizing overpriced food in the bread riot of 1801[183] and eyewitness accounts of the Bristol Reform Riots of 1831 also attest to the participation of women at a variety of levels. [*Fig. 2.16*] Some middle-class women at first verbally encouraged the protesters but were aghast at the destruction of property that followed. It was reported that 'not a few' of those confronting the authorities on the outskirts of the city at Totterdown were 'women of abandoned character whose violent language seemed well fitted to urge on the mob to desperation'. Women were also among the 170 prisoners liberated by rioters from Bridewell Prison, who horrified respectable witnesses by stripping off their prison clothes and leaving 'almost in a state of nudity', while 'others flung mud at Sir John Wetherell's carriage.[184] Rolinda Sharples's painting portraying the trial of Colonel Brereton, court-marshalled for his conduct during the disturbances, faithfully identifies a surprising number of female members of Bristol's polite society, some of whom actually attended the proceedings.[185] [*Colour plate 10*]

Conclusion

As the Atlantic economy expanded, we have seen that some middling women played an identifiably significant and at times innovative role in the distribution and promotion of new consumer products, the expansion of educational provision and the promotion of print culture. The marital status of such women varied. Widows for example, who made the decision to keep on running their husbands' businesses met that challenge with varying degrees of enterprise and success. [*Fig 2.17*] and this chapter shows how unjust it is to regard them as an undifferentiated and passive constituency.

As the city's economy became increasingly specialised and its professional and political networks more formalised, the evidence suggests that gender and class disparities were recast and more sharply polarised. In Bristol, for

2.15 Jane Cave Winscom first published her 1793 protest poem on the Bristol Bridge riot anonymously but later came out as its author. BRL B9420

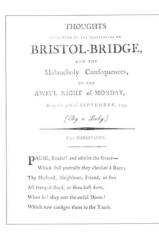

THOUGHTS
OCCASIONED BY THE PROCEEDINGS ON

BRISTOL-BRIDGE,

AND THE

Melancholy Confequences,

ON THE

AWFUL NIGHT of MONDAY,

Being the 30th of SEPTEMBER, 1793.

(By a Lady.)

Price THREEPENCE.

PAUSE, Reader! and admire the Grace—
Which ftill protrafts thy checker'd Race;
Thy Hufband, Neighbour, Friend, or Son
All tranquil flood, as thou haft done,
When lo! they met the awful Doom!
Which now configns them to the Tomb.

2.16 A respectably dressed working woman with a basket full of looted bottles can be seeing fleeing from the Charge of the 3rd Dragoon Guards in Queen Square, 1831 in this 1833 watercolour attributed to both Thomas Leeson Rowbotham and William James Müller. (BMAG M4621). ©*Bristol Culture*

example, although some women benefited from the rise of the permanent shop, the increasing regulation of space in the interests of improvement and social order, did marginalise and ultimately declass those other middling women who lacked the wherewithal to afford permanent premises. Indeed some market traders and women in declining trades such as tobacco pipe making were being jettisoned out of the middling ranks by the early nineteenth century. An initial comparison between *Sketchley's Directory* of 1775 and *Pigot's Directory* of 1830 suggests that, despite the proliferation of new

2.17 This early-nineteenth century trade card advertises Mrs. Elizabeth Ring's china shop.
BRO. *Bristol Museums, Galleries & Archives.*
See also colour plate 6

trades, middling women were in fact being ghettoised into a narrower range of occupations.

Nevertheless, women continued to work as small businesswomen into the early nineteenth century, swelling the numbers of what would later come to be called the lower middle class. But it seems likely they were disadvantaged by the establishment in 1801 of Bristol's Commercial Rooms, which formalised male networking amongst those who were not members of the older Society of Merchant Venturers. Businesswomen were further marginalised by the establishment of the exclusively male Bristol Chamber of Commerce in 1823.

By this time, the increasing dominance of the domestic ideal for women becomes more evident in the popular discourse and seems to have reshaped the way women could make their mark in the public sphere. Some of those who could afford to eschew paid work, especially those from Dissenting backgrounds, continued to play an engaged role in economic and political life under the guise of their philanthropic activities and concerned themselves with such issues as prison reform, debtors, the discipline and welfare of servants and the provision of housing for distressed women of middling rank.[180] Today, such women might be called social entrepreneurs and then, as now, their activities force us to question the designation of economic activity strictly in terms of remunerated work. Likewise, women's actual engagement in political life (be it through riot, participation in election rituals, or petitioning and patronage) is not fully captured by conventional categorisations of political activity.

Limited though most of them were by their lack of access to capital and education, by the demands of constant child-bearing and by the social expectations laid upon them, Bristol women should be seen not as passive ciphers but as individuals who responded to their varying circumstances in different ways. Whilst it is impossible to quantify with precision what impact women had on the institutions and culture of the city, it seems evident from even this preliminary exploration of the sources that both the economy and public life would have been much the poorer without them.

Women in Bristol 1835-1914

June Hannam and Moira Martin

If this were but in truth Aladdin's cave,
How much of toil and trouble we might save!
'We're very poor just now at Barton Hill:
Slave of the Lamp, arise and do my will!'
'Your pleasure, master?'
'Pay this little bill!'[1]

This poem was written for a fund-raising event organised by well-off families in Clifton to contribute to the building of a church in Barton Hill. It was one of many initiatives that illustrate the complex relationship between middle- and working-class women, so central to the history of women in Bristol throughout the nineteenth century. Barton Hill was a working-class area where hundreds of low-paid women were employed in the Great Western Cotton Factory. By contrast, Clifton was an affluent suburb of Bristol where women with substantial wealth could make an impact on public life. The numbers and influence of the urban middle classes had grown with industrialisation and the rapid development of cities. Changes in patterns of work and family life as well as in wealth highlighted the gulf between classes. And yet middle- and working-class women continued to interact in numerous ways. Middle-class women took an interest in social questions affecting the poor, including family poverty and work conditions as well as the spiritual and moral life of working people. Working-class women also sought help from middle-class women; in 1889, for example, striking cotton workers demonstrated on Sunday mornings outside churches in Clifton and Cotham, where the factory owners and their families worshipped, in order to draw attention to their struggle.[2] Strikes posed a challenge to notions of class cooperation that many middle-class women sought to foster, but other issues such as the suffrage campaign could bring women together across the class divide.

Women of all classes contributed to the prosperity of Bristol. Whether as workers or consumers, activists or dependants their presence helped shape the city. The labour of working women provided the foundation for the development of industries that were to sustain Bristol's prosperity. For the most part middle-class women were not engaged in paid employment, which implied a loss of status, but they did participate in the economic, political and cultural life of the city.[3] They instigated new forms of social action, often derived from their traditional roles as carers and moral guardians of the family, and thereby made their mark on the city.[4] They not only took part in mixed-sex bodies, but also formed single-sex groups which focused in particular on the needs of women and children. Indeed, the nineteenth century was the high point of a rich associational life amongst middle-class women through which they effectively redefined the place of women in local society and in the social space of the city.[5] The varied ways in which women made an impact on the city of Bristol in the nineteenth century, and their changing relationship to public life, will be explored in the following chapter.

Economic turmoil in the 1830s and 40s

The 1830s to the 1840s was a turbulent time for working people as they faced threats to their employment from trade depression and changes in production methods. Bristol had a diverse economy but did not experience industrial growth on the scale seen in the North. As the old staple industries of wool, brass and glass declined so new trades based on materials such as tobacco and cocoa flourished. Nonetheless, most industries were based on workshop rather than factory methods of production and this meant that productivity and wages were low.[6] Women's earnings were on average one third those of men and therefore women and girls were particularly affected by the low wage economy. Many were employed as outworkers, making clothing, boots and shoes and pins at home. Charleton's pin making firm in Kingswood, for example, employed about 110 female workers in the factory in 1841, while another 500 women and girls worked as outworkers.[7]

Although outwork continued in many industries, new forms of production were introduced in others. In the east of the city the Great Western Cotton Factory was completed in 1838. Employing 2000 workers, mostly women, it was the largest mill in the south of England.[8] [*Fig. 3.1*] The industrial development of this area continued with a tannery and later board mills and a cardboard box-making factory, while housing was built for the factory workers. Old and new industries formed the basis for the wealth of the industrial and mercantile elite, and many of the women who were most influential in the nineteenth century were members of these elite families.[9]

3.1 The Great Western Cotton factory by Samuel Loxton (1857-1922), a Bristol illustrator. BRL

Political movements in the first half of the nineteenth century

The 1830s and 1840s were marked by political as well as economic change. Working-class women were involved in the numerous protest movements in this period, although they are rarely mentioned in press and official reports and so can be difficult to find.[10]

Owenite Socialism

One movement which attracted women was Owenite Socialism, named after the textile manufacturer Robert Owen. He proposed that workers should live in agricultural communities with tasks, including child care, shared communally. An emphasis was placed on co-operative forms of manufacture and also of trading, with shops being set up to fund activities. Owen's followers established communities in the 1820s which developed a vision of a new world in which not only the structure of work would be changed, but also relationships between men and women, including marriage (and the legal restrictions on divorce). Lecturers preached this message throughout the country and the attempt to address sexual oppression drew considerable female support.[11]

The focus on community meant that all members of the family were attracted by Owenism. They attended Sunday assemblies in Bristol where there was an address, music, poetry and the singing of social hymns.[12] When Robert Owen spoke at a meeting in the city it was reported in the *Bristol Gazette* that at least 5,000 attended including many females and young persons.[13] Although women do not appear to have held office in the Bristol group, Emma Martin, née Bullock (1812-51) did come to prominence.[14] The daughter of a cooper who died just after her birth, she was independent-minded from an early age, joining the Particular Baptist sect at 17 and being part of a Bible society for 4 years. She set up her own Ladies' seminary at the age of 18 and three years later married a Baptist brick and tile maker. She ran her school, with her sister, giving her first public lecture on education in 1838. Emma Martin left her husband after he had dissipated her inheritance and then became involved in Owenism. Her talents were soon recognised and she became a lecturer paid by the Central Board, but this entailed a move to London and thereafter she had little further impact in Bristol.

Chartism

Chartism was another key working-class movement in the 1830s and 40s which aimed for political and social reforms.[15] The People's Charter of 1838 set out six points to achieve a more democratic system, including adult male suffrage. Women took part in the movement throughout the country but are rarely mentioned in books and pamphlets about Bristol Chartism.[16] Nonetheless they were clearly involved. One report of a meeting in 1838 noted that only about 500 attended and most of these were women and children.[17] David Jones claims that Bristol was one of those towns where Chartists had social and educational institutions for all members of the family. Women formed their own separate groups and often came together to pool their resources – for example, women employed at a pipe factory in Bristol joined with Chartist women to call for improvements in their work conditions.[18] The failure of the Chartist uprisings of 1839-40 was followed in Bristol by the setting up, with female assistance, of co-operative stores and women were also active in raising money for the wives and families of those imprisoned and deported. Jones notes that Bristol was one of many towns in which female organisations continued well after 1842.[19]

Anti-Slavery campaigning

Middle-class women were far more visible in social and political reform movements during this period and were certainly not confined by domestic concerns. The cause of anti-slavery quickly attracted female support.[20] Individual women became involved, sometimes working alongside male relatives and friends and at others forming their own, single-sex groups. This was a pattern that continued through the nineteenth century – both sexes worked together but increasingly women formed women-only spaces in which to make their mark.

Bristol was at the forefront of the anti-slavery campaign, partly because of its links with the slave trade and also because it had a high proportion of non-conformist professional families who were concerned with social questions. In 1840 a small group of Clifton women, predominantly from a Quaker background, formed the Bristol and Clifton Ladies' Anti-Slavery Society (B&CLASS) as an auxiliary to the British and Foreign Anti-Slavery Society that advocated the gradual abolition of slavery. They held meetings in members' houses, and raised funds for the parent society, but were reluctant to hold public meetings.[21] At the same time women from Unitarian families, who were as well educated as their brothers, joined their male relatives in support of the flamboyant American abolitionist, William Lloyd Garrison. He championed women's right to take an active part in the campaign and had the radical aim of immediate emancipation. Among those involved were Mary Carpenter (1807-77) and her sister Anna Thomas, who had married into the family that owned the Broad Plain Soap Works. They were the daughters of Lant Carpenter, the Unitarian Minister for Bristol. They were joined by Mary Estlin (1820-1902), the daughter of John Bishop Estlin, an ophthalmic surgeon who was a leading advocate of Garrison's views and was a friend and physician to Lant Carpenter.[22] [*Fig. 3.2*] Mary Estlin was a key figure in the abolitionist campaign, not just in Bristol but also nationally. She travelled around the country with her father giving talks and accompanied visiting American fugitive slave abolitionists such as Frederick Douglass and Sarah Parker Redmond on speaking tours.[23] She also transformed the Bristol and Clifton Ladies' Anti-Slavery Society. Appointed to its committee in 1851 she encouraged the development of a plan of action and persuaded members to support Garrison's more radical position.[24]

Women's political horizons, then, were not just bounded by locality but were national and global in scope. Religious, family and friendship networks brought them in contact with like-minded reformers who kept them well informed about international events, especially through correspondence. Mary Estlin, for example, was in frequent contact with Rev. George Thomp-

3.2 Mary Estlin and her father
John Bishop Estlin relaxing in
their drawing room, depicted by a
young relative in a letter home.
Estlin Collection. BRL

son, who promoted Garrison's views in England, and the American abolitionists, Rev. Samuel May and Maria Weston Chapman, the organiser of the
Boston Anti-Slavery Bazaar.[25] Homes were not just private 'havens' but 'open
and convivial spaces' where, by offering hospitality to political activists women
could extend their own knowledge and aspirations through lively discussions.[26] [*Fig. 3.3*] Many of the leading abolitionists, such as Samuel May, Maria
Weston Chapman and William Garrison, stayed with the Estlins and the
Carpenters. The African-American Frederick Douglass was hosted by the
Carpenters and spoke in the city to much acclaim in 1847.[27]

Women's position on race and class could be more radical than that of
some male leaders. Mary Carpenter tried to interest working women in anti-
slavery activities and was criticised by John Estlin who thought it was the
educated classes who would benefit the movement most. Mary Estlin was
forward-looking in her concern about the material problems faced by freed
slaves and in her interest in the long term impact of racism on their lives. By
1859 she was a member of the mixed race and gender London Emancipation
Committee which had been set up by George Thompson and two self-

3.3 The house of John Bishop and Mary Estlin where hospitality was given to anti-slavery campaigners from Britain and the United States, including freed slaves. BRL

emancipated African Americans, Ellen Craft and Sarah Parker Redmond. In 1863 she joined with the latter on the committee of the Ladies' London Emancipation Society which focused on the specific issues facing women and was in correspondence with radical women abolitionists in New York.[28] In the late 1870s she was a subscriber to *Anti Caste*, a journal edited by a Quaker, Catherine Impey of nearby Street, who hoped to build an international anti-racist movement.[29] Mary Carpenter also had a long-term interest in race. After meeting the Indian religious philosopher Ram Mohan Roy when he visited Bristol in 1833 [*colour plate 10*], she focussed on the position of women in India. She visited in the 1860s and encouraged Indian and British colonial administrators to train more women as teachers and to promote female education.[30] It has been suggested by Sandra Holton that women such as these developed a more radical outlook in their theory and their practice than others of their class and generation, and that this affected the ways in which they approached political and social movements later in the century.[31]

Purposeful lives – female philanthropy, 1850-1900
In the early-nineteenth century, as Gorsky notes, women tended to work in philanthropic organisations run by men.[32] In later decades, however, there

3.4 The Good
Shepherd Convent at
Arnos Court.
BRO 43207/29/19/2

was a growth of single-sex charitable societies that allowed women's authority and autonomy to develop, while women also contributed to shaping middle-class ideology both locally and nationally.[33] In setting up their own institutions and initiating new forms of voluntarism, many women encountered difficulties and restrictions, both in relation to working-class women and to their own lives, that led to their involvement in the women's rights movement. There was a close interconnection throughout the period between voluntary social action and a concern to address gender inequalities.[34]

Rescuing women from moral danger

Many of the early philanthropic initiatives had focused on 'fallen women', childbirth and the care of infants and this was to continue through the nineteenth century. The contribution of Roman Catholic women to this work, in particular that of religious sisters, has been neglected. Nonetheless, they provided one of the first examples in Bristol of women working in a single-sex group when the Good Shepherd Order set up the Magdalen House for 'penitent women' in 1851, next to their convent at Arno's Court.[35] This was to provide an alternative form of support for Catholic girls in moral danger, since it was considered essential that girls of good character should be treated separately from the 'fallen'.[36] [*Fig. 3.4*]

Another single-sex organisation was formed in 1855 when the Ladies' Committee of the City Mission decided to break away from the parent body and formed the Bristol Female Mission Society, with two women employed to work with prostitutes in St Jude's, St James' and St Michael's parishes.[37] A separate branch of the Mission, known as the Preventive Branch of the Female Mission Society, was set up in 1859. Many of the leading women of Bristol joined the Society, including Mrs Annie May and various members of the Quaker Sturge family.[38]

Frances Power Cobbe, who had come to Bristol to work with Mary Carpenter, publicised the work of the Female Mission in an article in the *English Woman's Journal* in 1861 and in her paper 'Friendless Girls and How to Help them' given at the Social Science Congress that year.[39] Recognising the need for secure employment as an alternative to prostitution, the Preventive Branch of the Female Mission Society opened a registry office and a home for vulnerable girls aged from 12 to 16 years. The aim was prevention rather than cure: providing girls with a place to live where they could be trained in domestic service and encouraged to lead an honest life. The founders of the Preventive Mission contended that 'The Home is intended for girls who are in need or moral danger, not on account of bad personal tendencies, but from neglect or evil surroundings. No girl who has lost character, by dishonesty or any other way is eligible'.[40]

Mary Carpenter: inspiring women's social action

Social networks and the ability of women to inspire others were central to philanthropic activity and to the development of women's rights. The most well-known social reformer who exemplifies this was Mary Carpenter.[41] Concerned about the problem of juvenile delinquency, which she encountered when teaching in a ragged school for poor children, she sought to change attitudes to young offenders. Mary Carpenter established industrial schools and reformatories in Bristol, including Kingswood Reformatory in north Bristol and Red Lodge Reformatory for Girls in the centre of the city. [*Colour plate 11*] She gained a national, and then international reputation for her work.[42] Reluctant at first, by the late 1850s she was prepared to read papers at annual conferences of the National Association for the Promotion of Social Science (NAPSS) and in 1861 gave evidence to the Select Committee on Poor Relief.[43] Mary Carpenter also had a lifelong interest in female education and was vice president of the Girls' Public Day School Trust.

Mary Carpenter was at the centre of a circle of like-minded reformers. She had already forged links with Unitarians in Britain and in the United States during the anti-slavery agitation. Among her friends were John Bishop Estlin and Matthew Davenport Hill, a founder of the NAPSS who came to Bristol in 1851 as a Commissioner for Bankruptcy.[44] She discussed her ideas about reformatories in correspondence with Hill and it was largely as a result of their work that the Industrial and Reformatory Schools Acts were passed. Women were attracted to work with Mary Carpenter in Bristol where they gained experience before moving on to other activities. Frances Power Cobbe, for example, gained a national reputation as a feminist writer and journalist.[45] Rosamund and Florence Davenport Hill worked in Carpenter's reformatories and were joined in 1862 by Catherine and Susanna Winkworth, who were later to take an interest in girls' education and in housing.[46] Agnes Beddoe also helped to run Carpenter's ragged schools and assisted her in setting up the Indian Society. The daughter of a clergyman from Edinburgh, she settled in Bristol after her marriage to John Beddoe, a physician and anthropologist. After Mary Carpenter's death in 1877 she became president of the Mary Carpenter Home for Working Girls and then established one of her own.[47]

Throughout the 1850s, 1860s and 1870s a number of industrial and reformatory schools were set up by Bristol women to care for girls who were considered to be in moral danger or who had been convicted of a criminal offence. These included The Industrial Home for Destitute Girls, Dowry Parade, founded in 1852 by Mrs Saunders whose daughter Emma acted as honorary secretary and taught at the home, though she is better known for her later mission work with railway workers.[48] The Sisters of Mercy established an industrial school for 'poor girls and women, most of whom are Irish', in 1854[49] and in 1856 the nuns at the Good Shepherd Convent in Brislington decided to convert their penitent home into a reformatory school for Catholic girls.[50] Other institutions were established by women for women. For example, the Park Row Asylum for Discharged Female Prisoners was founded in 1854 by Miss Sawyer from Henbury who was supported by a committee of ladies.[51]

Women's rights movement
Women's suffrage

Many women who wanted more influence over social questions, and who were frustrated by their own lack of rights and opportunities, became involved in the movement for women's rights from the 1860s onwards.[52] A key demand was for women to exercise the Parliamentary vote. This was an issue affecting all women, since it was their sex that prevented them from voting. It was also believed that the vote would enable women to bring about social change to benefit the poor.

The first women's suffrage petition of 1866, prompted by a new franchise

3.5 Anna Maria Priestman Agnes Beddoe, and Emily Sturge. All from Sarah Jane Tanner's *How the Women's Suffrage Movement Began in Bristol Fifty Years Ago*, Carlyle Press, 1918

bill, was signed by several Bristol women, including Susanna Winkworth, Florence Davenport Hill and Agnes Beddoe.[53] Three Quaker sisters who also signed, Margaret Tanner (1817-1905), Anna Maria Priestman (1829-1914) and Mary Priestman (1831-1914) were to play a significant role in the women's movement in Bristol but were not yet resident in the city.[54] Women's suffrage societies were formed throughout the country with Bristol becoming the fifth city to set up a committee in 1868 after a meeting in Matthew Davenport Hill's home.[55] Agnes Beddoe, Mary Estlin and Florence Davenport Hill were members from the beginning, while Anna Maria Priestman joined in 1870. [*Fig. 3.5*] At first called the Bristol and Clifton branch of the National Society for Women's Suffrage, its title was changed in 1869 to the Bristol and West of England branch. From 1871 it was associated with the Central Committee of the National Society of Women's Suffrage (NSWS) which was London based but brought together representatives from provincial groups.

As its work expanded to areas outside the city the Bristol Society took on an organising secretary in 1873 and opened an office at 53 Park Street, moving to 16 Park Street in 1876. In 1880 Helen Blackburn took over the role of secretary and ran the organisation from her lodgings at 20 Park Street. Blackburn was already well known at a national level. She contributed articles to the *Englishwomen's Review* and was honorary secretary of the NSWS from 1874-1880. While in Bristol she organised large demonstrations and embarked on speaking tours of the West Country. She is perhaps best known for her writings, including a history of the suffrage movement which contained many insights into the Bristol movement.[56]

3.6 This anti-suffrage cartoon was one of a number published in the unabashedly conservative *Bristol Magpie* and specifically addressed to Emily Sturge. It warns that domestic chaos would result when married women campaigned for the vote and portrayed suffragists as mannish and unattractive. *Bristol Magpie*, 15 March 1890. BRL

The suffrage campaign provided a different experience for participants. Gathering signatures for petitions and lobbying MPs were familiar tactics, but some women now found the courage to speak to large public meetings, often for the first time. Agnes Beddoe, Lilian Ashworth Hallett from Bath, Helen Bright Clark of Street and Emily Sturge were the main speakers for the Bristol society and often had to face hostile crowds.[57] [*Fig 3.6*] Support from family and friends could be crucial. Sisters in particular gave each other support, including those from the Sturge, Priestman, Tribe and Pease families who could be found in a wide range of interlinking women's rights and social reform campaigns.

Expanding opportunities for work and education
Women also had a set of other demands. These included access to secondary and higher education, opportunities for professional employment and a change in the legal status of married women. As early as 1862 a Bristol Nurses' Training Institution and Home was established to supply trained

nurses of good character. Unusually, half of the committee set up to take this forward were women, the majority of whom were wives of doctors.[58] Later initiatives were associated more closely with women's rights campaigners. In 1868 John Percival, head of Clifton College, set up the Clifton Association for the Higher Education of Women, a mixed-sex committee with Catherine Winkworth as secretary. The committee organised extension lectures by leading academics that were attended by young men and women from Clifton, including the Sturge and Winkworth sisters, Gertrude Savill and Mary Clifford, who was later to play a leading role in voluntary work. They often met in the home of John Addington Symonds, who lectured on the Renaissance, and his wife Catherine, the daughter of Lord North, where they found that the 'mental stimulus was of lasting value'.[59] Catherine Winkworth then acted as the driving force for the establishment of a university college in the city. Bristol's University College was finally set up in 1876 and was at the forefront of new ideas in being open to both sexes and providing scholarships for women.[60]

Campaigning to repeal the Contagious Diseases' Acts

Another key campaign, building on an earlier interest in prostitution, was the movement to repeal the Contagious Diseases' Acts, passed in the 1860s to control the spread of venereal disease in the armed forces in garrison towns. Police had been given wide powers to arrest women suspected of being prostitutes and to force them to undergo a medical examination. If they were found to have a sexual disease they could be confined to a Lock Hospital for nine months.[61] There was an outcry against the Acts, partly because of the threat posed to civil liberties, and a National Association, open to both sexes, was established to gain their repeal. Josephine Butler then set up a Ladies National Association (LNA) in 1869 which was more feminist in its approach, highlighting the injustice of punishing 'the victims of vice' and arguing that the Acts gave men power over women's bodies.

Respectable middle-class women needed courage to speak out about issues of a sexual nature, but in Bristol many were willing to do so and the city played a leading role in the campaign. The Priestman sisters, now living in Bristol, were close friends of Josephine Butler. Mary Priestman worked hard for the national organisation, sending the annual report to all subscribers, writing handbills to be used in national elections and, with her sister Margaret Tanner, helping to sort out problems with paid agents when Butler was ill.[62] Mary Estlin, Mary Priestman and Mrs Charles Thomas were members of the national executive and Margaret Tanner was national treasurer.

Compared to local groups that emphasised moral and religious issues, the Bristol LNA has been described as independent and feminist in character.[63] Some members, including Lilian Ashworth Hallett, Mary Estlin, Mary Priestman and Helen Bright Clark were already involved in the suffrage campaign and were speakers and office holders in both movements. Others, for example the Quakers Margaret Fry and Susannah Pease, were first attracted to women's rights through the LNA and later took up the suffrage cause.[64] Walkowitz has pointed out that the Bristol group had the highest persistence rate of subscribers in the country – 48% of subscribers in 1870 were still there in 1877 and 33% in 1884; the proportion of single women was also high and rose as time went on from 42% of all subscribers in 1870 to 49% in 1884.[65] The Bristol group came up with new initiatives. In 1877, for example, they took over the management of the Old Park Lock Hospital and organised a mission week of propaganda in surrounding towns.

Organising women workers

The Bristol LNA also reached out to working-class women and the labour movement, forming a separate branch in Bedminster with a lower subscription rate and persuading the Trades Council to pass a resolution of support.[66] There was a radical strain in the women's movement in the city in which working-class women were seen as 'voters, lobbyists and allies' rather than as the subjects of rescue schemes. An interest was taken in their wages and work conditions.[67] Anna Maria Priestman gave a paper on this subject at the Social Science Congress of 1874. She argued that women needed trade unionism and the vote to ensure that legislation such as the Factory Acts would not exclude them from skilled work.[68] This was a view shared by many middle-class feminists at the time. Helen Blackburn, for example, who supported trade union organisation, joined with Jessie Boucherett to form the Women's Employment Defence League in 1891 to fight against restrictive legislation.

Anna Maria Priestman had been inspired by an initiative of Emma Paterson who, in 1874, established the Women's Protective and Provident League as an umbrella group to encourage women to organise.[69] Unions were formed among skilled groups such as tailoresses, bookbinders and upholsterers which mirrored in most respects those of men, offering sickness and unemployment benefits and some support during disputes. In Bristol Anna Maria and Mary Priestman, Emily Sturge and Agnes Beddoe took a leading role in forming a National Union of Working Women, and both Helen Blackburn and Eliza

Walker Dunbar attended the Trades Union Congress as delegates to represent the union.

Eliza Walker Dunbar was the first woman to qualify as a doctor in the city. She linked her professional concerns as a paid worker to social questions and to women's rights. With the financial assistance of Lucy Read, she founded a dispensary for women and children in 1874 followed by the Bristol private hospital for women and girls, Berkeley Square, Clifton, in 1898.[70] [*Fig. 3.7*] She was attached to the Union of Working Women as a medical attendant and at the TUC expressed her ambivalent position as 'standing upon neutral grounds, being neither producer nor capitalist', but claiming that she was 'impelled to admire the strength which you have acquired through union'.[71] Union membership was always small but some working-class women gained experience as union officers, including Miss Merrick, who was president for six years until standing down in 1883.[72] Its main interest lies in the fact that it was an attempt by middle-class women to establish a different relationship with working women and to seek new strategies to improve their employment conditions.

Women at work: 1880s to 1914

Female workers remained crucial to Bristol's economic success. At the time of the 1911 census indoor domestic service and the clothing industry were still the largest employers of female labour, accounting for approximately 21% and 24% of all female workers in the city, with a further 10% in some form of domestic labour.[73] The figures for the clothing industry are likely to be an underestimate since home workers tended not appear in the census returns. Opportunities also opened up, especially for young, single women, to work in the new factories manufacturing sweets, tobacco, other food products and paper which developed rapidly in the late-nineteenth century. [*Fig. 3.8*] Approximately 22% of the female workforce was employed in these trades, including cotton workers. Products for which Bristol was to become well known, such as Wills' cigarettes, were largely dependent on an efficient, but low paid, female labour force to retain their competitive edge through to the inter-war years. As these factories expanded they moved out of the city; Wills tobacco, and Robinson's paper manufacturing firm, established new factories in Bedminster which brought distinctive characteristics to the locality and to the experience of the labour force which mirrored those of cotton manufacture in Barton Hill.[74]

3.7 The Read Dispensary for women and children, Hotwells, founded 1870 by Dr Eliza
Walker Dunbar. BRL K818 *Loxton Collection*

Sweated Labour

From the 1880s onwards the low pay and long hours of 'sweated' female
workers were the subject of government and other investigations.[75] These
concerns were reflected in a series of articles, written by the special commissioner of the *Bristol Mercury* in 1884, on the 'Homes of the Bristol Poor'. In
St Jude's, for example, he found women making boxes for Elfin matches at a
rate of 2d a gross, 'binding them up in bundles of three dozen, finding their
own string and flour for pasting on the ornamental paper and the picture of
an aerial sprite winging his way through the clouds'.[76] Earnings were rarely
more than 3/4d a week. A report on Bristol as part of the Royal Commission
on Labour's investigation into female employment in 1894, also found that,
unlike Leeds where new factories had been built, the clothing industry was
still largely carried on within the home. There were some small factories but
they were old, often poorly ventilated and lacked basic facilities such as cloak-
rooms and dining rooms. In the opinion of the inspectors they employed a

3.8 Women filling paper boxes with Fry's chocolates, *Commercial Bristol*, 1903-4, vol. 1-2, no. 10. BRL

'rough class of women', borne out by the high proportion of married women, 37%, who worked in them. Women married to skilled workers were more likely to prefer to work at home to retain 'respectability'.[77]

Factory Girls

Girls aged 18-25, from solid working-class families, were attracted instead by the 'modern' conditions in newer factories in the confectionery, tobacco and paper trades. These were the girls 'employers are most anxious to have' and the Commissioners claimed they were 'free to choose how and where they will work'.[78] Wills factory at Bedminster had good lighting, ventilation and sanitary arrangements, while a dining room with subsidised meals and a matron to deal with minor sickness and injury were provided on site. Alford suggests that employers understood the relationship between good conditions, the right type of worker and productivity and this was another way of expressing how 'cleanliness was next to godliness'.[79] This reflected the concerns of social reformers about the impact of the environment on moral and spiritual character. In 1883 a report in the *Bristol Times and Mirror* praised the good effect of Wills' factory on the workforce. 'Looking at these trim and tidy girls with smiling faces and nimble fingers, one instinctively feels that the system adopted must have a wonderful influence, for they are as far removed from the Midland and northern type of factory hands as can well be imagined'.[80] Female wages, however, were low – in 1894 women aged 24 were paid 12/6d a week compared to 24/- for men – and they worked a 50

3.9 Extract from 1911 Census for the Priestman family, showing the number of servants, their ages and the roles they performed

hour week.[81] This perhaps explains why, despite the improved environment, women workers in the newer factories expressed their discontent in the two periods of major unrest in the city, 1889-92 and 1910-14.

Nonetheless, young women were keen to work in the new factories, especially Wills. As the census data of 1911 suggests, 70% of female workers in these trades were aged under 25 with less than 5% being married or widowed.[82] To maintain the 'respectability' of their factories employers expected women workers to leave when they married. In contrast, in the cotton factory with its different traditions and practices, 40% of the female labour force were married or widowed.

Domestic Service

The largest single area of employment for women workers was still domestic service. A higher proportion of the labour force was in the older age groups compared with the new factory trades – 50% were aged between 20 and 40 – although they were largely single women. Most of the women engaged in social reform or in the women's movement had servants and it is worth noting how this enabled them to give their time and energy to public affairs. Households usually employed three to four servants. The Priestman sisters lived with their niece and in 1911 had five servants, described as a waitress, 33, a laundry maid, 39, a housemaid, 24, a cook, 29 and a sewing woman, 68. Elizabeth Sturge, aged 61, and her sister Helen aged 82 had three servants, a cook, 30, a parlourmaid, 30 and a housemaid 27.[83] [*Fig. 3.9*]

White Blouse and Professional Work

There were also more opportunities for girls from lower middle-class and working-class backgrounds to find paid employment as clerical workers, as shop assistants in department stores, as nurses and as teachers. [*Fig. 3.10*] The introduction of state schooling after 1870 meant more work for women from a variety of backgrounds since there were different routes to gain training. Numbers rose from 373 in 1881 to 1911 in 1911.[84]

A small number of women, who had benefited from the expansion of educational opportunities, were able to teach outside primary and secondary schools. As early as 1878-9 Mary Paley, the wife of Alfred Marshall, professor of Political Economy at Bristol University, delivered his lectures for a session and was paid to do so.[85] When the Marshalls left Bristol, Mary Fry (Mrs Abbot) took Mrs Marshall's place as lecturer in Economics for several terms.[86] It was highly unusual for a married woman to work full-time in a salaried position, but the number of single women appointed to teaching roles at the University College did increase. Marian Pease was appointed as Mistress of Method at the Day Training College and she later invited Hilda Cashmore to come and work there as a history tutor. Three women undertook research in chemistry at Bristol in the late-nineteenth century: Katherine Williams, Emily Fortey and Millicent Taylor; the last became a lecturer some years later.[87] An even smaller number of women qualified as doctors in the nineteenth century, including Ethel Tribe and Eliza Walker Dunbar.[88]

3.10 Pre-war advertisement of Bristol private commercial school for typing and shorthand. The headline addressed to parents, mentions children but those pictured are young adult women. *The Bristolian,* August 1913. BRL

1892.

THIRTY-THIRD REPORT

OF THE

Preventive Mission

(the Preventive Branch of the
Bristol Female Mission Society)

FOR THE

YEAR ENDING DECEMBER 31ST, 1892.

Bristol :
Henry Hill, Painter and Stationer,
21 St. John Street.

3.11 *Thirty Third Report of the Preventive Mission for year ending 1892*, pp.22-23. The Mission provided poor girls with support and training so they could enter domestic service. The subtext was to prevent them from falling into prostitution and crime. Annual reports contain valuable information on officers, subscribers and the aims and objectives of the organisation.
BRL, B12280

Women as Financial Patrons

Although most middle-class women did not engage in paid employment they used their access to personal wealth to contribute to the life of the city. Their money founded large projects, such as the Old Lock Hospital, the Read Dispensary and various industrial and reformatory schools.[89] The religious sisters who set up the convent in Dighton Street were from wealthy families and one of the founders, Diana Beauchamp, put £2500 of her own money towards the expansion of the convent in 1852, while Mary Ann Caley donated £1000 when she joined in 1846.[90] Women helped to maintain charitable institutions such as hospitals through regular subscriptions or one-off donations, with many supporting several organisations at once. This contributed to their civic status since names were published in annual reports.[91] The 1892 Annual Report of the Preventive Mission, for example, lists a donation of £20 by Mrs Pethick as well as the names of all the regular subscribers.[92] [*Fig. 3.11*]

Although under the law married men had control over their wives' income, in practice they often shared their interest in social questions and therefore married women had money at their disposal. Single women often had independent incomes derived from shares or, as Sandra Holton notes in her study of Quaker families, from money left to them through a female line of unmarried aunts.[93] Anna Maria and Mary Priestman, for example, were able to establish their own home in Bristol in the 1860s thanks to a legacy from their aunts in Malton, while Mabel Tothill and her sister Gertrude were left some money by their maiden aunts. They also inherited money on their father's death in 1910, some of which was used by Mabel Tothill to purchase property for the Barton Hill University Settlement in 1911.[94]

Bristol's Home Workers *and the* Royal Commission on Labour

June Hannam

Report on Women's Employment, 1894

The Royal Commission on Labour was set up between 1891 and 1894 to investigate conditions of employment in industry. It was prompted by the labour unrest of the 1880s which had drawn public attention to problems of low pay and long hours of work. Lady Dilke, president of the Women's Trade Union League, argued strongly that women needed to be represented. It was agreed, therefore, that four women would be appointed to act as Lady Assistant Commissioners to investigate women's work in London and provincial towns, including Bristol.

Clara Collet, a graduate who had worked on Charles Booth's survey of the poor in London, wrote the report on Bristol – reporting on the manufacture of clothing, boots and shoes, cotton, tobacco and confectionery in factories, workshops and at home. The extract reproduced here gives information on homeworkers. It shows that they might be married, widowed or single and that they often collaborated with other family members. It also shows that earnings could be better at home than in factories. ∎

Index Number.	Persons working.	Kind of Work.	Ordinary Prices.	Amount earned in re
272	Married woman and sister.	Trousers		On 9d. cords make pairs a day comfo give out finishin each, leaving 5 day (two persons 6d. cords make a day; give finishing, leaving
286	Married woman; another married woman as learner.	Men's and juvenile coats.	Range upwards from as low as 3d.—4½d. for juveniles, as low as 7d. for youths', and as low as 8d. for men's.	On 8d. work by can make six on 4½d. coats ca nine.
289	Married woman; little girl helps when back from school.	Trousers; and trouser finishing when she can get nothing else.	5d., 6½d., 7d., and 8d. For finishing gets 2d., 2½d., and 3d.	If finishing trouser each, can do on a day, working s a.m. to 9 p. interruptions. A woman could dozen comforta morning if sl nothing else to c
216	Widow; learner (aged 16).	Machines uppers; does samples and "bespoke" work.		On "Bal." boot fancy vamps at the dozen they make one dozen than a day. The is very quick an 8s. a week, leav 3s. 2d. a day.

'The doctor said the daily walk there and back would do her good'. An extract from the Royal Commission Report

Amount earned in a Day.	Average Earnings per Week, in ordinary Weeks (Gross, unless otherwise stated).	Cost of Trimmings to be deducted from Gross Earnings.	Hours per Day.	Cost of Sewing-Machine.	————
On 9d. cords make eight pairs a day comfortably; give out finishing at 1d. each, leaving 5s. 4d. a day (two persons). On 6d. cords make 12 pairs a day; give 1d. for finishing, leaving 5s.	- - -	- - -	Only 1½ hours on Saturday; could not say about the rest of the week.	Each pays 2s.6d. a fortnight.	Comfortable cottage and good garden at Winterbourne. Very bright and intelligent.
On 6d. work by herself can make six a day; on 4½d. coats can make nine.	15s. by herself -	7d. -	Averages from 8—8 and 8—4 on Saturday, but works short hours on some days and long on others.	- - -	Worked in a factory three years ago; could not earn so much; was only a baster then, and machinists got the money. Does not baste at all now; machines without basting. Had little money left from factory wages after paying for the children to be looked after.
If finishing trousers at 2d. each, can do one dozen a day, working from 6 a.m. to 9 p.m., with interruptions. A young woman could do one dozen comfortably in a morning if she had nothing else to do.	Could not say ; was so often slack.	1d. in 1s. -	? - -	- - -	Used to work in a factory; had plenty of work and women to baste; often took 30s., out of which she paid 3s. 6d. to a girl. Left six years ago; had been there 20 years. Only did machining then.
On " Bal." boots with fancy vamps at 4s. 6d. the dozen they could make one dozen in less than a day. The learner is very quick and earns 8s. a week, leaving her 3s. 2d. a day.	Generally more than 16s. nett for herself.	1s. a week -	8—7. ¾-hour interval for dinner. Half day on Saturday.	- - -	Has one child; her assistant looks after the housework. Unusually clear-headed and capable. Works for a shoemaker who is not a " Society " man, but he gives her regular work, and with a child to keep she could not afford to live on 6s. a week strike pay; sufficient if she were a factory girl. Worked in a factory nine years; was paid 16s. a week, day-work, the last three years.

Royal Commission on Labour, Report of Miss Orme on the Employment of Women, 1894. BRL

From 'foot soldiers' to social leaders

By the late-nineteenth century middle-class women were increasingly influential in civic life. Their work with voluntary charities enabled them to take on leadership roles in both the private and public sector. Religious zeal and commitment to a 'civilising mission' motivated many, but charitable work also reinforced their social standing and moral authority. This was acquired in both single and mixed-sex organisations, including the highly significant Charity Organisation Society (COS).

Charity Organisation Society

Set up in London in 1869, the COS disseminated new ideas about the treatment of poverty. It criticised indiscriminate almsgiving and insisted instead on a 'scientific' approach that would distinguish between the 'deserving' and the 'undeserving' poor. The latter were to be consigned to the harsh discipline of the workhouse. A Bristol branch of the COS was set up in 1872 by Gilmore Barnett, with a Ladies' Committee made up of women from leading families.[95] Although Martin Gorsky and Frank Prochaska have argued that women's role in mixed-sex organisations was confined to home visiting and fund raising, by the late-nineteenth century women in Bristol participated far more extensively in the committee structure of groups such as the COS. They also began to hold leading positions. There were no female office holders in the COS in 1890, whereas by 1896 Miss Catherine Woollam was a vice president and Miss Norah Fry was honorary assistant secretary, a post held for two years from 1898 by Miss Elizabeth Sturge and then by Miss M J Ogilvie.[96] Elizabeth Sturge later recalled that she had been attracted by the more systematic approach encapsulated in the COS.[97] Given its moralistic approach it is more surprising that one of the leading members was Mabel Tothill who, despite becoming a socialist, continued her work with the COS and later the Civic League until the First World War.

Women's Philanthropic Organisations

It was easier for women to assume leadership positions and to come up with new initiatives when they formed their own organisations. Agnes Beddoe set up the Bristol Emigration Society in 1883 to help orphaned children from industrial schools and workhouses to emigrate to Canada where they would be put to work on farms.[98] Influenced by the pioneering work in London of the housing reformer Octavia Hill, Susanna Winkworth tried to tackle problem of inadequate and insanitary housing in Bristol by purchasing houses in Dowry Square, Hotwells and letting them to tenants. In 1874 she was mainly responsible for setting up the Bristol Industrial Dwellings Company, which had a number of male shareholders, while the Jacob Wells Dwellings and Brandon Buildings were designed and built to a high standard and rented out to suitable tenants.[99] Ada Vachell was inspired by her encounter with organisations in London, in particular the West London Mission and the 'Guild of the Poor Things', which she visited in 1895. Here those who were disabled were enjoined to 'endure hardness as good soldiers'.[100] On returning to Bristol Vachell set up the Guild of the Handicapped to help children and adults suffering from physical disabilities and later set up a school for disabled children at Broad Plain, St Philip's.

Temperance reform was also supported by both middle-class and working-class women, although the movement tended to be dominated by men until the 1870s. Bristol had a branch of the British Women's Temperance Society and of the splinter group, the Women's Total Abstinence Society. In 1878 Sarah Terrett, the wife of a butcher and a member of the Bible Christian Church, set up the White Ribbon Army in Bedminster to campaign for temperance and to support those trying to change their lives, and it won the support of local politicians such as Sir Joseph Weston and Mark Whitwell. Terrett was one of a growing number of women who were prepared to speak in public and to take on the role of preacher as well as reformer.[101] As Helen Meller has shown, temperance reformers tried to influence leisure by providing for wholesome recreation.[102] Women set up clubs for working girls, encouraged young women factory workers to sign the pledge and supported Bands of Hope for children. There was a harsher side. Some campaigned against the provision of alcohol in the workhouse, whether as a reward or as a Christmas treat, while others joined in campaigns to moralise the poor, such as the Shaftesbury Crusade. Mrs Tribe and her daughter Mabel, for example, who were members of the Total Abstinence Association, set up women's meetings and a girls' club in St Philip's as part of this crusade.[103]

From the late 1880s women engaged in voluntary social action increasingly saw the value of working together to increase their effectiveness. They formed local associations and unions, such as the Association for the Care of Friendless Girls, as a way to co-ordinate their work. When in 1892 Bristol hosted the national annual conference of these local unions, 30 organisations for the care of women and children were listed in the Bristol area. In 1895 the various local groups associated together under an umbrella group known as the National Union of Women Workers (NUWW). This should not be

WOMEN AND THE CITY

confused with trade unions or with working women since it represented middle-class women engaged in voluntary social work. Mary Clifford from Bristol played a key role in the establishment and development of the new organisation, later becoming its national president. Like Mary Carpenter before her she inspired women to join her in voluntary work. One of these was Miss Deane, the first secretary of the Bristol Civic League, who recalled meeting Mary Clifford just after leaving school:

> The joyous thing about my first personal contact with her was that she asked me to do something; she asked me to act as a steward at the Council of the National Union of Women Workers who were holding their meeting at Bristol for the first time. It brought me at once into touch with the women who were then pioneering all the women's questions of the day…the real power of her influence in my life was the encouragement to 'go on and do'.[104]

The daughter of a vicar, Mary Clifford helped her father in his parochial work as well as getting involved in the female Preventive Mission. After her father's death she began to visit the workhouse and was encouraged to stand for election to the Barton Regis Board of Guardians in 1882. She stood in a long line of Bristol women who were not just influential at a local level, but who helped to shape national policies and initiatives.

Party politics and local government

Party politics

Party politics provided another outlet for women's energies from the 1880s. Although the male electorate had increased, paid canvassers were prohibited by law and therefore the main parties had to re-consider their organisation and their strategies. The Conservative Party formed the Primrose League to encourage members to give active support. In 1884 women were admitted to a separate Ladies Grand Council, although at a local level both sexes worked together in habitations. These were often set up and run by women who were instrumental in attracting new members.[105] In Bristol the honorary secretary of the Redcliffe Habitation was Miss Davidson, while Mabel Hill, the daughter of the MP for Bristol South, Sir Edward Hill, was president of the South Divisional Council of the Primrose League.[106] For a short time in the 1890s Mabel Hill also edited the section of the *Bristol South Gazette* that dealt with politics.[107]

Women in the Liberal Party were organised separately in Women's Liberal Associations (WLA). These were later affiliated to the national group, the Women's Liberal Federation, formed in 1887, which gained a reputation for its feminism. Anna Maria Priestman and Emily Sturge set up a WLA in Bristol in 1881, one of the first in the country, which was closely linked to the women's movement.[108] Active members included Mary Priestman, Helen Sturge, Eva Tribe, Helen Bright Clark, Helen Blackburn and Sarah Jane Tanner who were all involved in the LNA and the suffrage campaign. They disagreed with those who wanted to keep the suffrage movement separate from other causes and believed that the demand for the vote and liberal goals were inextricably linked. Nonetheless there were tensions over the Liberal Party's lukewarm support for women's suffrage and women had to make diffi-cult choices when party loyalties and feminist priorities clashed.[109]

Roles in local government
The local Government franchise of 1869 enabled many widows and single women of property to vote in municipal elections. With its high proportion of single women, Bristol had the second largest number of women electors of any city. Women voters could, therefore, make a difference, especially in the affluent areas of Clifton and Redland.[110] They were not able to stand for the City Council, but women could be candidates for election to the School Board and to Boards of Guardians, elected bodies that ran state schools and the Poor Law at a local level. Both dealt with questions that could be seen to fall within the sphere of women's competence and interest – education and relief of the poor. Feminists argued that women needed to be represented on public bodies in order to articulate women's concerns.

Some women were elected to the Bristol School Board as independents, including Helena Richardson, but others were put forward as official Liberal candidates, including the suffragists Alice Grenfell and Emily Sturge. At 32 years of age Emily Sturge was the youngest member of the Board when elected in 1879. She promoted and supported initiatives such as the Day Training College for women, a truant school, technical education, evening classes and penny dinners. From 1883 she was also a member of the School Council of Redland High School. After her death from an accident in 1892 her sisters (Elizabeth and Helen) were asked if they would like to stand for election to the School Board, but they each declined and Marion Townsend was elected in her place. She served alongside a Conservative member, Miss Georgina Taylor and later alongside another Liberal, Mrs Louisa Swann.

Women had long been involved in attempts to expand educational opportunities for women in Bristol and were involved as school governors and council members as well as on the School Board. Catherine Winkworth, for example, was one of five female members of the first council of Clifton High School and was a governor of Red Maids' School.[111]

Poor Law work was initially less congenial to women but Mary Clifford, who started as a workhouse visitor, encouraged others to get involved. She had been persuaded to stand for the Board of Guardians by Thomas Pease, who was the chairman and the father of three daughters who were politically active, Rosa, Marian and Dora. Clifford claimed that she 'went upon the Board of Guardians to protect old women who seemed oppressed, and quickly found big matters calling for attention, such as the education and training of children, classification to promote purity, nursing of the sick, emigration, and legislation on various new matters'.[112]

In 1882 four women were elected onto the Barton Regis Board of Guardians, with Bristol returning more women Guardians than anywhere outside London and Edinburgh.[113] Those elected proved popular with the voters. Mary Clifford served for 25 years, Alice Winkworth for 37 years and Catherine Woollam for 27 years. The first cohort of women Guardians were either unmarried or widowed, but after 1894, when the property qualification for public office was abolished, it became easier for married women and working-class women to stand as candidates and in 1895 twelve women were elected. Again several of these women served as Guardians for many years.

Women had to deal with hostility from male guardians. One, for example, opposed the influence of women over workhouse management since they 'had never experienced the vicissitudes of life, and had never earned any money by their own exertions'.[114] Against all the odds, however, women did manage to influence policy. Mary Clifford in particular could draw on her experiences in a number of organisations, including the NUWW, the LNA, the Women's Guardian Society, and campaigns for women's suffrage, housing reform and temperance, to get across her point of view. She took the lead in developing policies with regard to children who were in poverty. As the *Manchester Guardian* stated in her obituary, 'She developed the boarding out system for orphan and deserted children and the emigration of suitable children to Canada; and the Act of 1889, which denied idle and vicious parents restitutional rights over their children just at the most important period of their training, really derived from her'. Similarly, Catherine Woollam was a senior member of the COS and a leading member of the Clifton

District Nurses' Association and she was instrumental in replacing pauper nurses with qualified staff in workhouse sick wards.

Many female Guardians shared the dominant view that a deterrent Poor Law, with its threat of the workhouse, would encourage the poor to work hard and remain independent of the state and believed that moral reform was the means to achieve this. At times, however, women could promote policies which seemed harsh even to other Board members. Clifford's attitude to old-age pensions, for example, was unpopular. She considered that pensions would undermine family responsibility and the work of charitable organisations and spoke in opposition to them at the Royal Commission on the Aged Poor.[115]

On the other hand women Guardians were concerned to improve the lives of the poor and were interested in rehabilitation rather than deterrence. They thought that this could best be achieved by classifying inmates of the workhouse according to age, sex, family circumstances, health, moral status and behaviour. They pressed for improvements to be made in the treatment of children, the sick, the aged, and the 'feeble-minded' and argued that remedial treatment was the most appropriate for children and young people, who would benefit from training and a more familial model of care. The removal of children from the workhouse was a priority and this was achieved through boarding out (fostering) and emigration, but also through the creation of separate children's homes. Women Guardians were also concerned about women and girls who had illegitimate children and efforts were made to protect young female inmates from the dangers of associating with 'disreputable women'.

Women Guardians, therefore, contributed to the development of alternative forms of care based on the twin ideals of 'home' and 'family'. The desire to introduce 'home elements' into institutions was not new, but in their role as Guardians, women now had the power to shape the nature of the most important state institution – the workhouse.[116]

Working together for socialism and trade unionism

Many women thought that they had something unique to offer the community and should remain independent of party politics in their day-to-day activities. This was not accepted, as noted above, by some Liberal women and was subject to an even greater challenge with the revival of socialism in the late 1880s. Socialism provided a different space for a minority of middle-class women to work with, and on behalf of, working-class women and a different

Mike Richardson and Sheila Rowbotham

New Women *and* Bristol Socialism

Helena Born and Miriam Daniell

In the late 1880s two remarkable 'new women', Helena Born (1860-1902) and Miriam Daniell, née Wheeler (1861-1894) joined Bristol's socialist movement. They played a central part in the upsurge of militant new unionism that reached out to unskilled and semi-skilled workers and they courageously rejected conventional women's roles.

Born encountered Liberal Radicalism at Oakfield Unitarian Church in Clifton, joining the Bristol Women's Liberal Association in 1885. The B.W.L.A. included prominent supporters of women's rights and maintained links with the radical wing of the women's suffrage movement internationally. It would teach Born to organize.

Artistic and fiery, Miriam Daniell was less involved in the B.W.L.A., but already interested in socialism when she and Helena Born became friendly in 1888. Daniell's enthusiasm was infectious and they walked for miles through muddy fields talking excitedly about the American Transcendentalists, Walt Whitman, William Morris and Edward Carpenter. Relief work during the floods of spring 1889 made them aware of working-class conditions and by that autumn both women had gravitated to the Bristol Socialist Society .This was a small, but intensely active group of Marxists and Christian Socialists, who combined their eclectic politics with self-education and warm fellowship fostered by dances, poetry and much singing of glees.

Daniell's personal circumstances changed dramatically after she fell in love with a student from Edinburgh, Robert Allan Nicol, and brought him back to her marital home. She left her husband and went with Nicol to working-class St Philips where they created aesthetic simplicity amidst the bees-waxed bare boards at 9 Louisa Street and an over-attentive rat.

Born, Daniell and Nicol were involved that autumn in supporting striking iron workers at John Lysaght's, then at Barton Hill Cotton Factory where 1,700 workers, mainly women, went on strike on October 21. The ad hoc Strike Committee soon found itself defending a host of workers from brush makers to pipe makers, inspired by the successful mobilization of the gas workers and dockers. Charismatic Daniell turned into a popular speaker; diligent Born did the accounts.

In January 1890 Nicol became secretary of the Bristol Gasworkers and General Labourers' Union. The strikes faltered. Nicol and Daniell wrote a pamphlet, *The New Trade Unionism*, arguing for equality between the sexes and inner, spiritual transformation alongside class militancy. Daniell became pregnant and faced humiliating ostracism as an unmarried mother. In August all three emigrated to America where baby Sunrise, portent of a new dawn, was born in November.

Class and gender inequality proved far more resilient than the idealistic enthusiasts had expected. It was left to a younger generation of socialist new women to take up where they left off. Among them were Enid Stacy, Katharine St John Conway and Gertrude Dix; influenced by the pioneering rebels, they would take quite different paths. ∎

Based on Mike Richardson's *The Bristol Strike Wave of 1889-1890*. Pamphlets 21 & 22, Bristol Radical History Group and Sheila Rowbotham *Rebel Crossings: New Women, Free Lovers and Radicals in the US and Britain, 1880 to 1914* (Verso, London).

BRISTOL STRIKERS ON PARADE.

A MONSTER PROCESSION.

On Saturday afternoon the great demonstration, in which skilled and unskilled labourers of Bristol united, took place, a monster procession through the city being followed by a mass meeting on Durdham Down. It had been arranged that those who took part in the celebration should assemble in the Cattle Market, that enclosure having been placed at their disposal for the occasion by the Mayor. Some persons who visited the spot soon after one o'clock came to the conclusion that the demonstration would not be very large, as at that time the Cattle Market presented no appearance of active preparation. This, however, was matter for small surprise as work does not cease on Saturdays till one, and then the employés had to get their dinner. Just before two preparations commenced, some of the banners belonging to the different labour societies being brought on the scene; and the men soon came trooping in, so that by the time at which the procession was announced to leave the Cattle Market there was a muster of many thousands. Mr T. J. Dauncey, secretary of the Trades Council, was entrusted with the duty of marshalling the labourers and others who took part; and, as all the arrangements had been carefully considered on the previous night by the organising committee, the large body of workers was quickly formed in order. Much satisfac-

Cotton workers at Barton Hill's Great Western Factory
BRL. *Loxton Collection*

REMARKABLE DIVORCE SUIT.

In the Divorce Division yesterday Mr. Justice Barnes had before him the case of "Daniell v. Daniell and Nicol." The petition was that of the husband, a solicitor, of Bristol, for a divorce by reason of his wife's adultery with the co-respondent, Mr. Robert A. Nicol, formerly a medical student at Edinburgh. Both the respondent and the co-respondent were stated to have strong Socialist views. There was no defence.

Mr. Pritchard appeared for the petitioner, Mr. Edward Tuckett Daniell, who deposed that he was married to the respondent, Elizabeth Miriam Daniell, at Clifton, on the 15th of July, 1881. They subsequently lived together at Westbury. He was a solicitor practising at Bristol. He lived with his wife happily until 1886, when she had to undergo an operation. She went to Edinburgh for the benefit of her health, and there she made the acquaintance of the co-respondent, Mr. Robert Allan Nicol, a medical student. In September, 1888, the co-respondent came to Bristol and stayed with witness.

Did your wife hold views about Socialism?—Very strong views. She used to take a leading part in demonstrations. Mr. Nicol used to share those views.

Examination continued—His wife suggested he should leave his house and go and live in the poor parts of Bristol. At that time he did not think there was anything improper between his wife and Nicol. He remembered her being summoned in reference to a pamphlet concerning Messrs. Fry's relatives with their workmen. He objected to the pamphlet and the mis-statements it contained. There was a statement that it was written by Miriam Daniell and Robert A. Nicol, and he took steps to stop it, as he objected to it. She was extremely annoyed at this, and said she would leave his house. She went to stay with some Socialist friends in Bristol against his wish and consent. That was in October, 1888. Shortly afterwards she, Miss Goen ta friends, and the co-respondent took a house and lived together in the slums at Bristol, they all holding the same views. They were connected with some Union in Bristol. He offered to make her an allowance of £1 a week while she was living in the slums, and more if she left that style of life. She had a salary in connection with the Union, and painted and wrote. In August, 1889, all three of them went to Boston, his wife saying that there was a wider sphere of usefulness in America. He wrote to his wife.

The letter was read, in which he asked her what her relations were with Nicol. He said he believed in her purity of motive, but knew what sentimental friendship would lead to. She replied denying that there was anything wrong between them. But a subsequent letter contained admissions.

His Lordship said it would be better to have some of the passages read. It might be she was merely with the co-respondent as she held eccentric views on marriage.

Mr. Pritchard said in the letter she said there was no blame in the fact of her living with Robert Nicol for nearly a year. She denied having committed adultery with him at Bristol, but that in America they "declared themselves openly." "Free love," she wrote, "is better than legalised marriage." It went on to say that there was one child, a daughter, which was called "Sunrise." All the rest was a statement of their views about marriage. The co-respondent also wrote stating that he was the father of the child, and that he would be happy to forward any documents as to the birth of "Sunrise," he adding, "I remain, with best wishes, yours truly, Robert A. Nicol."

Lizzie Hughes deposed that she was present at the marriage. In June of last year she had to go to America, and in the course of that visit she went to Boston. There she saw Mrs. Daniell and Mr. Robert Nicol. They were living together, and a child was with them.

His Lordship granted a decree *nisi*, with costs.

Remarkable Divorce Suit
His wife suggested he leave his house and go and live in the poor parts of Bristol...She denied having committed adultery... with [Robert Nicol] in Bristol but once in America 'they declared themselves openly. 'Free love', she wrote 'is better than legalised marriage.'

way to conceptualise social problems. It also provided more opportunities for working-class women to play a role in public life.

Working women take action: the labour disputes of 1889-1892
When less skilled workers throughout the country demanded better pay and conditions, 1889-92, women also made their voices heard.[117] In Bristol there were two key disputes – the strike at the Great Western Cotton factory in 1889 and a strike at Sanders confectionery works in 1892. The labour unrest attracted some middle-class women to give active assistance, including Helena Born and Miriam Daniell. They helped by producing and circulating leaflets, raising money, addressing large meetings and leading deputations to employers.[118]

The 1889 cotton workers' strike brought two other women into the socialist and labour movement – Enid Stacy and Katharine Conway, both schoolteachers, who were in All Saints church when the strikers arrived after parading through the city. They determined there and then to help them. Enid Stacy, whose family was committed to Christian socialism, joined the Bristol Socialist Society and then the Independent Labour Party (ILP). She played a key role in the strike of confectionery workers and, as a talented speaker, played an important part in the 1895 Bristol East by-election.[119]

For a few years Enid Stacy and Katharine Conway engaged in trade union organising and propaganda work for socialism, while also directing attention to the specific needs of the female worker who was often neglected within a male-dominated movement. During the Sanders dispute, for example, Stacy fought to ensure that the women's union organisation would not be absorbed by the strike organisation committee, which by then was run largely by men.[120] In her speeches and her writings she persistently tried to link feminism and socialism.[121] By 1895, however, all of these women had left the city. Enid Stacy, who had been dismissed from her job as a school teacher, took up paid employment as a full-time propagandist for the ILP at national level. Katharine Conway married one of the ILP leaders, John Bruce Glasier, and went to live in Derbyshire where she continued to be active in socialist politics. After the labour unrest, in Bristol as elsewhere, it was difficult to sustain trade union organisation amongst women workers; nonetheless, the foundations had been laid for more sustained organisation just before the First World War.

The unrest showed a growing gulf between women who were interested in employment conditions of working-class women. At the 1892 annual conference of the NUWW, which met in Bristol while the strike at Sanders was taking place, Mary Clifford agreed that union organisation was important for resolving differences, and promoting understanding, between employers and worker, but she deplored strikes. She offered to visit the women on strike and to pray.[122] Others were prepared to take more direct action, walking in processions with the strikers, taking part in deputations to employers and speaking at open-air meetings. Isabella Ford, a middle-class Quaker and social-ist from Leeds, whose paper on the need for trade unions had stimulated debate at the conference, left the room after the discussion to march through the streets with the women on strike.[123]

The Bristol Union of Working Women

The different approaches were also exemplified by two small trade unions that catered for women workers in Bristol. The Bristol Union of Working Women that had been established in the 1870s, was still in existence. The Priestman sisters set up a soup kitchen in 1889 to help the cotton workers on strike, but they did not taken part in any direct organising work. By the 1890s the secretary was Mary Talbot, an Admiral's daughter, who was described by Emily Sturge as 'diffusing benevolence'.[124] Mary Talbot thought that trade unions were there to raise wages, which was preferable to almsgiv-ing, but deprecated strikes and claimed that her organisation worked for the benefit of employers and workers. On the other hand she noted that the rules made provision for strike pay.[125] Nonetheless, a rival group, the Bristol Associ-ation for Promoting Trade Unionism among Women, was formed during the labour unrest and by the 1890s the secretary was Caroline May, the daughter and sister of clergymen, who was close to the socialist movement. She was assisted by Fanny Paul who had been a member of the older women's union.[126] They both argued that their aims were different since they saw strikes as a key weapon in the fight for improved wages and conditions.

Women's Co-operative Guild

Other organisations provided the opportunity for working-class women to express their views and to act collectively outside the workplace. The Railway Women's Guild, comprised of the wives and daughters of railway workers, had a strong presence in Bristol since the president of the local branch, Emily Webb, who was a Poor Law Guardian, was also president at a national level.[127] The most significant group, however, was the Women's Co-operative Guild (WCG), formed in 1883. Originally established to spread the ideals of the co-operative movement, the Guild quickly expanded its remit and became involved in political campaigns to improve women's lives. It drew attention

Mrs. Fidkin.   Mrs. Treble.

Miss C. May.   Mrs. Greenland.

Mrs. Drew.   Mrs. Jaques.

BRISTOL GUILDSWOMEN WHO HAVE SERVED ON THE CENTRAL
COMMITTEE OR THE S.W. OR W. SECTION.

3.12 Leaders of the first Bristol branches of the Women's Co-operative Guild. Caroline May (*middle row, left*) was also involved in women's trade unionism. Edward Jackson, *A Study in Democracy*, Manchester, CWS, 1911. BRL

WE WANT OUR MOTHER'S TO JOIN THE CO-OP STORE

3.13 Campaigning to form a branch of the Women's Co-operative Guild in Kingsland Road, a poor district. Edward Jackson, *A Study in Democracy*, Manchester, CWS, 1911. BRL

to the needs of mothers, including maternity benefits and improved housing, and also took up took up more controversial issues such as divorce law reform and women's suffrage.[128] The first Bristol branch was established at Newfoundland Road in 1890 and this was quickly followed by three more.[129] Office holders were usually wives of leading co-operators, but the first president was a single woman, Dora Pease, who was responsible for bringing Caroline May into the movement in November 1891. [*Fig. 3.12*]

Caroline May, who was described as one of the most strenuous workers for the Guild, set up the Bedminster branch in 1892 which soon had a membership of 73.[130] Education was one of the objectives of the Guild and in Bristol speakers covered a range of subjects including women's health, children under the Poor Law, women's suffrage, slaves in Zanzibar and the relief of Armenians. Guild members also sought election to the management committee of the wider co-operative movement where they drew attention to the conditions of work of female employees in co-operative stores. Another initiative was to use an organiser from Head Office to attempt to expand the co-operative movement in one of the poorer areas of the city at Kingsland Road. A week's campaign was undertaken in 1906 when bills were distributed and 'concerts, lantern lectures and teas' were organised, while the co-operative store was stocked with goods that might appeal to those on low incomes. [*Fig. 3.13*] The campaign had only limited success but a branch of the WCG was formed with 30 members.[131]

Into the twentieth century

In the decade leading up to the First World War middle-class women continued to take an active part in dealing with social questions in the city. Their own organisations were now well established and they were also active in mixed-sex groups such as the COS. Now that local authorities had a greater role in dealing with social problems, the COS amalgamated with the Civic League of Personal Service and Public Welfare to form the Bristol Civic League. Its aims were to 'promote public welfare by means of public service' and to provide trained and experienced visitors, many of whom would be women, to help local authorities. Women held key roles in the League. Miss A.T. Thompson was secretary, while Mabel Tothill and Miss Townsend wrote important reports on its work just before the war.[132]

Experienced women Guardians were joined by new members who would make an impact on civic life, including Emily Smith and Rosa Pease, both single women. Emily Ann Webb, Jane Tillett and Mrs Lloyd, who were

MRS. TILLETT. MRS. LLOYD. MRS. WEBB.

(Three early Labour Women Guardians of the Poor. Mrs. Webb is now a City Councillor and Justice of the Peace).

3.14 Labour Women Guardians of the Poor: Mrs Tillett, Mrs Lloyd and Mrs Webb. Samson Bryher, *An Account of the Labour and Socialist Movement in Bristol*, 1929

married working-class women connected with the labour movement, were also elected and brought a fresh set of attitudes. [*Fig. 3.14*] Regardless of class and political allegiances, women had a number of concerns in common, such as support for temperance or for improved hospital facilities. Rosa Pease became Chair of the Board of Guardians in 1920, while Emily Webb and Emily Smith both went on to become JPs and city councillors and Smith later became an alderman. All three women served as elected members for decades. The abolition of School Boards in 1902, however, reduced women's scope for holding public office. They now had to rely on co-option to the Education Committee which many saw as less satisfactory – there were only two women co-opted in 1913.

After 1907 it was possible for women to stand for election to the City Council but they had no success. Three women put themselves forward: Helen Sturge as a Liberal candidate and Lilian Maude King and Emily Smith as Independents. Emily Smith (1859-1944), the daughter of an Anglican vicar, was motivated by her Christian beliefs to serve the community and belonged to a wide range of organisations including the Civic League, the Clifton branch of the Junior Imperial League and the Bristol branch of the Soldiers' and Sailors' Association. She was also active in single-sex groups that promoted women's involvement in social and political questions, including the NUWW, the Women's Local Government Society and the Bristol Suffrage Society.[133]

Emily Smith argued that women of all classes were needed in municipal government because there were 'so many, many subjects with which women are peculiarly fitted to deal…education, housing, feeding of schoolchildren' and they would provide a connecting link between municipal and social work'.[134] For her, therefore, party politics had no place in municipal politics. And yet her own position was complex and ambivalent. She was, for instance, a committed supporter of the Conservative Party, taking part in the Women's Unionist Association and acting as honorary secretary and then treasurer of the Conservative and Unionist Women's Franchise Association.[135]

Barton Hill University Settlement
Since it was difficult to gain election or co-option to public bodies, women who wanted to make a difference looked for other strategies to improve working-class lives. One new initiative was the establishment of the Barton Hill Settlement in 1911. Congregationalists had already set up a settlement in 1890 at Broad Plain House, St Philip's, with George Hare Leonard as resident warden, which provided clubs and a crèche for the infants of working mothers. In 1909 staff and students at University College decided to set up a University Settlement and it was later agreed that Hilda Cashmore should be the warden. After graduating, Cashmore had worked at Chesterfield Settlement with Violet Markham and in 1904 she was appointed as lecturer in Modern History at the Bristol Day Training College.[136] Many of the female students that she and her friend, Marian Pease, taught were enrolled as members of a social service guild. This involved 'serious reading on social questions' and some 'practical work' and the University Settlement provided the basis for the practical training of professional social workers.[137]

Barton Hill was a good choice as a location for the new Settlement. The local population needed support and links had already been made with working-class men and women in East Bristol. Marian Pease, whose father had been a proprietor of the Great Western Cotton Factory, had set up the Cotton Girls' Club in 1880 and gained experience of the lives of girls and young women. She had been helped by Mabel Tothill, who was also the honorary secretary of the East Bristol Branch of the Civic League. The Settlement opened in 1911 and the first three residents, Cashmore, Tothill and Lettice Jowitt, were all Quakers. Jowitt, one of nine daughters of an established Quaker family, was a lecturer at the Day Training College. Miss May Stavely, another lecturer at the College, who was President of the newly-formed Bristol Association of University Women, also lent her support.[138] The contribution of such women to social research and to social and educational work is evident in the University Settlement. Although they were referred to locally as 'the Settlement ladies', there was a considerable degree of cross-class collaboration. As Gleadle argues, this was often easier for women to achieve than for men, though from the first the Settlement attracted both male and female members.[139] Professor Leonard lent his support and the Workers' Educational Association and representatives from trade unions, friendly societies, the Co-operative Society and the Adult School were involved from the start.

The first three female residents used their wealth and education to help those without their advantages. Fund-raising enabled the Settlement House to be purchased in Ducie Road, but any expansion needed substantial financial contributions from individual women. In 1912 Mabel Tothill bought a freehold property at 63 Barton Hill Road and the following year an iron hall was built to provide accommodation for boys' activities. Alice Carver's generosity led to the addition of a wooden structure in 1914 and an open-air school for children with TB. She also gave a legacy to pay off the loans for building work. In 1919 Tothill bought four more cottages on Barton Hill Road and gave them to the Settlement.[140]

The Settlement had support from the local authority, especially for new initiatives that involved children, including the Open Air School, Schools for Mothers and an After Care Committee which linked with local schools. The Toynbee Room and library became the meeting place of the local WEA where lectures were given on a wide range of subjects. Margaret Bondfield, a prominent trade unionist and socialist, stayed at the Settlement when she visited Bristol during the 1912 dispute at the Cotton Factory. She was very impressed by the staff there, especially Hilda Cashmore, noting that 'The Settlement opened a soup kitchen for the strikers and the Warden was most helpful in ensuring that both sides at least had each other's point of view'.[141] The following year Cashmore left Barton Hill to become Warden at Ancoats Settlement in Manchester.

Working for Socialism

The thorny question of whether women should seek their goals through mixed-sex political parties or through their own, single-sex organisations came to a head in the decade preceding the First World War. This was a period in which the Labour Party gained a more significant presence in national and local politics and when the women's suffrage movement reached its height. In Bristol the development of socialist and independent labour politics provided some working-class women with a space in which they could engage in political activity.[142] Miss Gregory was treasurer of the Bristol Socialist

1 Emma (d.1590), daughter of Henry Brayne Esq, with her second husband Charles Somerset (d.1598) and an unnamed daughter, are depicted on their tomb at St James' Priory. Brayne was a London tailor who purchased the Priory lands after the Dissolution. Emma (one of his two daughters) brought half of this property to Charles Somerset, a younger son of the Earl of Worcester. Heiresses, like Emma, were often crucial in the transmission of property through marriage. That her daughter's name goes unrecorded is not unusual.

2 *The Tomb of Martha and Robert Aldworth (d.1634)*, watercolour print by Edward Cashin, 1825. (BMAG M2268a). *Bristol Museums, Galleries & Archives.* Alderman Robert Aldworth, a Merchant Venturer, owned Bristol's first sugar processing house, and sugar loaves are carved at the base of the tomb. Martha 'his lovinge and belov'd wife'– portrayed as equal in size yet at a lower elevation than Robert – partnered him in taking on apprentices. St Peter's Church was gutted by bombing in the Second World War and the tomb did not survive

3 Elizabeth Gorges (1578-1658) married Hugh Smyth of Ashton Court in 1596 and then her cousin Ferdinando Gorges in 1629. She was actively engaged in the running of both her husbands' estates. As Gorges' widow she rented out the decayed premises of Sir John Young's Great House to John Knight Jr. (1616-1679) on the site of what is now Colston Hall in Bristol. Elizabeth and her sister-in-law Helena Smyth, and Elizabeth Appleton Challoner, all helped finance Knight's sugar refinery – the first in the city to use Caribbean sugar. (BMAG 3010). ©BMGA Culture

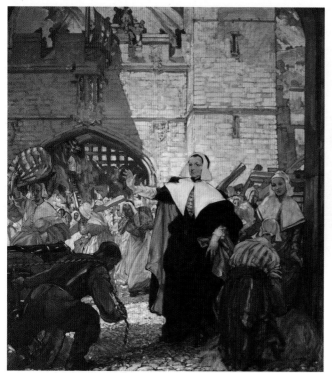

4 *Mistress Dorothy Hazzard and the Women of Bristol defending the Frome Gate against Prince Rupert, 1643*, an oil painting by Gerald Edward Moira (1918). (BMAG K521). *Bristol Museums, Galleries & Archives.* There is no contemporary depiction of this scene when, in July 1643, Dorothy Hazzard, a prominent Bristol religious radical, led a group of 200 women and children in defence of Frome Gate against an assault by Royalist forces. The painting owes much to the artist's imagination

5 Women market traders feature in the margins of many 18th and early-19th-century portrayals of the Bristol cityscape as well as in this romanticised Victorian recreation of Georgian Bristol. Detail from *Bristol High Cross* by Samuel Griffiths Tovey, 1841. (BMAG K763). *Bristol Museums, Galleries & Archives*

OPPOSITE ▶
8 Samuel Coleman, *St James's Fair, Bristol*, oil on canvas, 1824. (BMAG K3530).
Bristol Museums, Galleries & Archives
This portrayal of the annual fair a decade before its closure contrasts the bawd leading a young country girl to the brothel at the right of the painting with a respectable Quaker couple selling pamphlets (including an antislavery tract) and other items. See also Rolinda Sharples' portrayal of the fair on the front cover, showing women as entertainers and sellers of earthenware. In both paintings women are also portrayed as consumers

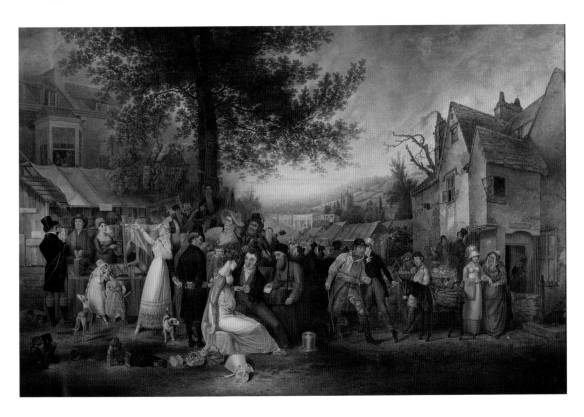

6 This enamelled portrait plaque is possibly Elizabeth Ring (1740-1816) at the age of 60. Ring worked with her husband Joseph in the manufacturing and retailing of china goods at the Water Lane Pottery in Bristol's Temple parish. Widowed in 1788 she continued to run the pottery in partnership with two male partners. In 1807 she operated an independent china and glass business at 9 Bridge Street which moved to 8 High Street in 1814. On her death, she bequeathed her business to her two daughters Elizabeth and Sophia and the firm remained in family hands until 1855. (BMAG LEAA21.9 Applied Art). *Bristol Museums, Galleries & Archives*

7 The Welsh Traders Book records those mainly female Welsh traders whom Bristol Corporation licensed to trade on the Back in Bristol (*aka* the Welsh Back).
BRO, F/M/We/ 1776-1807.
Bristol Museums, Galleries & Archives

9 *The Artist and Her Mother*, a portrait of Rolinda and Ellen Sharples by Rolinda Sharples, 1816. (BMAG K1064). *Bristol Museums, Galleries & Archives.*
Both women were accomplished artists

10 This detail from *The Trial of Colonel Brereton* by Rolinda Sharples, 1833 shows some of the women represented attending the trial. Note too the presence of the Hindu reformer Raja Ram Mohun Roy who was a friend of the Estlins and Mary Carpenter. (BMAG K1074). *Bristol Museums, Galleries & Archives*

11 *Mrs Mary Carpenter and her First Reformatory Girl, Annie Woolham, at Red Lodge, October 10th, 1854*, oil painting by George Edmund Butler, 1922. (BMAG K4578). *Bristol Museums, Galleries & Archives*

12 This painting of *Ann Yearsley Bristol Milkwoman and Poetess* by Joseph Manning, 1829, shows Yearsley as an untutored rustic. (BMAG M4069). *Bristol Museums, Galleries & Archives*

13 *Miss Annie Kenney*, by Winifred Bourne Medway c.1910. (BMAG K4330). *Bristol Museums, Galleries & Archives*. A leading member of the Women's Social and Political Union Kenney (1879-1930) became the paid organiser for Bristol and was living at 23 Gordon Road, Clifton when she sat for this painting. Little is known about Winifred Bourne Medway

14 *Portrait of Dame Clara Butt* (1872-1936) by Reginald Edward Higgins, c.1906. Clara Ellen Butt was an internationally famous opera star who worked closely with the composer Edward Elgar and captured the public imagination. Raised in Bristol, her talent was first spotted by the headmistress of the South Bristol High School which she attended in the 1870s. (BMAG K4362).
Bristol Museums, Galleries & Archives

15 *Peggy Ann Wood* (1912-1998) actress and co-manager of the Little Theatre, Bristol, by Arthur Wilson Gay, 1949.
University of Bristol Theatre Collection, ©*ArenaPal*

16 A British nurse looking very much 'the new woman' shakes hands with an Australian soldier in a wartime celebration of imperial solidarity.
The Journal of Bishop's Knoll Hospital Bristol 10 March 1917 Vol.1, no.5.
BRL 2181

17 Post-war election flyer for Mabel Tothill.
UBLSC and BRO 44562/3.
Bristol Museums and Art Galleries

18 Sherrie Eugene, Bristol's first black female broadcaster, on location at the newly-erected Pero's Bridge Bristol c.1999.
Courtesy Sherrie Eugene-Hart

19 Bristol's three women M.P.s with two members of the Board of Knightstone Housing Association who exemplify a growing coterie of well-educated women in Bristol's public life. From left to right: Sally Britton (Knightstone Housing Association), Valerie Davey M.P. (Lab Bristol West), Dawn Primarolo M.P. (Lab. Bristol South), Jean Corston M.P. (Lab. Bristol North) and Stella Clarke (Knightstone Housing Association) 19 March 1999.
©*Bristol Evening Post*

20 *Dawn Primarolo MP* by Richard Brazier 2010. Primarolo rose to become Paymaster General in 1999 and later held Cabinet Posts under successive Labour Governments. She retired from the Commons in 2015 and in that year was awarded the DBE.
Courtesy Houses of Parliament

3.15 'You can do much by your presence at our meetings'. Advertisement for the Bristol branch of the National Union of Women's Suffrage Societies. *Bristolian*, June 1914

Society, while Jane Tillett, wife of the trade union leader Ben Tillett, often chaired meetings.[143] Jane Tillett was elected to the Board of Guardians and was a representative on the Right to Work committee where she spoke on the feeding of schoolchildren. The other socialist group, the Independent Labour Party, with 600 members in 1911, was one of the largest branches in the country but before 1912 women did not play a prominent role.[144] They were more likely to become involved in labour politics through the Women's Labour League (WLL), a group established to encourage women to give support to the Labour Party. The Poor Law Guardian Emily Webb was one of the Bristol leaders. WLL members went out canvassing during elections, helped to organise women in trade unions during the labour unrest 1910-14 and collected money for striking miners in the Rhondda.[145]

Campaigning for the vote
The suffrage movement also revived at the turn of the century and reached

June Hannam and Moira Martin

Women *and* Cultural Life

Women in the nineteenth century were poets, artists, novelists, travel writers and translators. They played an important part in shaping the cultural life of the city and in some cases gained a national and international reputation for their work. Catherine Winkworth, for example, produced skilful translations of German hymns that continue to be widely used today. She also translated two biographies of founders of sisterhoods to help the poor and needy – the *Life of Pastor Fliedner* (1861) and the *Life of Amelia Sieveking* (1863). Her sister Susanna also translated German texts, including *The Life of Nebhur*. Women's literary and artistic interests were often varied. Alongside her publications on social questions Mary Carpenter also wrote a book on *Morning and Evening Meditations for Everyday in the Month* (1848) and memoirs of her father, Lant Carpenter, as well as producing a number of paintings. Amelia Edwards, an adventurous traveller, was also a novelist, artist, historian and Egyptologist. She was born in London but moved to Westbury-on-Trym in 1864 at the age of 33. She travelled extensively in Egypt from the 1870s and wrote about her experiences as well as publishing history texts and a translation to help scholars of Egyptian antiquities. One of her best known books was *A Thousand Miles Up the Nile* (1877) which she also illustrated. Amelia wrote numerous novels and poems. Her last novel, *Lord Brackenbury* (1880), was a run-away success that ran to 15 editions.

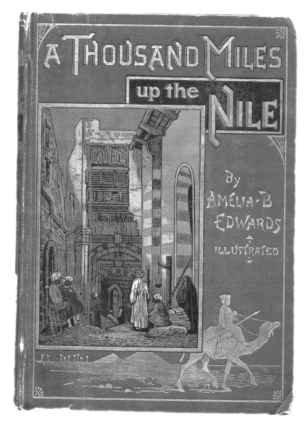

A less well-known traveller from Bristol, Eliza Bush, sought to follow Christ's footsteps in the Holy Land, and published a book about her experiences in the Middle East, Greece, and Turkey. Here she went to a mosque to see and hear the 'howling dervishes' and then to spot the Sultan, who she described as a

> plain, unpretending-looking man, more like a London banker than a luxurious Turk.

Writing fiction was perhaps the best way to reach a wide audience and at the same time could provide middle-class women with a much needed source of income. Women often wrote short stories that

'Miss Ellen Terry...in The Dead Heart', publicity card.
Michigan State University

were a key feature of many newspapers and journals in this period, as well as turning out full-length novels. Emma Marshall, the mother of seven children, was a novelist who was part of a literary circle in Clifton that included J.A. Symonds. After 1878, when her husband's bank failed, she had to become a 'hack writer', taking every commission that was offered, in order to help clear the family's debts. Brierley and Reid suggest that in Bristol she was most well known for her historical novels which had a local setting, in particular *In Colston's Days* (1907), which was dedicated to Symonds.

Emily Young lived in Clifton before the First World War and (though they were not published until the 1920s) wrote a series of novels based on close observation of Clifton Society. Young won prizes for her work and her novels were republished by Virago in the 1980s. Along with her husband Arthur Daniell, a solicitor, she supported women's suffrage and together they put on a feminist play.

The suffrage campaign encouraged women to express their ideas in novels, plays and poetry and Miss Ramsay, secretary of the Bristol suffrage group in the 1870s, wrote one of the earliest suffrage novels: *Miss Mildred's Career: A Tale of the Women's Suffrage Movement* (1874).

A small number of women also made a public impact through their role as entertainers. Kate and Ellen Terry appeared frequently at Bristol's Theatre Royal while Clara Butt [*colour plate 14*], who grew up in Bristol, gained an international reputation as a singer. Such women made it morally more acceptable for females to perform in public, but care was needed to protect their reputations and respectability – the Terry sisters were chaperoned by their parents into their 20s... ■

out to a wider group of women.[146] [*Fig. 3.15*] The Women's Co-operative
Guild invited numerous speakers on suffrage while one of their leaders, Annie
Martin, a member of the Women's Liberal Association, was an activist in the
suffrage movement.[147] The Bristol branch of the National Union of Women's
Suffrage Societies (NUWSS) made more efforts to involve working women.
Selina Cooper and Sarah Reddish, working-class organisers from Lancashire,
were invited to Bristol in 1904 for a week's campaign when they held numerous meetings and addressed members of the WCG and the Shop Assistants'
Association. Such initiatives were short-lived. NUWSS committee members
were still drawn largely from Clifton and were less radical in their political
views than their nineteenth-century predecessors. There is little evidence after
1904 that they tried to broaden their membership to include working women.
It was the development of militancy after 1906 that gave the suffrage
movement greater prominence and that provoked controversy. A Bristol
branch of the Women's Social and Political Union (WSPU), the militant group
led by the Pankhursts, was formed in 1907 with Annie Kenney appointed as
a paid organiser. A charismatic speaker, she had a devoted following in Bristol
and inspired others to come into the city to work with her. [*Colour plate 13*].
Local supporters included Victoria Simmons of Clifton, one of twelve
children from a vegetarian family, who joined the WSPU with her mother
and sisters after hearing Annie Kenney speak, and Lilian Dove Wilcox, a
widow from Bedminster, who took over as honorary secretary of the Bristol
branch when Annie Kenney left the city in 1911.[148] The Priestman sisters,
now in their 70s and members of a suffrage group that was unique to Bristol,
the Women's Reform Union, also gave help to Annie Kenney and supported
the WSPU financially until 1912.[149]

The WSPU were adept at gaining publicity. They sold copies of their
newspaper, *Votes for Women*, on the street and took actions that led to arrest
and imprisonment. Teresa Garnett, for example, while holding a horse whip,
accosted Winston Churchill when he left Temple Meads station and spent a
month in Horfield prison where she went on hunger strike and was forcibly
fed. As militancy escalated after 1912 numerous buildings were destroyed,
including the University Sports Pavilion.[150] In contrast to some towns there
is little evidence that socialist women were involved in this campaign although
the WSPU did try to attract working-class support by holding meetings
outside factories in the lunch hour.

The NUWSS was keen to distance itself from WSPU militancy, but did
adopt more flamboyant methods, including demonstrations and a Suffrage

Pilgrimage in 1913.[151] The plan was for members of local federations (formed from suffrage societies) to walk from different parts of the country to converge in London for a mass rally in Hyde Park on 20th July. Mabel Harriet Cross, aged 41, the wife of a Clifton solicitor, was the organiser of the Bristol contingent. She was honorary secretary of the Bristol WSS and organiser of the West of England Federation. She was helped by Sarah Jane Tanner, aged 57, from Westbury on Trym, who produced a history of the Bristol suffrage movement as well as writing suffrage songs to existing tunes, and Mrs Hicks, also the wife of a Clifton solicitor.[152] The crowd were usually good natured but there was a difficult situation when the pilgrims reached Twerton, a working-class district in Bath. During a meeting some of the 'Pilgrims were badly mobbed by hooligans…Miss Tanner was knocked down and much bruised and Mrs Cross had to escape, disguised in a man's coat and hat, from the back of a house in which they had taken refuge'. Nevertheless, next morning they marched off 'with banners flying, accompanied by many sympathisers'.[153]

Socialist and suffrage campaigning in East Bristol
Since 1912 the NUWSS had also changed political tactics and had agreed to support the Labour Party where a sitting MP was hostile to women's suffrage. In 1913 the National Union's Election Fighting Fund (EFF) committee decided to support a labour candidate in East Bristol where the MP, Charles Hobhouse, was a Cabinet member and anti-suffragist.[154] The EFF sent Annie Townley, a socialist and wife of a textile worker from Blackburn, as a paid organiser and she soon gained support from working-class women in East Bristol. This was vital since the local NUWSS committee gave little help-three of its members had resigned over the pact with the Labour Party.[155] Annie Townley worked through a separate group, the East Bristol Women's Suffrage Society, whose secretary was Mabel Tothill.[156] There was further help from ILP members, notably Walter and Bertha Ayles [*Fig. 3.16*], who had come to Bristol in 1909 when Walter was appointed organiser for the ILP. Bertha Ayles was already employed as a part-time organiser for the Women's Labour League and was soon involved in the Bristol WLL as well as becoming chairman of the Bristol ILP in 1912.[157]

Annie Townley made an immediate impact. She gained support for her cause from various groups within the local labour movement, including trade unions, while working women's organisations such as the WCG, the WLL and the Railway Women's Guild were reported as 'rallying with enthusiasm for the fight'.[158] By May 200 friends of women's suffrage had been enrolled. Members of the Bristol East ILP women's group went out canvassing every Wednesday and Annie Townley proclaimed that registration work had been a great success, 'especially among the committee of the National Union branch themselves who never before had heard Labour speeches, or met Labour men'.[159]

The campaign became even more intensive after July when Walter Ayles replaced Alderman Frank Sheppard as prospective candidate. Ayles was crucial in persuading the local labour and socialist movement to take women's suffrage seriously since he was personally committed to women's rights.[160] The momentum of the campaign, including regular meetings and joint labour and suffrage meetings was kept up until the outbreak of war when active propaganda came to an end.

Conclusion

Women continued to make their mark on Bristol's economic, cultural and social life throughout the nineteenth century. What was distinctive at this time was women's high profile engagement in voluntary social action and political reform campaigns. It was not just the sheer numbers involved and the breadth of their interests that was noteworthy, but also the exciting initiatives and new ways of working that deserve more attention. In this period reform movements were by no means always London-centred. New ideas could start in the provinces. Bristol was at the forefront of developing many new initiatives, including reformatories for juvenile delinquents, emigration societies for children and homes for friendless girls. From a local base women built on religious, family and friendship networks to bring themselves into the heart of national and international reform movements, including anti-slavery work and the campaign to repeal the Contagious Diseases' Acts. Women worked closely with men but also formed their own groups where they gained experience in leadership, as well as organisational skills, from working together with other women.

These high-profile women who engaged in social action were drawn largely from middle-class families in Clifton. Nonetheless, by the end of the period working-class women had also begun to make their voices heard both through their own organisations, such as the Women's Co-operative Guild, and also through the women's suffrage campaign. At the same time they began to participate in the growing mixed-sex socialist and labour movement. In the twentieth century tensions over loyalties to class, sex and party were exacer-

3.16 Walter Ayles, Bristol ILP
councillor and his wife Bertha,
organiser for the Women's Labour
League, pictured at the opening of
the ILP headquarters, Kingsley Hall,
Old Market, Bristol. They were both
suffrage supporters.
*Souvenir of the Opening of the Kingsley
Hall*, 1911. BRL, B24623

bated at a time of wide ranging social, economic and political changes.
Women continued to work together as women in order to achieve social
reforms, but they now had to develop a way to work with local authorities,
who had an expanded responsibility for welfare services, and with paid professionals. Also, once partial enfranchisement had been achieved in 1918 many
women turned to formal party politics to achieve their goals which could
make it difficult to work with other organisations. The spaces in which women
were able to continue to play a role in Bristol's civic life in the twentieth
century, and some of the tensions between them, will be explored in the next
chapter.

Bristol Women in the Twentieth Century

Madge Dresser and June Hannam

Two world wars, economic depression, the growth of the Labour Party, the development of a welfare state, and the rise of a consumer society were just some of the momentous changes affecting women in the twentieth century. In 1914 women still did not have the vote, were barred from most professions and had little control over their fertility. By 2000 most formal restrictions on their access to work, education and political participation had been lifted, and divorce and birth control had become commonplace. How far did these reforms affect the ways in which women could shape their city? To what extent were there continuities as well as discontinuities in their position despite the upheavals of war? How far were women successful in challenging gender inequalities that hampered their attempts to be 'active' citizens?

The First World War

Described as a 'total war' the First World War required women as well as men to be involved in order to ensure success.[1] Women were needed to undertake paid work to release men for the armed services, while welfare work and fund raising took on a new meaning at a time of conflict. Many suffrage campaigners hoped that by demonstrating their capabilities and 'service' to the nation women would strengthen their argument for the vote and would gain greater equality in the workplace and in the home.[2] Although historians such as Arthur Marwick have also claimed that war promoted formal equality between the sexes, more recent studies suggest that the impact of war on women's position was complex. Individual women gained new experiences at the workplace, but were often seen as temporary workers at a time of national emergency. War also highlighted the importance of women's 'traditional' role as mothers and homemakers to ensure a stable family life.[3] Nonetheless, in the short term, women had an expanded role to play in civic life which in turn was important for the national war effort.

Attitudes to war

When war was declared the immediate response of women who were engaged in public life was to offer their services for any relief work needed on behalf of women and girls or members of the armed services. In common with other parts of the country members of the Bristol National Union of Women's Suffrage Societies (NUWSS), including Mabel Tothill, Helen and Elizabeth Sturge, Miss Pease and Sarah Jane Tanner, became involved in the Prince of Wales Relief Fund in order to help women who had lost their employment at the outset of war. Mabel Tothill was honorary treasurer of the Fund's Committee for Women's Employment and used the Barton Hill Settlement as a workroom and training area for unemployed women, in particular seamstresses. Before it was wound up early in 1915 it was used to make garments for distressed Belgians and others.[4]

Women War Workers

As more men were needed to fight the demand for women workers steadily increased. Munitions workers gained the greatest publicity. They were entering a male preserve and were also producing goods rarely associated with femininity – weapons of war. Women were known as 'dilutees' since the tasks they performed were subdivided into component parts and were not directly comparable to those of male workers.[5] In Bristol, where the manufacturing base was diverse, women worked in a range of war-related industries. For example, they were engaged in the manufacture of aircraft at Filton and Brislington, where they stitched canvas over wooden frames and coated it with 'dope' to tighten the fabric.[6] [*Fig. 4.1*] They were employed as munitionettes at Strachan & Henshaw's iron works, and in making motor cycles for army contracts at Douglas Motors of Kingswood. They also took jobs in the Avonmouth Gas Works and made glycerine for explosives at Thomas & Co. Soap Works.[7] Women were also directly substituted for men in non-industrial occupations, working as conductors on trams and buses, as postwomen, as railway clerks and as ambulance drivers.[8] [*Fig. 4.2*]

Even occupations identified with women could provide a different experience of work in the context of war. Nurses, for example, now treated wounded soldiers from the front line as existing hospitals increased the number of beds available for casualties. The work expanded as new hospitals were established, including the Beaufort Hospital at Fishponds and Bishop's Knoll which was set up specifically for Commonwealth troops.[9] [*Colour plate 16*] These required many more trained nurses as well as members of the Voluntary

4.1 Women doping aircraft wings at Filton in the First World War.
Duncan Greenman Collection, OW77

Aid Detachments. Women were also attracted into the armed services and the Women's Land Army, whose members showed their pride in the work they had done when 600 women marched in a parade in front of the Colston Hall towards the end of the war.[10]

In the press women were praised for their 'splendid patriotism' in coming forward to help the war effort, including their 'magnificent' voluntary work.[11] Nonetheless *The Bristolian,* now re-named *Bristol & The War,* introduced a note of criticism: 'but frankly the women of the working class do not seem to be doing all they might' despite being offered good money for work that is 'not unduly hard, and for hours that cannot be considered excessive'.[12] Underneath the rhetoric of patriotism, therefore, there were class tensions and a failure to acknowledge the low pay and poor conditions of women's war work. The 'dope' that was used in aircraft manufacture, for example, was highly inflammable and toxic, 'causing giddiness, headaches and fatigue', while women in the gas industry were injured from leaking mustard gas.[13] Pay in Bristol was low compared to other regions, especially in 'traditional' women's trades,

4.2 'Lady conductors' substituting for men on Bristol tramways.
Bristol & the War, Jan-Feb, 1917. Vol. 11, no. 31. BRL

where wages could be as little as 9/- to 11/- a week. In this context, despite the fact that industrial disputes were illegal, female textile workers in the Great Western Cotton Factory took strike action in 1916 to obtain a rise in wages. Many were now members of the National Federation of Women Workers (NFWW) but a special fund was also set up to assist non-union members.[14] Help came from women in the University Settlement, the Women's Co-operative Guild, the Women's Labour League and the Railway Women's Guild. On this occasion the employers had to concede and make a settlement.[15] Although women's wages overall had increased by the end of the war they still received less than men, even for similar work.[16] For example fourth-class examiners at a Bristol shell factory received a third less than the men.[17]

Patriots and Peace Activists

The solidarity women experienced as women when they fought together in the suffrage campaign was difficult to maintain after the first few months of war. Some displayed a fervent patriotism. Emily Smith, for example, a Conservative in politics, was honorary secretary for a time of the Bristol branch of the Women's Defence Relief Corps, which aimed to 'train women to be good citizens'. [*Fig. 4.3*] Its civilian branch sought to provide women to work in jobs that would release men to fight, while the semi-military section was designed to aid in recruiting men for the armed services and to train women in stretcher bearing, signalling, scouting and the use of arms'.[18]

Others were committed to working for peace. When Aletta Jacobs, a Dutch suffragist, organised a Women's Peace Congress at the Hague in May 1915, Mabel Tothill, Marianne Hill, Mariabella Fry and Marion Pease, all Quakers and suffragists, wrote to the press to defend the Congress against criticisms in the *Western Daily Press* that they were reckless and aiding the Germans.[19] As a result of the Congress a new group, the Women's International League (WIL) was formed in Britain and the Bristol branch had 82 members by 1916.[20] Members were drawn largely from the pre-war suffrage and socialist movements and included the secretary, Miss Baretti, members of the Fry, Sturge and Pease families, all Quakers, and the socialists Mabel Tothill, Annie Townley and Hannah Higgins.

The WIL was part of a fervent mixed-sex movement for peace which included Quakers, the Union of Democratic Control and the Independent Labour Party (ILP), all of whom shared the common aim of working for a negotiated peace, for a just settlement after the war and for the establishment of an international organisation for the maintenance of peace.[21] Peace campaigners did not seek to disrupt the war effort itself but they encountered fierce hostility. The University of Bristol came under attack for being pro-German and staff of the Barton Hill Settlement, including Mabel Tothill, were accused by Dr Geraldine Hodgson, in a letter to the press, of using the Settlement for 'semi-secret' peace activities.[22] This caused a flurry of excitement in the city and led Mabel Tothill to write to the editor of the *Western Daily Press* to apologise for using Settlement notepaper on behalf of the peace group, Fellowship of Reconciliation, and assuring readers that she was no longer associated with the Settlement.[23]

Socialist women were at the centre of peace activism, distributing literature and speaking at meetings. Mabel Tothill, along with the ILP councillor Walter Ayles, was one of the most high profile peace activists in the city. She attended annual conferences of the WIL and was president of the Bristol Peace Council. In 1916 she took on even more controversial work when she became honorary secretary of the Bristol Joint Advisory Committee for Conscientious Objectors, set up by the ILP to support men who refused to fight. She produced

4.3 Members of the Women's Defence Relief Corps in Bristol, drilling in uniform. *Bristol & the War*, February 1916. BRL

leaflets to draw attention to the plight of those imprisoned for their views and towards the end of the war spoke on public platforms to argue for their release.[24] Her own view of patriotism was very different from that of Emily Smith. She wrote that despite problems of unemployment and poverty, in England the majority enjoyed 'a large measure of liberty of thought, speech and action'. 'If we are true patriots' we will stand by 'those who have surrendered their physical freedom to secure freedom of soul'.[25] With so many ILP men imprisoned a space opened up for Mabel Tothill, Annie Townley and Hannah Higgins, along with a new recruit Lucy Cox, to take on important positions within the organisation and they ran the branch throughout the war.[26]

Voluntary Relief Work

Voluntary relief work – a traditional focus for women's energies – was needed now more than ever before. For some the welfare of soldiers took priority. Mrs Georgina Budgett, for example, the wife of a director of a grocery firm and secretary of the Bristol Red Cross, came up with the idea of sending parcels of food to prisoners of war with a card inside to ensure that the prisoner had received the parcel and it had not been stolen. Georgina Budgett organised an army of female volunteers to generate money for the scheme and they managed to raise £40,000 a year.[27] The initiative was then adopted elsewhere in the country.

War also highlighted the importance of maternal and child welfare. This provided an outlet for women, especially suffragists, who wanted to support the war effort through preserving life rather than destroying it. Harriet Cross, secretary of the Bristol NUWSS, was a key figure in setting up maternity centres and Schools for Mothers, and became superintendent of the School in Bedminster.[28] She sought financial and practical support from members of the NUWSS by drawing attention to the links between her work with mothers and the development of the nation. Harriet Cross claimed that 'the mothers of the nation are its best assets…and we as a nation need to be taught this' since they were building up future citizens 'to secure and safeguard to them the land their men were fighting for'.[29] As well as monitoring the health of babies and providing advice on child care the Schools encouraged thrift and making do with scarce resources.

The local authority was also prompted by war-time conditions to take an interest in maternal welfare. This opened a temporary window of opportunity for women's groups, including those representing working-class women, to become involved in official bodies dealing with welfare. The WIL, the Women's Co-operative Guild (WCG) and the Railway Women's Guild, for example, were all asked to send a representative to the local committee set up to administer welfare centres. The socialist campaigner Annie Townley welcomed this initiative but also took the opportunity to argue that mothers needed the vote to safeguard their interests in a Parliament of men.[30]

Women Patrols and Police

Members of pre-war women's groups not only held different views about the war itself, but also about women's work and the female worker. Class was a key issue here. The National Union of Women Workers (NUWW), for example, welcomed the opportunities that the war presented to expand women's paid work and to demonstrate their capabilities. But they also expressed concerns about the moral welfare of working-class girls, an issue raised frequently by government, employers and the press during the war.[31] These complex issues came to the fore in the establishment of the Bristol Training School for Women Patrols and Police, the first in the country.

The Bristol branch of the NUWW played a key role in this initiative. After hearing an address on women patrols in London a committee was formed of the NUWW and other interested groups to raise funds for a training school which was finally opened in September 1915.[32] Active members of the committee included the pre-war suffragists Helen Sturge, Rosa Pease and Emily Smith, who was president of the Bristol NUWW. Dorothy Peto, director of the training school from 1917, provided energetic leadership and later

4.4 Dorothy Peto, director of the Training School for Women Patrols and Police. *The Bristol Training School for Women Patrols and Police, Annual Report*, 1917. BRL B18020

became head of the women's branch of the Metropolitan Police.[33] [*Fig. 4.4*]

The School had two objectives which linked both paid and unpaid work. The first was to train women volunteers to patrol the streets, railway stations and parks to help safeguard 'wholesome recreation' and to promote a 'higher standard of self-control' in young women.[34] The school worked in partnership with the Civic League in order to find placements for trainees. The second objective was to train women as a preliminary step to their joining the paid police force, although it was not until the Police Act of 1916 that women could be given full powers of arrest. Recruits came from all over the country and were then employed in varied capacities – as patrol volunteers, as paid assistants to specific police forces, as police in munitions factories where they were under government control and, in a small number of cases, as policewomen under the control of the chief constable.[35]

The chair of the Watch Committee and the chief constable welcomed the patrols but were less convinced about the employment of women police.[36] Nonetheless by 1918 eight women were employed as uniformed constables. Bristol prided itself on being the first city in the country to employ a woman detective in 1916, followed by a second in the following year.[37] They were to be engaged in solving all classes of crime, not just those involving women and children. This was highly controversial and led to a statement from the Metropolitan Police that claimed that:

> It is sometimes unsafe to trust a woman with an important investigation where young men are concerned. They are swayed by emotion. They can't help it; it is in their nature, and they have been known to fall in love with the man they have been sent to watch.[38]

This response showed that beliefs about the different natures and capabilities of men and women were still deeply rooted, despite the war, and would continue to affect their public roles in subsequent years.

Between the wars

In 1918, after many years of struggle, women over 30 were given the right to the Parliamentary vote, while the municipal franchise was also extended. It was not until 1928, however, that women finally achieved equal voting rights with men. During the first election when younger women went to the polls headlines in the press speculated about the impact of the 'flapper vote'.[39] But how far were women able to take advantage of these changes? They were still hampered by a male-dominated political culture and by an emphasis in the media on their primary roles as wives and mothers. Economic depression reinforced these views and made it difficult to build on war-time changes.

Women and Employment

At the end of the war women were expected to leave work if their employment was needed for returning service men. This was not necessarily welcomed by women workers. Miss Howarth, regional organiser for the NFWW in Bristol reported that 80% of women would want, and needed, to stay in their present jobs rather than returning to their old ones unless the latter were made more attractive. She thought at least half of women in industry were dependent on their earnings and 30% of them had dependants.[40] Nonetheless it was difficult for women to retain their positions, especially when unemployment increased. Early in 1920 the Bristol branch of the International Union of ex-servicemen, through deputations and demonstrations, put pressure on employers to dismiss female workers. The Tramways Company was a specific target and on some occasions women conductresses were manhandled. Torn between sympathy for ex-servicemen and its female employees, the Company reluctantly dismissed its women workers.[41]

Unemployed single women then found that they were not entitled to either Poor Relief or unemployment benefit unless they accepted low paid work, especially in domestic service.[42] It was more difficult for married women to find employment in manufacturing; the closure of the cotton factory in 1925 reduced the demand for married women's labour and firms producing food, tobacco and paper still preferred to take on single women.[43]

By the time of the 1921 census private domestic service was again the occupation with the highest number of female workers. Although the method of recording occupations had changed since 1911, making any direct comparison difficult, the figures suggest that in 1921 women workers were still concentrated in private domestic service (7488), tobacco (6294), confectionery (4466) and tailoring (4434).[44] There was an increase in 'white blouse' work, a trend that had already begun before the war, with women employed as clerical workers, telegraphists and typists. The number of women in the professions steadily increased and they gained more influential posts, especially in education and medicine. In 1920, for example, at Bristol University, Helen Wodehouse was appointed as chair of education, the first woman to hold such a role, and in 1928 Winifred Lucy Shepland was appointed as the first woman Registrar of any university.[45]

A number of doctors followed in the pioneering footsteps of Eliza Walker Dunbar. They were responsible for focusing on areas that were often neglected, such as paediatrics or mental health, and for introducing innovations in treatment. Elizabeth Casson (1881-1954), for example, was engaged in charitable work with Octavia Hill before she decided to study medicine at the age of thirty and was the first woman to obtain a doctorate from Bristol University in 1926. She gained a national reputation for her work with mentally ill patients. In 1929 she founded a private clinic, Dorset House, for those with limited means where she developed new ways of treating patients through occupational therapy. She also organised a psychiatric clinic at Bristol General Hospital and took honorary posts as a consultant in occupational therapy at Southmead and at Ham Green Hospital.[46]

Politics

After the war, electoral reform and the passing of the Sex Disqualification Removal Act in 1919 provided an opportunity for women to play a wider role in public life. Bristol appointed its first women magistrates in 1919 from among those who had given many years of their life 'in the service of the city'.[47] They included Emily Webb, a Poor Law Guardian since 1900, Emily

Smith, an active member of women's organisations, the Kyrle Society and the Civic Society and Miss Townsend, a long-time co-opted member of the Education Committee.[48]

The NUWSS hoped that more women would stand for local elections and formed a Women's Citizen Association to encourage them to do so. Echoing pre-war arguments, Elizabeth Sturge emphasised the special qualities that women would bring to municipal government and criticised the fact that 'party politics were considered of more importance than the needs of the people'.[49] In Bristol, however, party political rivalry was fierce. The growth of the Labour Party led to an anti-socialist reaction and a Citizens' Party was formed from Conservatives and Liberals in 1926. In this context, if women were to have any success they had to stand for a specific party.[50]

Bristol did not have a woman MP until Lady Apsley in 1943, but a small number of women were successful in gaining seats on the City Council. Between 1919 and 1939 there were 18 different women councillors, eleven from the Labour Party and seven from the Conservative/Citizen parties.[51] The highest number in any one council was 10 in 1939. The six women elected in the 1920s had all gained experience of public work in the pre-war period.[52] The first was the socialist Mabel Tothill (1920), elected despite her controversial peace activism during the war. [*Colour plate 17*] She was quickly followed by the Conservative Emily Smith (1920) and Lilian Maude Pheysey (1920) for the Labour Party. Pheysey, a mother of eight, had been active in the Mothers' Union, the Workers' Education Association and the Bristol Temperance Society – a rather different set of activities than most labour women. She was also a JP and, in 1932, became the first female alderman, followed by Emily Smith in 1933.[53]

To what extent did women on the council make a difference and in what way? They were constrained by party loyalties and priorities, and rarely acted together as women to challenge gender inequalities. Nonetheless they pursued a range of social and environmental issues. The Conservative Edith Robinson campaigned for the council to purchase Oldbury Court estate to provide healthy leisure facilities for local people.[54] There was only one woman councillor on the Housing Committee but women did maintain pressure on the council to tackle housing problems throughout the period. Emily Smith was successful in her campaign for a lodging house for single women with limited means in St Pauls, while others raised issues of the water supply, street lighting and overcrowding.[55]

Labour women were the most vociferous in pursuing welfare questions, but it was difficult to get measures passed when the Labour Party did not have a majority until 1937.[56] Nonetheless, in 1921, Lilian Pheysey was instrumental in persuading the council to cover over part of the River Frome in order to provide employment for unemployed men and to improve the sanitary condition of the local area.[57] She also campaigned for green areas and public baths and washhouses. Some welfare issues did challenge gender inequalities. Mabel Tothill, for example spoke frequently about the provision of public conveniences which would have made it easier for women to move freely outside the home but this was rejected on the grounds of cost.[58] A similar demand was made in Kingswood when pressure was exerted on the council by the Women's Co-operative Guild, but again the issue was deferred because of the expense.[59] This suggests that it was more difficult for working-class women to make their voices heard than it had been during the war. The WCG, for example, no longer had a co-opted member on the Maternity and Child Welfare Committee in 1926, despite protests from the Labour Party, while a request from the WCG for representation on the Kingswood Milk Committee was also denied.[60]

Women were still able to play an important role in the Poor Law and its associated welfare institutions. By 1929 there were 20 women guardians, compared to eight during the war, and two of them had served as chairman: Miss Rosa Pease in 1920 and Miss Lydia Phelps in 1928.[61] Women Guardians were particularly well represented and active on committees concerned with the welfare of women and children, such as the Home Allowance Committee, the Girls' and Women's Protection Committee and the Children's Committee. Indeed they often chaired these sub-committees. However, they were also well represented on the Finance and General Purposes Committee, so could not be said to be marginalised.[62] In a period of severe economic distress Labour women guardians focused on the needs of the unemployed. Mrs Florence Batt's motion in 1922 that there should be more generous relief for the unemployed in the winter was carried, but subsequent attempts to increase the scale of relief were unsuccessful.[63] When Public Assistance Committees (PAC) replaced Boards of Guardians in 1929 women's participation declined. But by 1938, in contrast to some cities, women seem to have recovered their influential role and constituted a third of the Bristol PAC.[64]

The Women's Movement
Earlier histories suggested that once the vote had been won, the feminist movement fragmented and there were few concerted attempts to challenge

gender inequalities until the Women's Liberation Movement of the 1960s.[65] Recent histories, however, have drawn attention to the growth and vibrancy of a range of women's organisations in the 1920s and 30s.[66] These included women's groups within the main political parties, and also non-party political organisations such as the Women's Institute, the Townswomen's Guild (which developed from the NUWSS), the Mother's Union and the National Council of Women (formerly the NUWW). Some were reluctant to use the label feminist and an emphasis was placed on the importance of women's role within the home, but they did campaign for a series of reforms to improve women's lives, including the provision of birth control advice.[67]

The education of the new woman voter was a key aim of all these groups. They invited outside speakers and encouraged members to give talks and to participate in political activities. Both the Women's Liberal Federation and the Labour Party women's sections, for example, held a mock council or parliamentary meeting with members taking different roles in order to encourage younger women to stand as candidates.[68] They wanted women to see the connection between local politics and their home lives and to give women a space to express themselves. Annie Townley, for example, argued that Labour women's section meetings enabled housewives to meet together in the afternoons and to share their problems, many of which were overcome when they realised that others had the same difficulties and 'where for an hour she can feel the sense of responsibility as a citizen'.[69] Individual women also pressurised the Labour Party to support issues of importance for women. The councillor Kate Gleeson, for example, organised a series of conferences in Bristol in the 1930s on infant mortality and pressed for more birth control information. In 1934, after a heated debate, it was agreed that the Labour Party would provide a room in their premises for Harriet Cross to give contraceptive advice.[70] The Conservative and Unionist Association Women's Section, with nearly 8,000 members in 1937, focused more on fundraising and political canvassing.[71] There were still over 7000 members in 1975.

Other organisations were based on specific occupations or industries. The Electrical Association of Women (EAW), for example, was comprised of women who worked in the industry and also the wives of male employees. The EAW sought to promote the use of electricity in the home to ease the burden on housewives and campaigned for women to influence house designs. Dorothy Newman, the energetic chair of the Bristol branch, pushed for the building of an all-electric house, opened in 1935, which brought her to prominence at a national level.[72] Such groups did not work in isolation –

the EAW, for example, was affiliated to the National Council of Women (NCW), the Institute of Voluntary Welfare Workers and the Venture Club. The latter, a female equivalent of the Rotary Club, was formed by professional women in Bristol in 1920 and was the first of its kind in the country. The aim was for women who worked 'to exchange ideas', to work for the common good, and to 'widen the spirit of comradeship'.[73] When Vicky Tryon (1897-1977), a GP, was president she encouraged the Club to help the unemployed, to support homeless women in Bedminster and to take an interest in children without mothers.[74] In 1930 Venture Clubs merged with the Soroptomists Clubs, a movement begun in America in the early 1920s. The Soroptomists also worked closely with the EAW, the NCW and the Federation of University Women on projects such as funding public lodging houses and the provision of ambulances.[75]

Welfare Work

Although the state took increasing responsibility for welfare during the twentieth century, women still had a role at local level as Poor Law Guardians or as co-opted members of welfare committees, as well as in voluntary organisations. Outside the framework of party politics women worked together on welfare issues, in particular housing where the poor state of Bristol's housing stock was a cause for concern. Hilda Cashmore of Barton Hill University Settlement formed a branch of the Garden Cities and Town Planning Association (GCTPA). Just prior to the introduction of the 1919 Housing Act, the City Council consented to the creation of a Women's Advisory Committee and asked Miss Townsend to be responsible for it. She was supported in this work by Mrs Falk of Barton Hill University Settlement and Mrs Burman of the Women's Co-operative Guild. The Advisory Committee produced detailed recommendations for new houses and although these were accepted by the Housing Committee many of the recommendations were not implemented.[76] When the economic crisis of 1921 resulted in cut backs to subsidies for house building Cashmore, as Chair of the GCTPA, launched the House Famine Campaign and a mass meeting was held at the Colston Hall in 1923 to encourage the council to build more homes. Following the Labour Government's Wheatley Housing Act of 1924 Bristol Council built 7000 homes.

International interests

Welfare was not the only area in which women sought to make an impact. The interest in peace and international relations that a minority of women

4.5 The Tuckett family, from left to right: Angela Tuckett, her brother Coldstream, father Richard Clayton Tuckett, and elder sister Joan c.1920. Born in Clifton, Angela later qualified in 1929 as Bristol's first women's solicitor. *Courtesy Erynne Baynes*

had shown during the First World War continued into the inter-war years with many more becoming involved in organisations such as the Peace Pledge Union. Marge Evans, a Labour Party activist, criticised her party for being too parochial in the 1920s but claimed that international events at last became centre stage in the 1930s with the rise of fascism in Germany and the Spanish Civil War. The anti-Fascist and pro-Communist sympathies of Angela Tuckett (1906-1994), Bristol's first woman solicitor, led her to visit Spain and Greece in the 1930s and to co-found Bristol's Committee for the Defence of Spanish Democracy before going on to be a nationally important organiser in the labour movement.[77] [*Fig 4.5*]

Women were active in helping refugees from these areas. Dr Elizabeth Casson, for example, joined with Quaker and Jewish women in the city in taking in German refugees. She provided physicians with work as nurses for board and lodging in her hospital.[78] Although women, and men, in the peace movement remained committed to the idea that international conflicts should not be solved by war, events in Germany and Spain did make them reassess their immediate strategies. Once war was declared in September 1939 most gave their support to the war effort.

Second World War

The Second World War can be viewed as even more of a total war than the first, with civilians now facing danger from aerial bombardment.[79] Women were once more needed to play a key role, but there was again ambivalence about how to use them.[80] This time, however, as Sue Bruley notes, we are fortunate that more first-hand accounts of women's experiences are available than there were for the 1914-18 conflict.[81] In Bristol these include Joyce Storey's *Joyce's War*, VAM, *The Diary of a Bristol Woman*, and Ethel Thomas, *War Story*.[82]

Employment

Women were direct substitutes for men as porters and ticket collectors on the railways, as readers of gas meters and as policewomen. They were also recruited for heavy industry in a range of tasks, including welding, work in iron and steel furnaces and in the canning factory north of Avonmouth where they filled five-gallon cans with petrol for the war effort.[83] [*Fig. 4.6*] During the Second World War women were used more extensively in the armed services. Although they were not employed in any combatant capacity, the local press recognised the significance of what they did, noting that while it was men who bombed Germany and Italy it was the 'WAAF who make their work possible'.[84] Alongside tasks associated with women, such as canteen and clerical work, they also trained as mechanics, drivers and wireless operators. In 1941 members of the WAAF at Avonmouth were used to fly barrage balloons so that men could be relieved for other duties.[85] Some women found themselves facing enemy fire. At a reunion Diana Walker, who was employed to fly Spitfires from Filton to other airfields as part of the Air Transport Auxiliary, recalled how she was shot at by a German bomber and also 'by our own anti-aircraft guns over the Bristol Channel'.[86] As concerns about labour shortages increased married women were encouraged to take up employment in war-related industries, in particular on a part-time basis, with the mayor of Bristol emphasising the 'homely' jobs that were available.[87] Given the difficulties that mothers faced over looking after children, the Education Committee, exceptionally, approved new schemes for the care of children of war workers.[88] Government propaganda also urged other women to help those who went to the factory. [*Fig. 4.7*] Indeed, for most women it was relatives who stepped in. Joyce Storey's sister-in-law looked after her small daughter while she went to work at the Magma Products in Warmley, 'a big engineering firm with huge war-time contracts' where she had to ensure that lubricating fluid was always kept running into two large milling machines.[89] She welcomed the opportunity to have more money, but not all married women were keen to take on employment. V. A. Mound's diary for the period

4.6 Engine fitters working on the 152 Beaufort aircraft at the Bristol Aeroplane Company Filton during WW2. *Courtesy Duncan Greenman Collection*

showed that she was preoccupied with family issues, including her teenage daughter's education. When she was asked to join the staff at the Bristol Aeroplane Works because they were short of typists she noted 'I like doing voluntary work, but feel I cannot undertake regular employment with a fairly large house to run, and both daddy and Joyce to cater for'.[90] In 1943, to 'appease the Labour Exchange' she took work in a solicitor's office, mornings only, but suffered from 'nervous debility'.[91]

Voluntary Work
Voluntary work provided another outlet for women's energies. The women's section of the British Legion, whose national president was Lady Apsley, and the Women's Voluntary Service, established by Lady Reading in 1938, aimed to organise women for national defence. Their activities were based on

4.7 1941 Poster urging women who could not go into factories to help those who could. Bristol Air Raid Protection and Health Department, Bristol. BRO Ma5261. *Bristol Museums, Galleries & Archives*

women's 'traditional' domestic and caring roles but, as Caitriona Beaumont argues, they did give housewives and mothers 'the opportunity to contribute in a very active and public way to the war effort'.[92] The Bristol WVS branch had over 1500 trained members by April 1940 and they soon provided vital services, including helping with evacuated children, organising clothing depots and running canteens.[93] Bristol was the fifth most heavily bombed city during the Blitz and feeding the fire and casualty services as well as those who had lost their homes took organisational skills and hours of hard work.[94] In 1941 over 2,000 people were being fed on a daily basis. The Housewives' Service, set up as a group within the WVS, had 9000 members by 1941. They provided clothing, bedding and furniture and often used their own cars to transport those affected by bombings. They were instrumental in helping to increase blood supplies for transfusions and it was reported in 1944 that over 50,000 blood donors had been signed up.[95] There was also a Women's Home Guard who helped to organise a 'mock invasion of Bristol' in 1942.[96]

4.8 Bristol women in the Land Army and in the W.V.S. sorting clothes for displaced civilians. *Western Daily Press*, 11 December 1942 and 19 February 1942. BRL, B1094

It is significant that the WVS was included in a *Western Daily Press* series on women war workers and was praised as a 'wonderful organisation'. [*Fig. 4.8*] Volunteers not only provided food and sorted clothes, activities traditionally defined as female, but they also took on tasks that 'crossed gender boundaries' and involved physical danger, such as driving ambulances or civil defence duties during the Blitz. The *Western Daily Press* singled out the women of 'Report and Control', who wore the distinctive CD on their berets, who sat at telephones during the raids and who 'bravely stuck to their posts, coolly carrying on despite the danger'.[97] Nurses were also put in danger as they stayed with patients trapped by debris, leading to assistant Matron Lilian Stevens and sister Violet Frampton being awarded the George medal for outstanding bravery.[98] [*Fig. 4.9*]

Politics

The war-time coalition did provide a space for women to act together in the interests of women, outside party political rivalries.[99] The Bristol branch of the Women for Westminster group, that aimed to increase the number of women elected to national and local government, held lectures on questions such as housing and maternity and child welfare.[100] The Standing Conference of Women's Organisations in Bristol, which represented 33 women's groups, lobbied for women to be co-opted onto council committees and took a keen interest in plans for post-war reconstruction.[101]

Although women were welcomed more readily into a range of occupations

4.9 This 1950 cartoon highlights the contribution housewives and nurses had made to the war effort. *Bristol Evening Post*, 4 January 1950. BRL

in the Second World War, there continued to be an emphasis on the importance of their role as mothers and housewives. Once the war was over married women were expected to withdraw from full-time employment and, when there was a labour shortage, they were encouraged to work on a part-time basis for 'pin money'. It is hardly surprising therefore that this discouraged women from identifying as workers with the consequence that they were less likely to join trade unions, aspire to long-term careers or take part in political life.

Post-war Bristol

Even after the war, the institutions and ideas that governed Bristol's public life continued to marginalise women right up until the end of the 1970s. Ordinary women's experiences, needs and priorities were still discounted in the prevailing discourse and the social networks which ensured the continuance of old elitist practices proved remarkably resilient. But changes were undeniably afoot. The transformation of the economy, the creation of the welfare state and Britain's entry into the European Union all helped to create the circumstances for a concerted challenge to gender discrimination by the early 1970s. But it isn't until the late 1980s that one can discern a meaningful shift in the *status quo* as older certainties about the way the city should develop came increasingly under pressure.

Women and Employment 1945-1970

 The post-war period saw a rise in married women's paid employment which at first sight suggests a general trend towards the equalisation of women's economic position in relation to men. But as Jane Lewis has observed, aside from a minority of women entering professional careers, 'the most striking characteristics of women's paid jobs have remained low pay and low status.'[102] The boom in Britain's economy just after the war initially masked the structural decline in Bristol's diverse manufacturing base and this decline not only affected the industrial working class as a whole, but had a disproportionate impact on women in particular. And though the expansion of Bristol's service sector in this period did begin to transform and widen women's employment opportunities, sex segregation still continued to inform and limit their experience in the labour market.

Certainly, Bristol women were 'rapidly expelled' from traditionally male jobs when peace returned.[103] Lady Apsley, M.P. for Bristol Central, had observed that perhaps a third of the women employed wanted to build on their war-time experience and continue to work and train both within and outside the Armed Services. But the (all-male) Council of Bristol's Chamber of Commerce blandly assumed that *all* war-time women workers 'would only be too glad to return to their homes' to make way for returning servicemen.[104]

Though the lack of a consistent set of gender-sensitive statistics measuring women's employment over this period makes it hard to give a precise picture of women's employment (especially of women in casual and part-time work who were often not captured in official statistics), it is clear that the male bias in employment in the manufacturing sector was a particular hallmark of Bristol in the 1950s. In other words, fewer women seemed to have been employed in paid labour than nationally, especially in manufacturing, moving one commentator to observe that 'attitudes to female employment [in Bristol] have apparently not simulated those of the nation.'[105] Those women who were employed in industry were mainly unskilled and, as before the war, still concentrated in food and tobacco and in the paper and printing trades. Wills remained the dominant employer in the field [*Fig. 4.10*], but Packers Chocolate (later Elizabeth Shaw), Robertsons Jam, Smiths Crisps, St Anne's Board Mills, Messrs. Mardon Son and Hall and E.S. and A. Robinsons were still important local industries, and particular areas in the city were deeply affected by their relationship with them.[106] In Barton Hill, for example, over a third of all girl school leavers in the early 1950s worked at the printers Mardon Son and Hall (who made cigarette cards for Wills) and E.S. and A. Robinsons.

4.10 Wills Tobacco
Factory Bristol, 1963.
Wills Magazine, October
1963. BRL

Barton Hill's old Cotton Factory, which by then had been converted to both
the production of paper bag printing and light electrical accessories, employed
500 women and girls.[107]

Most women who did waged work outside the home were in the service
sector and it was this sector which hugely expanded in a number of different
directions. In the late 1940s, both private and public employers were anxious
about the shortage of female clerical workers (their gender was taken as a
given).[108] As the economy recovered from the war and Bristol became a
regional centre for industry and commerce, women found jobs as shop assistants and clerks in Bristol's new Broadmead shopping centre and as typists
and secretaries in the proliferating array of office blocks which by the 1960s
had begun to punctuate the city's skyline.[109] Nurses and nursing assistants
were recruited locally and from Ireland and the Caribbean to staff the city's
expanding hospitals. Press features of the time with such titles as 'Mrs. Mopp
gets Mechanised' and 'Girls in Banking' attest to the high degree of sexual

4.11 J.S. Fry & Sons'
typing pool.
BMAG TC3106.
*Bristol Museums,
Galleries & Archives*

and age segregation operating in the service sector.[110] Black women workers
in Bristol faced the added obstacle of racial discrimination even after it was
made illegal in 1968.[111] Older married women, especially those decanted from
the declining number of manufacturing jobs, were siphoned off into the most
poorly paid jobs as office cleaners, whilst the spread of mechanised accounting systems and the demand for shorthand typists afforded somewhat better
but still limited pay and prospects for younger and better educated women.
[*Figs. 4.11 and 4.12*] Though Bristol women reportedly comprised nearly a
fifth of all those employed in engineering and electrical goods and a third of
those in the chemical industry in 1961, many of these would have been
employed as clerical, cleaning or canteen staff rather than in production.
Women tellingly comprised only 10% of those working in the city's largest,
most dynamic and well paid industry, namely aerospace, which by 1971
employed 26,000 workers.[112]

Women in post-war Bristol continued to work as they had for centuries as
shopkeepers and in the distributive trades. The overwhelming majority were
small businesspeople, but Vera Hughes, who founded Mail Marketing International in Park Street in 1950 grew her Company into an important employer
in the city by the 1960s. The continuing exclusion of such women from established male business networks (such as the Council of the Chamber of
Commerce, the Commercial Rooms, the Society of Merchant Venturers, the
Constitutional Club, the Clifton Club and the Masons) led them to form their

Secretaries are getting better than ever!

More and more bosses are buying* them

PHILIPS

See the complete range at our Bristol Park Street showrooms or 'phone for a BTD man to demonstrate Philips at your office.

BTD

*You can hire a Philips—or any office machine under the BTD Contract Hire Scheme. Find out about it!

The best service to businessmen in Wales and the West.

BTD Office Equipment, 32 Park Street, Bristol 1. Tel. 21104.   and at Cardiff, Swansea, Newport

4.12 *Business News West of England Vol. 2*, September 1972. BRL

own networks.[113] The Bristol Club of the National Federation of Business and Professional Women celebrated their 20th anniversary in 1963. It's not clear if this is the same organisation which referred to itself until 1998 as the 'Bristol Ladies Business Group,' but its very name is symbolic of women's continuing marginalisation in this era.[114]

The expansion of both higher education and the welfare state, however, afforded more opportunities for women to train and work in the professions, as teachers, social workers, doctors, administrators and the like. Both the creation of the NHS and the Department of Child Health at Bristol University finally afforded Dr. Beryl Corner the recognition and financial security her male colleagues had long taken for granted. Before the war, she had struggled to find a post and had taken an honorary position at the Bristol Children's Hospital, but in 1945 became one of Britain's first women consultant paediatricians and the first woman elected to the British Paediatric Association. A year later, she founded Britain's second special baby care unit at Bristol's Southmead Hospital and went on to gain an international reputation for her innovations in the treatment of the newborn.[115]

A small but increasing number of well-educated women were employed as middle level officers in Bristol's City Council. The most established figure was Bristol's city archivist, Elizabeth Ralph (1911-2000) whose 40-year career began in 1937. A devout Anglican like Beryl Corner, she was a member of the National Association of Local Government Officers and in 1957 became the first woman chairman of the National Society of Archivists. Having played a major part in preserving the city's records during the war, she subsequently published respected works on the archives and history of the city, campaigned for the preservation of historic buildings and also served as the archivist to the Society of Merchant Venturers.[116] Bristol's first female Principal Medical Officer, Sarah Walker, was appointed in 1957 and predictably her brief was maternal and child health.[117] It would not be until 1967 that the first woman of colour, Carmen Beckford, a Jamaican, would attain a professional municipal job. She had the newly created post of voluntary liaison officer. Her high profile and difficult brief was to better 'community relations' at a time of increasing racial tension between Bristol's small but growing ethnic minority population and white Bristolians.[118]

Given the limited powers Beckford had, it is tempting to wonder what role tokenism played in some of the more visible public appointments of women (and ethnic minorities) made in this period. In 1970, Bristol University elected its first woman Chancellor, the Nobel Prize winning chemist, Professor Dorothy Crowfoot Hodgkin.[119] But her appointment belied the fact that though the number of women academics at Bristol University had by then risen from 23 in 1950 to 38, the actual proportion of female to male academic staff had in fact declined from 11% to 6% over the same period.[120] The newly established Bristol Polytechnic had only 29 female lecturers out of a total of 413 academic staff in 1973[121] and most female academics in the city were still concentrated in the city's two teacher training colleges, only one of which, St. Matthias, had a female principal.[122]

Women in political life 1945-c.1970
Though, as we shall see, relatively few women were represented in formal political office, women continued to engage in public affairs in a variety of other ways.[123] The Bristol Women's Labour Committee which had 27 sections aimed to promote the participation of more women councillors and to this end held a meeting shortly after the war.[124] The Bristol Women's Conservative Association headed by Lady Apsley, had swelled to some 12,000 members in 1950 and still served, as they had before the war, as important fund raisers and canvassers for their party.[125] The above-mentioned Standing Conference of Women's Organizations (which by 1950 represented 'about 40 different women's groups in the city') campaigned that year for cleaner food, and better 'cloakroom facilities in schools'[126] and seemed to have effected the reform of some council by-laws on food hygiene.[127] The Bristol Women's Club (affiliated to the American-based International Congress of Business and

4.13 Lady Janet Inskip (1897-1974), magistrate, philanthropist and pioneering reformer in the treatment of young offenders, she was one of few publicly prominent women in early post-war Bristol

Professional Women's Clubs) composed of 'such varying types as doctors of philosophy, hairdressers, lawyers, housewives, secretaries and teachers,'[128] pronounced itself opposed to pay discrimination, and also aimed 'to get women more involved in politics' and public life.[129]

A few mainly middle- and upper-class women did engage in public life as individuals in their own right, as members of public boards or through other voluntary work. Fifteen of Bristol's 78 magistrates were women by 1950, but they were the exceptions to what was still an overwhelmingly male-dominated elite. Even by the late 1960s, only seven out of the 130 people identified in an authoritative study of Bristol's most influential people were women.[130]

Undoubtedly one of these was Lady Janet Inskip (1897-1974),[131] who was characterised as a latter day Mary Carpenter for her pioneering work with young offenders in the city.[132] The wife of the solicitor Sir John Inskip, leading light of Bristol's Citizen Party, Lord Mayor of Bristol and later Director of Bristol Newspapers and the United Western Press, Janet Maclay Inskip had been raised in relatively progressive circles. The daughter of a Presbyterian Glasgow shipbuilder who served as Minister of Shipping in Lloyd George's War Cabinet, she, unusually for her day, went on to higher education, attending the pioneering Westfield Ladies College in Hampstead.[133] She moved to Bristol on her marriage in 1923 and became a magistrate in 1934. [*Fig. 4.13*] Appointed as the chair of the Juvenile Court Panel of Magistrates in Bristol during the war, Lady Inskip as she was by then called, continued to campaign for progressive reforms in the treatment of marginalised young people for nearly a quarter of a century. Her expertise was recognised by the Home

Office (who had appointed her to their advisory Council for the Treatment of Offenders in 1944). A patron of the Ashley House probation hostel for boys, the founder of Bristol's Prisoners' Aid Society, and a member of many public boards, she was also President of Bristol's Folk House, an informal education centre 'for the workers' whose premises she had probably purchased. It was she who personally funded the post-war cleaning and restoration of Bristol's magnificent Abbey Gate, the Norman Arch by Bristol Cathedral.[134]

Generally speaking though, the fifties and sixties were not a time of widespread female involvement in public life. It has been argued that Bristol women from both middle-class and traditional working-class backgrounds, still did not generally see themselves as 'political' or even primarily as 'workers'.[135] Unionisation was lower for women than for men though one notable exception was at the Fry's Chocolate Factory at Keynsham which employed many Bristol women. Here in 1951, 2000 women came out in protest at the employment of female non-union labour.[136] Women's reluctance to identify as workers, even though many worked throughout their lives, beginning as full- time workers when single and then returning as part-time workers after having children, stemmed from the continuing assumption that a woman's place was in the home and that married women's paid employment was either a temporary prelude to marriage or done for 'pin money.' Women were less likely to identify with the ethos and priorities of male-dominated trade unions. Yet, as the consumer society took off in the sixties, their often fierce desire to work in order to have some money of 'their own,' would, increasingly propel many married women into part-time employment. That, and their advocacy that the family allowance be paid to wives not to husbands, would increasingly challenge the very traditional sexual politics to which they themselves subscribed.[137]

Women in formal political office
Despite the prevailing apathy, a small but active coterie of women from both the Labour and Citizen Parties, did serve as councillors throughout the period with 6 of the 9 women councillors elected in 1945 describing their occupation as 'married women' or 'housewives'.[138] Though 1963 saw the much vaunted appointment of Florence Brown as the first woman mayor[139] in the city's 800 history (the post of Lord Mayor had replaced that of Mayor in 1898), only a fifth of all councillors in 1950 were women and the proportion fell nearly to pre-war levels in 1964. As the following table shows, even fewer held the

Women Councillors and Aldermen in Bristol 1939-1997[141]				
Year	Women Cllrs	Total Cllrs	Women Aldermen	Total Aldermen
1939	10	85	1	28
1950	17	85	5	28
1964	12	85	4	28
1973	18	56	4	28
1987	16	68	6	26 (Hon. Post)
1997	18	68	9	37 (Hon. Post)

more powerful position of council alderman which persisted until 1973. The reasons for this gender imbalance had to do with both male resistance and female diffidence. Vera Cox, the Southwest Regional Organizer of the Labour Party, did try to get women to play a more active role in local politics in the late sixties but it was clearly an uphill battle.[140]

So what of the women who did break the mould and become local councillors? Of these, Jessie Stephen (1893-1979), is perhaps the most distinguished.[142] Though she did not come to Bristol until she was in her late forties, her extraordinary life before then shaped the contribution she ultimately made to the city. Born in Scotland to a socialist working-class family, she was organizing domestic workers like herself by the age of 16. By 1913 she served as one of the Pankhursts' militant suffragettes 'assigned to drop acid into pillar boxes dressed in her maid's uniform'[143] and went on to become an early member of the Independent Labour Party, where as a single woman she campaigned for birth control education. Stephen then variously worked as government advisor in the Ministry of Reconstruction, as a journalist and as a union organizer, and served as a councillor in both Bermondsey and Portsmouth, founding her own secretarial agency.

She moved to Bristol in 1944, having been appointed as the first woman area union organizer of the National Clerical and Administrative Workers' Union for south Wales and the west of England, and later worked for the Broad Quay branch of the Co-operative Wholesale Society. In 1952, the year she became the first female head of Bristol's Trades Council, she began a six-year stint as Labour councillor for Bedminster (1952-1958) and later represented Brislington from 1962-1965, campaigning all the while for improved housing and social services provision. She sat on the Boards of various hospitals, the Bristol Co-operative Society and on the National Assistance Board Appeals Tribunal and had a national profile as a member of the National Women's Advisory Committee of the Trades Union Council and of the

4.14 Florence Brown, Bristol's first woman Lord Mayor revisits Wills' Tobacco Factory where she previously worked. *Wills Magazine* 1963-1965. BRL

Executive Council of the Clerical and Administrative Workers Union. An avowed women's rights campaigner, she spanned both first- and second-wave feminism, chairing the first meeting of Bristol's Women's Liberation Movement in the early 1970s. In 1977 she received an MBE for her services to trade unionism.[144]

Three other women politicians merit our particular attention, the first of whom, Alderman Florence Brown, was a Labour ally of Stephen's. Born in Bristol, Brown had worked at Wills as a tobacco stripper before the war, became a shop steward and subsequently a trade-union supported councillor in 1936. Most remembered for her appointment in 1963 as Bristol first female Lord Mayor, more work is needed to document her political career. [*Fig. 4.14*] An activist who worked to recruit working-class women (including Marge Evans) into the labour movement, she was a staunch advocate of extending welfare provision and noted for her particular interest in the education of disadvantaged and disabled children. Until recently, both the 'Florbrow' Family Group Home in Stapleton and a special school in South Bristol bore her name.[145]

The very fact that she, a working-class woman, was awarded an honorary degree from Bristol University in 1965, alongside Lady Inskip and the social-work pioneer Agnes Field, signalled a symbolic shift towards the inclusion of working-class women in the public sphere.[146] By contrast, Mercia Evelyn Castle who became the second female Lord Mayor in 1968, was much more in the mould of Bristol's traditional Conservative elite. [*Fig. 4.15*] A magistrate and Citizen Party councillor, she seems more identified by her interests in

4.15 Mercia Castle, Bristol's second female Lord Mayor. *Illustrated Bristol News*, Vol. 14, no.195, July 1968. BRL

4.16 Helen Bloom and her husband Sidney in the Lord Mayor's Mansion, Bristol, 1971. BRO 40826/LOR/27/6. *Bristol Museums and Art Galleries*

golf and bridge than by any passion for social reform. Nonetheless, she served on various Hospital Boards and Council Committees, chaired the Board of Winford Orthopaedic hospital, and received an OBE in 1960 for her public works.[147]

Arguably, Bristol's most prominent female politician during the sixties and early seventies was Helen Bloom, née Strimer (1901-1987) who in 1971 became the city's third female Lord Mayor and its first Jewish one.[148] [*Fig. 4.16*] She began as a Labour councillor in 1945 and retired in 1979 just as second-wave feminists were beginning to transform the Party's political landscape. Strimer first lived with her extended family in the poor district of St Philips and St Jacobs where her Austrian-born father worked as an 'Ostrich feather dresser'. She attended the Hannah More Board School in Barton Hill and was an active member of Bristol's Hebrew Congregation in Park Row whose debating society introduced her to political issues.[149] She and two of her four sisters, Berta (later Sacof) and Jeannette (later Britton), founded the Bristol branch of the Fabian Socialist Society, commonly described as the intellectual wing of the Labour movement, and were engaged in refugee work during the war before becoming Labour councillors.[150] Like the reform-minded Sturge,

Priestman, Tribe, Pease and Winkworth sisters of the previous century, the Strimer sisters supported one another in their public campaigns.[151] A personal friend of Jennie Lee and Aneurin Bevin, Helen Strimer was the first sister to be elected to the council in 1945 when her occupation was then listed as 'snuff blender.'[152] She represented the Avon Ward in 1945 and from 1964 (as Mrs. Helen Bloom), St George East. Like Brown and Castle, her main political focus was on the provision of health care in the city and she served on the Board of Bristol's teaching hospitals. Married at 49 to an affluent local businessman, she remained a Labour activist into her 70s, working for women to take on a more active political role, 'but gracefully admitt[ing] that not having had children herself had enabled her to take on far more responsibility than she could otherwise have done.'[153]

1969-1979: increasing economic instability
Bristol became an altogether less settled, more diverse and dynamic place by the end of the 1960s. Immigration from the New Commonwealth had added to Bristol's cultural vibrancy. But increasing class and racial tensions made themselves evident as structural changes in the economy challenged the city's traditional job base, its provision of public services and its rather parochial sense of itself. Women's representation on the local council rose to a third by 1973 but just as Avon County Council, established in 1974, was poised to take on many of Bristol Corporation's powers.

Meanwhile, the economic structure continued to transform in favour of service and higher technology industries and larger corporations. As London firms and government offices relocated to Bristol, and as globalisation became more evident, the power of local government to control how the city developed was further diminished.

The 1970s saw a dramatic collapse in the city's traditional manufacturing jobs with the absorption of such iconic Bristol firms as Wills by international corporations. In all, some 40 industrial firms either closed or left Bristol with an estimated loss of over 4000 jobs.[154] Over a third of tobacco workers and nearly half of workers in the paper, printing and packing trades lost their jobs and women in these industries were two times more likely to be laid off than men.[155] Those hit hardest by this collapse lived in such outlying council estates as Knowle West, Hartcliffe and Southmead (where unemployment was estimated at 10%) or the inner city area of St Pauls, where Black and Minority Ethnic (BME) unemployment rates were thought to be far higher still.[156] Plainly, for these groups especially, reliance on the male breadwinner bringing in a family wage was no longer quite so viable a strategy.

By 1981, more than 82% of Bristol's female workforce were employed in the service sector. By that same year, more women than men were employed in education, medical and dental services, retailing, business and miscellaneous services.[157] Though most service jobs were low level, an increasing proportion of girls were staying on at school and achieving the qualifications needed to access jobs in the higher end of the sector.[158] The number of women in higher education between 1962 and 1980 trebled. Most were still going into teacher training and the Arts, and less than half as many women as men obtained degrees in 1970. Parity would not be achieved until 2000.[159] We know of few Bristol women who achieved notable success in the commercial and technical fields before 1990. Those who had seem to confirm Selina Todd's observation that individual talent notwithstanding, a middle-class background was still an important prerequisite for high achievement.[160]

For example, Mary Perkins, née Bebbington, was a Bristol Fairfield Grammar School girl, whose father owned the optical business Bebbington and Perkins. She gained her degree in Optometry at Cardiff University and in 1967 returned with her new husband to Bristol where they bought out the family firm and capitalised on the city's booming consumer climate. By 1980, they sold what had become a regional chain of 23 shops for £2 million. Four years later, she reportedly hit on the idea of selling two pairs of glasses for the price of one in the Bond Street shop she and her spouse co-owned in Bristol, thus launching the beginning of Specsavers. This grew into the largest opticians' chain in the world and made Mary Perkins Britain's first woman to become a self-made billionaire.[161] [*Fig. 4.17*]

Similarly, Jenny Body, whose mother was one of Bristol's first female pharmacists, had attended Bristol's select Redland High School for Girls. She had a summer placement as a clerical worker at British Aircraft Corporation (later Airbus) where her father was employed as an aeronautical engineer. In 1971, she became the first woman to secure an engineering apprenticeship at that company, went on to distinguish herself there in the fields of wing design and technology management and later became the first woman president of the Royal Aeronautical Society.[162] But her potential might never have been realized had she not had the background she did.

Women's liberation in Bristol: the rise of second wave feminism and its impact on the city c.1968-1979

The rise of the Women's Liberation Movement in Britain coincided with the

4.17 The Bristol-born Mary Perkins, co-founder of Specsavers with her family. *Courtesy Specsavers*

period of increased economic instability referred to above. It was initiated by a new generation of women, who, though often highly educated, found themselves in a society where sex discrimination was still perfectly legal and traditionalist attitudes about a women's place still widespread.[163] Women in the broad left felt increasing dissatisfaction with the attitudes they encountered in the Labour Party and the trade unions especially with regard to community organisation and gender roles. Some turned to more radical groups such as the Communist Party or such New Left groups, including The International Marxist Group and the Socialist Workers Party to press for more radical policies. But here too women came up against what they would come to term as 'sexism' on the part of their male comrades.[164]

Bristol's Women's Liberation Group was one of the earliest to be founded and played an active part in the movement's national development. By 1971 there were 36 Women's Liberation Groups in Britain, 30 of which were in England. These loosely federated groups formulated demands at a 1971 National Conference which famously included: financial independence for all women, equal pay, equal access to jobs and education, free contraception and abortion on demand, and free 24-hour nursery provision. By 1978 the demands had expanded to include equal legal and financial status, the right to a self-defined sexuality, including an end to discrimination against lesbians, and

4.18 Ellen Malos c.1973 in the basement of her Redland home which served as the headquarters of Bristol's Women's Liberation Movement and where temporary refuge was first provided to victims of domestic violence. *UBLSC (DM2123-FA-Arch-Box43)*

freedom from sexual intimidation and violence regardless of marital status.[165]

One of the features distinguishing the 'Women's Lib Movement' from the earlier suffrage movement was its use of 'consciousness raising sessions'. These open-ended informal and often emotionally intense meetings promoted the sharing of quite personal individual experiences in order to articulate a new understanding of how the 'personal was political.'[166] The Bristol group epitomised this process, beginning as a small group of women who met in each others' houses to 'talk about themselves, their problems and their position in society.'[167]

Composition of the early WLM group in Bristol
Aside from the former suffragette Jessie Stephen and the playwright, author and poet Angela Rodaway (1919-2012),[168] the original group consisted mainly of highly educated and cosmopolitan incomers in their twenties and thirties. Their backgrounds ranged from respectable working-class to professional and their political orientation, though decidedly to the Left, varied considerably. One central figure in this network, Ellen Malos (an Australian) was a committed socialist married to a University of Bristol academic. [*Fig. 4.18*] Her own aspirations to do a PhD were initially curtailed by her family respon-

sibilities and the prevailing culture around women's employment. By 1969, she and fellow Australian Lee Capaldi, both members of the trade unionist National Joint Action Campaign for Women's Equal Rights, were among the first organisers of the Bristol WLM as were the Swedish painter Monica Sjöö, the poet Pat V.T. West, and the artist Beverly Skinner. Early recruits included single parents who became 'politicised ... due to their experiences of isolation, discrimination and lack of childcare' and married women such as Janet Brewer and Marilyn Porter who had come to feminism by way of the House-wives' Register. Another was Betty Underwood, a long-time member of the Communist Party who had grown progressively disillusioned by its 'lack of "enlightenment" regarding women's issues...' They initially met in each other's homes and their focus was on workplace rights and the problems of 'unsup-ported mothers.' Though most resided in the middle-class areas of Clifton and Redland, Underwood, who chaired the second national conference of the Women's Liberation Movement in Skegness in 1971, lived in the council estate of Knowle West.[169] By then Bristol members included the Londoner Suzie Fleming who made a distinctive (if divisive) contribution to the WLM as an early proponent of 'Wages for Housework.' This campaign highlighted the crucial importance of women's work within the home and argued that as such the State should pay for it.[170]

What impact did the Women's Liberation Movement have?

In some respects the propagandising, lobbying, campaigning and networking tactics of the Bristol WLM were reminiscent of those employed by the evangelical reformers in the previous century. But their passionate irreverence, their explicit discussions of sexuality, and their flair for provocative creativity as exemplified by their 1973 revue 'Sister Show' made them far more contro-versial in a socially conservative city where even women thought women's rights were mainly 'for those that get left behind'.[171] At first traditionalist women's groups invited WLM speakers to their meetings as a novelty turn, good for 'a bit of a giggle.'[172] But the Bristol WLM group soldiered on, speak-ing to unions, women's clubs and schools, organizing courses, attending rallies and battling out their positions on a variety of issues. Their numbers nearly trebled to a hundred women by that year.[173] With new groups proliferating throughout the Bristol area, for example Weston, St Pauls, Westbury, Knowle, Portishead, Olveston and Kingswood, their influence soon extended beyond the formal membership.[174] Their campaign to counter the Tory attempt to stop family allowances being paid directly to women[175] and their engagement with anti-poverty and housing groups such as Child Poverty Action, Shelter, and the Claimants' Union, further broadened their appeal. So too did their campaigning for the passage and implementation of the Equal Pay Act (1970) and the Sex Discrimination Act (1975).[176] The Social Security Act of 1975 which, building upon the 1971 Divorce Act 'guaranteed some income for divorced and separated British women', was also relevant to their concerns.[177] The rise of largely female-headed single parent families, which characterised this period, provided a new constituency for the feminist movement. Bristol's WLM members also networked with both the Labour Party and with the growing number of women employed as state or voluntary service providers. They had become increasingly politicised by the growing social disparities within the city and by their own exclusion from power in their respective organizations. In 1972 the first Labour Women's Rally in the South West Region was organized at Transport House to raise awareness about women's concerns. In November 1975, Robertson's Jam, one of 'the major private employers of women workers in Bristol', was challenged by its largely female and unionised workforce for contravening the new Equal Pay Act.[178] Two years later, an increasing number of women in the public service sector participated in protests against cuts in public spending.[179]

One of the more enduring achievements of second-wave feminism in Bristol was to establish the need for a shelter for women victims of domestic violence. The absence of such provision for women, especially those with dependent children in the early 70s, had led to the establishing of the 'Bristol Women's House'. Between 1973 and 1977 this was located in the basement of Ellen Malos's Redland home providing pregnancy testing, legal advice and accommodation for 4 of the 23 women and 26 children who sought its protection from domestic violence. The Women's House finally moved from Malos's basement in 1973 to Union Street and subsequently to other venues in the city. This led to the formation of Bristol Women's Aid in 1974 which tirelessly pressured Bristol City Council through lobbying and a High Court case to provide dedicated refuges. The first of these was established in the city in 1976, the year that the Domestic Violence Act was also passed.[180] Nicola Harwin, who began as a Bristol Women's Aid worker in 1979, later became head of the National Women's Aid Federation, whose headquarters were for a time in Bristol. She reckoned that the experience accrued by Bristol Women's Aid subsequently informed government investigations into domestic violence and helped to pioneer the multi-agency approach now routinely adopted for tackling a range of abuse-related issues.[181]

Waterside leisure showpiece

How an artist sees the future of E Shed

Bristol artist Mrs. Anne Hicks has prepared a drawing to show what could be done with the massive E Shed in the City Docks.

She believes it would be an ideal building for all kinds of activities, such as a yacht club with a restaurant or as a theatre.

"So long as the building is not pulled down I don't really mind. It's a super building and has so much potential," Mrs. Hicks told the Evening Post today.

"They only want to pull down E Shed to make way for a road, which is ....

4.18 1971 Drawing of EShed by the Bristol Docks from an original painting by Anne Hicks. Hicks's visualisations of how the then declining Docks could be transformed into a public space for cultural and leisure activities were central to the successful campaign to save them from demolition. *Bristol Evening Post*, 3 October 1972. *Anne Hicks Collection*

Academics at Bristol University, the University of Bath and the newly formed Bristol Polytechnic, provided much of the personnel and intellectual energy behind the local movement. By the mid-70s they pioneered Women's Studies courses for the public as well as for university students, established research networks and began to publish feminist work including a feminist anthology *Half the Sky* (1979) whose impact went well beyond Bristol. Many went on to become leading authorities in their respective fields, their research building on their grass-roots political engagement.[182] Significantly, Anna Pollert and Marilyn Porter's pioneering sociological case studies of the lives of women employed in Bristol's traditional tobacco and printing industries still remain the only substantive investigations of working Bristol women in this period.[183] In 1990, Malos, by then at the University of Bristol, co-founded with Gill Hague the activist-based Domestic Violence Research Group, which became the University's Gender and Violence Research Centre.[184] Yet despite all this energy, the Bristol WLM never had sufficient funding to support a permanent women's centre in the city.[185]

Organized labour and feminism in this period were not the only avenues by which Bristol women became engaged in grass-roots politics. From the late sixties, environmental campaigners of both sexes began to organize in protest against a massive road building programme initiated by the council. The Slade-trained artist Anne Hicks and her husband Jerry were part of a small group of campaigners (which included George Ferguson and the architects Jean and Stephen MacFarland), who successfully opposed the council's plans to fill in the Docks with concrete and office blocks.[186] [*Fig. 4.18*] In 1971 Dorothy Brown, a Scottish-born architect, founded the Bristol Visual and Environmental Group. She used her own finances and research in her robust campaigns which proved instrumental in saving the Avon Gorge and some 400 historic buildings in the Old Market area and elsewhere in the city from destruction.[187]

Protest against council policies also began to propel more local working-class women into the public sphere in order 'to better their daily lives in the city and to fight their economic and political marginalization.'[188] Women figured disproportionately in grass-roots protests in Totterdown against the road scheme affecting their area whilst others in Barton Hill and Southmead protested against unresponsive management of council estates. Pat Dallimore from the deprived Knowle West estate, tried with other tenants on the estate to combat the disproportionately high food prices charged by local stores by establishing a cooperative food purchase scheme. Later, in the mid-1990s, she was involved with Mary Smith to effect a drug prevention campaign.[189] Jamaican-born Olive Osborne, who worked variously as a nursing assistant and hairdresser, ultimately lobbied Parliament to ban the fraudulent pyramid selling schemes then afflicting people in her community. She went on to found the first literacy classes and after-school enrichment sessions for black children in Bristol, and founded the Bristol Community Growth and Support Association in 1975, providing welfare support and advice to inner city residents.[190] Princess Eldoris Campbell (1939-2015), also from Jamaica, similarly began her activism in the 1970s, becoming Bristol's first Black staff nurse in 1974 after she successfully challenged the discriminatory policies then routinely employed at Bristol's Glenside Hospital.[191]

The Thatcher years: 1979-1990

The gap between winners and losers in Bristol's economic transformation intensified during this period. New opportunities in the professions, management and business arose for those women with the confidence and cultural

Bristol's First Women MPs Madge Dresser

Violet Meeking Bathurst (Lady Apsley) Cons., Bristol Central, 1943-1945
Dawn Primarolo Labour, Bristol South, 1987-2015

The careers of Violet Meeking and Dawn Primarolo make an instructive contrast. Violet Meeking came from a privileged, landowning background and married into the aristocratic Bathurst family; by her thirties she was confined to a wheelchair.

Primarolo [*Colour plate 20*] came from an aspiring working-class family and had to combine motherhood and paid employ-

ment throughout her political life. Both were mothers and, whilst Apsley was widowed, Primarolo was twice married and spent some time as a single parent. Though their class backgrounds, political allegiances and life experience were worlds apart, both were engaged Parliamentarians, concerned in their various ways with the status and pay of women their health, environment and welfare. ∎

Lady Apsley as political wife campaigning in Bristol on behalf of her husband Lord Apsley (pictured by car). ©*Top Foto.co.uk*

Dawn Primarolo (in white dress) picketing BP petrol station in Bedminster, Bristol c.1986.
BRO 41232/IM/Ph/4. *Bristol Museums, Galleries & Archives*

'We want more women for the ATS'.
Western Daily Press, 13 February 1938, *BRL*

Dawn Primarolo MP, Hartcliffe estate, Bristol c.1990.
Thanks to Dawn Primarolo and Claire Radford

capital to exploit them. The triumphs of Mary Perkins's co-founding of Specsavers, Jennifer Bryant Pearson's establishment of the hugely successful JBP Public Relations in 1984 contrast with the fate of those hit by the continuing long-term collapse of Bristol's traditional industries. In 1980 the St Anne's Board Mills, which had produced cigarette packets for Imperial Tobacco, closed with the loss of 1800 jobs and between 1980 and 1987 some 6000 jobs were reportedly lost in the St Anne's and St Philips area alone.[192] Low-skilled male, and older female, workers living in Bristol's outlying council estates and in the inner city could not easily be absorbed into the expanding service sector. The urban disturbances in St Pauls and Southmead in 1980 further highlighted the social disparities in the city. Racial discrimination, though no longer legal, was still prevalent. The general and long-term unemployment rates in the 'St Pauls neighbourhood', which had the highest concentration of black residents, were approximately three times as high as those in the wider city.[193] Low paid and more casual jobs were 'characterised by a much greater concentration of black workers and, particularly in the services, of women.'[194]

Becoming visible: the changing political landscape

The 1980s saw, according to Keith Bassett, a 'significant New Left faction' of 'younger and more middle-class Labour councillors' in both the Bristol Council, and the Avon County Council. Many were 'attracted by the more socially inclusive municipal socialism' espoused by Ken Livingston's Greater London Council. It is worth adding that many of them were women from modest backgrounds who were often the first of their family to have access to higher education and who were inspired by feminist ideas. Although not all were members of New Left organisations, most did challenge the council's prevailing focus on attracting outside capital in the interests of growth and championed instead 'a more radical counter-capitalist strategy, emphasizing indigenous growth, expansion of cooperatives and "restructuring for labour" rather than the needs of capital.'[195]

Dawn Primarolo is perhaps the most prominent example of someone who began as a union and community activist, gained a degree as a mature student and went on to a political career. But there were others too, such as Pat Roberts and Jenny Smith. Both were Northerners who arrived in Bristol with their husbands in the 1970s. Smith became a Labour councillor for Stockwood from the 1980s after combining years of community activism in the poorest areas of the city with raising a family and studying as a mature student. A Quaker, her political career reportedly began 'when a number of Bristol charities approached her to help bring about change in local authority practices'. As a Labour councillor, she campaigned on housing, travellers' rights, and lobbied continuously for policies supporting marginalised Bristolians.[196] Roberts, a social worker, though directly involved in the abortion campaign of the late 1970s, and one of the many Bristol women who went to 'embrace the base' at Greenham Common in 1983 in protest against Cruise missiles there, did not focus exclusively on feminist issues when she became a councillor in 1988.[197]

But feminism did inspire a younger Labour councillor, Pam Tatlow, to lead the successful campaign in the mid-1980s to establish a dedicated 'Women's Committee' within Bristol City Council. The idea, first mooted in the early 1970s and adopted in the 1980s by the Greater London Council, specifically sought to involve a wider range of women in the political life of the city, including those from ethnic minorities, the disabled and perhaps most controversially lesbian and bisexual women whose public presence in Anti-Rape and Reclaim the Night Marches and Demonstrations were a hallmark of the 1980s. [*Fig. 4.19*] Though designed as a cross-party affair, the very concept of a Women's Committee was opposed, albeit unsuccessfully, by Conservative women councillors such as Joyce Fey (Henleaze) and Gwyneth Hebblethwaite (Redland)[198] and other opponents of the Labour Left. Its implementation signalled a shift in the council's political culture. When, for example, the Committee hosted an International Women's Day event in the Council House in 1987, an unprecedentedly wide range of grass-roots groups attended, ranging from Asian women's groups to gay activists. They were not only addressed by national and local women politicians but serenaded by feminist musicians amid a colourful exhibition of historic women's trade union and suffrage banners.[199]

Though riven with factionalism and political rivalry, the Women's Committee's provision of financial subsidies for grass-roots groups from the late 1980s and into the 1990s, established important new networks of connection between local government and previously marginalised sections of the city's female population.[200] In particular it afforded funding to women from the South Asian community to organize independently of their existing communal structures, affirmed gay women in the public arena and explicitly recognised that safety, transport and childcare problems needed to be addressed in order to ensure women's participation in civic life. When Tatlow was succeeded in 1991 by Labour councillor Diane Bunyan, the shift in political culture initiated

Down Among the Women Madge Dresser
Community Activism in Knowle West

The late twentieth century saw a rise in grass roots community activism especially in Bristol's inner city and outlying Council housing estates. Women played a leading role in trying to redress the social inequalities experienced in their own locale and through this some were drawn into a wider involvement into politics and public life.

The Knowle West estate (first developed in the 1930s) housed many Bristolians decanted by slum clearance schemes from Bristol's city centre. By the 70s the estate was suffering from a dearth of shops and social facilities and poor public transport. By the 1980s it was hit hard by job losses in manufacturing, especially with the decline of cigarette making and the closure, in 1990, of the Imperial Tobacco factory (formerly Wills's). All these things impacted on women's lives and those of their families. Unemployment reportedly reached over 30%. The women's writers workshop and Knowle West against Drugs (KWADS) featured here are two of a number of initiatives organised in response to the social conditions affecting people on the estate.

Knowle West Against Drugs Meeting (KWADS) c.1994.
Courtesy Knowle West Media Centre

Knowle West Against Drugs
Mary Smith OBE, founding member of Knowle West Against Drugs (KWADS):

> Heroin hit the streets of Knowle West [in 1994].... It hit all of the families at the same time. It was just like a wave that washed over this estate. We were already poor and unfortunate before that and... apparently...we died five or ten years earlier than anybody else in the country, in Knowle West.

> We [in KWADS] marched to Downing Street, you name it, and we went all over the place. It was such a powerful experience because nobody could tell us what to do. We weren't paid by anybody at all. Nobody paid our wages, so we could say what nobody else could say. No councillors could say it, no officials could say it, no head of the NHS. Nobody could say what we could say because we were unpaid and we were passionate. We did reforms in prisons and schools; whatever you could think of, we changed things.

Denise Britt with Home Secretary Michael Howard, 1995.
Courtesy Knowle West Media Centre

'Nobody could say what we could say because we were unpaid and we were passionate'

Pat Dallimore 'The Silver City'

...Leaving the streets of dogs, kids and
        broken glass,
We came to lanes and fields of
        green,
a new world, where birds sang
        Gasping for breath we made our
        way up a narrow winding path,
to the top of the hill.
Resting our bicycles in velvet grass,
We stood and looked at Bristol
        for there it lay, a silver city,
gleaming majesty.
The sun-reflected light made
diamonds of the factories,
houses and council flats' windows.
Cathedral, churches, looked dull
and small, but rock solid, the
        foundation still of the silver city

Pat Dallimore (*left*) at a women
writers' workshop.
Pat Dallimore was a local writer
and radio commentator who
campaigned with fellow Knowle
West residents for better
facilities on their estate.
*Courtesy Knowle West Media
Centre*

Shush – Mum's Writing (Bristol: Bristol Broadsides, 1981)

Mary Smith (paper in hand) with
Michael Howard leaving Filwood
Community Centre, September 1995.
Courtesy Knowle West Media Centre

4.19 WLM demonstrations in Bristol c.1987. These photographs show the loose coalition of different groups allied to the movement. Suzie Fleming, founder of the Wages for Housework Movement is pictured in the bottom image, extreme right. *University of Bristol Library, Special Collections*

by the Women's Committee was evident but incomplete. Bunyan recalls: 'I cleared the Council Chamber by breastfeeding my daughter, I was oblivious [to the fact] that they all had walked out'.[201]

As late as 1993, the proportion of women councillors had not exceeded

1970 levels. [*See table page 163*] Nonetheless, the emergence of women as more powerful players in the city's political life gained momentum as the millennium approached. It was exemplified by the appointment of Lucy de Groot as the Chief Executive of Bristol City Council (1995-2000), the installation of Councillor Barbara Janke as leader of the Liberal Democrats and the election of two more women M.P.'s, namely Jean Corston in 1992 (Bristol East) and Val Davey (Bristol West) in 1997. [*Colour plate 19*].

Outside local government, individual women in Bristol continued to make ground-breaking initiatives, most notably perhaps in the field of health. After her own experience of breast cancer, Penny Brohn (née Tamblyn, 1943-1999), a Clifton-born lecturer at Bristol Polytechnic, founded, with Ann Pilkington, the Cancer Help Clinic in 1980 (latterly the Penny Brohn Cancer Help Centre). Their promotion of more patient-centered 'alternative' approaches to cancer treatment excited both controversy and emulation and helped to challenge existing clinical practice.[202] In 1988 Bhupinder Sandhu, who had come from India to England in 1963, became the first female paediatric consultant to be appointed in Bristol since Beryl Corner some forty years previously.[203] Based at the Bristol Children's Hospital, Sandhu built up a children's gastroenterology unit there whilst taking an active role in the Labour Party and various public bodies. In the 1990s Professor Jean Golding conceived and founded the internationally famous 'Children of the Nineties' project at Bristol University which followed 14,500 women and their children for an unprecedentedly comprehensive long-term study on health and life style, which at the time of writing is still ongoing.[204]

The 1990s saw both the continuing expansion of the leisure and financial sectors of the economy whilst more traditional industries came under ever-increasing pressure. Women played central roles on both sides of the longest running labour dispute in the city's history. This began in 1993 when the venerable printing firm Arrowsmith (founded in 1854) dismissed its workers who had been resisting management reforms and wage cuts since the 1970s.[205] Victoria Arrowsmith-Brown had taken over the management of Arrowsmith from her father in 1993. University-educated and socially liberal, her priority was to rationalise production techniques and reduce costs in order, as she saw it, to preserve the firm's existence in the face of global competition.[206] Opposing her in the public arena were Dawn Primarolo and Jean Corston who condemned Arrowsmith's treatment of its workers as part of a Thatcherite strategy to downgrade worker rights.[207]

4.20 Annabel Lawson
Jeremy Rees and John
Osborn, the three
founders of Arnolfini
c.1961.
Courtesy Arnolfini

Women and cultural life in post-war Bristol

Despite the increasing recognition of the importance that the creative industries had already made to the city's regeneration after the war, little is known about the contribution women made to the city in this regard.

By the sixties, Bristol's emerging creative scene was marked by its left-leaning counter-cultural origins, and as such afforded some limited space for women to enter it, especially those who had gained some confidence through the new educational opportunities now available to them. The graphic designer Annabel Lawson, for example, was in 1961 one of the three co-founders of the Arnolfini Gallery [*Fig. 4.20*] which by 1975 had relocated to the Docks and became a major provincial arts centre. Significantly this decidedly alternative cultural revival gained momentum in the 1970s and 1980s, just as the corporate and growth-driven policies of the Council were coming under increasing criticism.

'*Bristol Boys made more noise*', than women in Bristol's burgeoning popular music culture but there were some women who made their mark as performers and as patrons. Gill Loades, who was Bristol's first woman DJ at Bristol's Dugout club in the 1970s, has since documented its development. She and others credit Pamela 'Ki' Longfellow, the wife of the rock star Vivian Stanshall, as the moving force behind the establishment of the Thekla (aka the 'Old Profanity') in 1982, a converted ship which became an important focal point for music, comedy and theatre in Bristol.[208] Clare Wadd and her partner Matthew Ward provided another outlet for alternative music by way of Sarah Records, an Indi label and fanzine which lasted from 1987 to 1995. The songwriter and singer Beth Gibbons co-founded the group 'Portishead' that was so crucial to establishing 'the Bristol sound' in the early nineties.[209] But it would not be until later in the decade that Bristol had its first female full-time professional DJ, Roz Scordilis aka 'Queen Bee'.[210]

Women certainly featured more significantly in Bristol's increasingly lively literary culture. Internationally renowned writers such as Dorothy Reynolds, Angela Carter, Philippa Gregory, Julie Burchill, Catherine Johnson and Helen Dunmore, and poets U.A. Fanthorpe and Libby Houston, were at some points influenced by their time in Bristol and in turn raised the city's profile.[211] By the 1980s the mainly autobiographical writing of working-class Bristol women such as Joyce Storey, Victoria Hughes and Pat Dallimore, who also had a regular guest spot on BBC Radio Bristol, were given a public platform by small independent publishers.[212]

Women also played a central role in bringing theatre to wider audiences before and after the war. The Bristol Unity Theatre Club (allied with the New Left Book Club) was organised by the Communist solicitor and qualified pilot Joan Tuckett (1895-1957), sister of the above-mentioned Angela Tuckett, who produced its worker-run theatrical productions in Bristol from 1936 and throughout the Blitz. On May Day in 1944, 7000 people stood at Queen Square, the site of the 1831 Bristol Riots, to watch 'Now is the Day,' a pageant Joan based on Samuel Bryher's *An Account of the Labour and Socialist Movement in Bristol*.[213] Bristol's Little Theatre, possibly inspired by the American Little Theatre movement which championed promoting theatre to popular audiences, was co-managed by Peggy Ann Wood (1912-1998) [*Colour plate 15*] and her husband Ronald Russell. Based at Colston Hall for nearly 30 years they staged no fewer than 900 productions including 50 world premiers between 1935 and 1963 and Wood ran the theatre and its repertory company the Rapier Players single-handedly during the war.[214]

By the 1970s, the left-leaning street theatre movement emerged and women such as Liz Jones and Linda Crowe, along with David Illingworth and Tony Robinson, formed part of the original Avon Touring Company. In 1986 Sheila Hannon co-founded the long-running Show of Strength Theatre Company, which she now heads, and in 1998 was instrumental in opening the theatre at Bedminster's newly renovated Tobacco Factory.[215]

Though largely consigned to cover 'the women's angle,' female journalists such as Barbara Buchanan, Daphne Hubbard, Helen Reid, and Quita Morgan had begun to feature more regularly as columnists and reporters in the post-war papers with Buchanan winning Britain's woman journalist of the year in 1967 for her campaigning features on cervical cancer.[216]

It took longer for women to establish themselves in public broadcasting. Jenni Murray, of Radio 4's iconic *Women's Hour*, began her early radio career at BBC Radio Bristol in 1973 highlighting women's issues around the same time that Jan Leeming first presented a women's programme for HTV. Kate Adie also began as a studio technician before doing farming programmes for Radio Bristol and progressing to BBC TV as a television presenter in 1979. Susan Osman too worked at HTV in the early 1980s before becoming a lead presenter for BBC West's News team in 1991.[217] Sherrie Eugene, the Bristol-born school leaver of working-class parents from Dominica, also began her remarkable career at HTV in 1982, first as a signer for the deaf and then as the region's first black female presenter and newscaster, marking a new watershed in women's representation in the region.[218] [*Colour plate 18*]

Women also worked in television as members of various independent television production (often community-oriented) companies, such as Forum Television in the 1980s and 90s. FEM FM, the UK's first women-run radio station, was licensed to broadcast from Bristol for a week in March of 1992 and specifically aimed to promote both gay and straight women's entry into radio broadcasting.[219] Increasingly women made inroads into the commercial television sector. Icon Records co-founded by Laura and Harry Marshall, went on to become one of the biggest independent production companies in the UK and established Laura as part of Bristol's reconfigured and still largely male commercial and arts elite.[220]

Other women were also beginning to find posts higher up in the city's more established cultural institutions. Sara Davies began as part of the management team of Bristol's new arts centre the Watershed, and progressed as freelance journalist and broadcaster to become a distinguished radio producer for Radio 4 in Bristol. In 1987 the Bristol Old Vic hired Phyllida Lloyd as its first female associate director and among her many local and later national successes, it is notable that she directed the stage and screen musical of the Abba musical 'Mamma Mia', originally written by another Bristol resident, Catherine Johnson. Tessa Jackson took over as the Director of the Arnolfini in 1991, whilst Jane Krish who came in 1992 to run the Wildscreen Festival of Wildlife Film and Television reportedly transformed it by 2000 '... into the biggest and best respected international event of its type'. Gillian Thomas was hired as chief executive of the Science Centre At-Bristol in 1996 and was awarded an OBE for her efforts in 2000.[221]

By the millennium's end, women's public visibility was noticeably increasing. Britain's first women Anglican priests were inaugurated in Bristol

Cathedral in 1993 and women continued to be co-opted into an increasing variety of public and voluntary boards and professional and managerial posts in the city. Some of those who had begun in Bristol's alternative arts scene gained public prominence in other fields. Jekka McVicar, for example, became an internationally recognised horticulturalist and co-proprietor of Britain's largest culinary herb farm near Bristol.[222] But women were still underrepresented in senior positions of power. In 1998 the Bristol Initiative was set up with big business backing to regenerate a city it saw as socially and politically divided. To this end it identified and co-opted 170 of the region's 'great and the good in all sectors' to serve on its board. Only 15 (10.5%) of these were women which makes an interesting comparison with the 1962 survey of Bristol notables, previously mentioned, in which 5% of the city's 130 most influential people were women.[223] So, although the more recent list does reflect the wider opportunities for women by then available, including as it does CEOs and managers of large companies and voluntary agencies, all of whom appear to have been graduates, the continuing gender disparity is telling. Significantly, at least 8 of those women named in 1998 had come up through the ranks by way of their involvement in the 'soft' areas of education, health and the media. And even within such areas, the glass ceiling had yet to be cracked. More women featured as governors at the city's two universities for example but still constituted only 20 out of the 257 Professors at the University of Bristol in 2000.[224] Discrimination was even more marked in the commercial arena where women were until 2003 still formally barred from becoming members of The Society of Merchant Venturers.[225]

The century in retrospect

Thus although the twentieth century was distinguished by the entry of women into a broadening range of public roles and the removal of formal barriers in both politics and the workplace, deeper structural and cultural barriers still prevented women's from a full and equal participation in public life. Despite their increased entry into paid employment and increased access to higher education, women still shoulder the bulk of unpaid work within the home as carers and organisers of domestic and community life. The enduring and complex relationship between home, work and civic life thus continues to pose particular pressures for women.

Yet even to measure women's contribution to the city strictly in their relation to established institutions arguably replicates a patriarchal agenda. Women have continued to make innovative contributions to Bristol life

4.21 Zehra Haq (right) c.1987. Haq, born in Singapore came to Bristol after her marriage. She founded the Barton Hill Asian Women's Association, based at the Barton Hill University Settlement, which later became Dhek Bhal, an important provider of support and services for the city's South Asian residents. *Courtesy Dhek Bhah*

outside the established power structures. More research is needed before we can fully assess how women's increased presence as both formal and informal activists and workers has shaped the modern city. The evidence so far suggests women in community-based and/or single-sex organisations frequently challenged existing policy priorities, foregrounding issues previously sidelined or ignored by traditional political and economic institutions. There seems too to be a discernible continuity of concern here which reaches far back into the past. Though not necessarily informed by explicitly feminist values, the issues they have raised often grew out of their experiences in the domestic sphere. They seem disproportionately identified with schemes supporting social welfare, especially regarding children, the mentally ill, the disabled and the elderly,[226] [*Fig. 4.21*] and education, in campaigns for green spaces and historic buildings, and in protests against sexual violence within the home and in the streets. Women's initiatives in these and related areas continue to raise important questions about how we define what is significant to our collective lives.

Notes

Introduction

1 Definitions of 'civil society' and 'the public sphere' are the subject of a vast literature beyond the scope of this book. For our purposes we shall take 'civil society' to include those areas between the household and the State where people might come together. These would include for example, the workplace, religious congregations, voluntary associations and commercial and cultural organisations of varying sorts. Such distinctions are especially problematic before the late eighteenth century when the household and workplace often overlapped. As a rough demarcation, we are focusing on the impact women had outside their duties within the household as housewives and mothers, though we are aware that this is a porous distinction. The very notion of work takes for granted not only unpaid domestic work within the home but the labour of female family members in workshops and shops. We are mindful of the emergence of what Jürgen Habermas has called 'the public sphere' in the late seventeenth century in England where there was a proliferation of new arenas for public participation. See Jürgen Habermas, *The Structural Transformation of the Public Sphere*, trans. by Thomas Burger and Frederick Lawrence (Cambridge, Mass: MIT Press, 1989); Craig Calhoun (ed.), *Habermas and the Public Sphere* (Cambridge, Mass: MIT Press, 1992).

2 For example, see Kathryn Gleadle, 'The Imagined Communities of Women's History: Current Debates and Emerging Themes, a Rhizomatic Approach,'*Women's History Review*, 2, 4 (2013), pp.524-540; Leonore Davidoff and Catherine Hall, *Family Fortunes. Men and Women of the English Middle Class, 1780-1850* (London: Routledge, revised ed. 2002); Anna Clark, *The Struggle for the Breeches. Gender and the Making of the British Working Class* (London: University of California Press, 1995); Kathryn Gleadle, *British Women in the Nineteenth Century* (Houndmills, Basingstoke: Palgrave, 2001); Krista Cowman, *Women in British Politics, c.1689-1979* (Houndmills, Basingstoke: Palgrave Macmillan, 2010).

3 Kathryn Gleadle, 'British Women and Radical Politics in the Late Nonconformist Enlightenment, c.1780-1830', in Amanda Vickery (ed.), *Women Privilege and Power: British Politics, 1750 to the Present* (Stanford, CA: Stanford University Press, 2001), p.151.

4 For an overview, see Barbara Caine, *English Feminism, 1780-1980* (Oxford: Oxford University Press, 1997); June Hannam, *Feminism* (Harlow: Pearson Education, 2012).

5 Linda McDowell, *Gender, Identity and Place: Understanding Feminist Geographies,* (Cambridge: Polity Press, 1999) offers an overview of developments in a gendered geography of place.

6 Examples of British regional studies include: Eleanor Gordon and Gwyneth Nair, *Public Lives: Women, Family and Society in Victorian Britain* (London: Yale University Press, 2003), on middle-class women in Glasgow; Deirdre Beddoe, *Out of the Shadows: A History of Women in Twentieth-Century Wales* (Cardiff: University of Wales Press, 2001); Krista Cowman, '*Mrs Brown is a Man and a Brother': Women in Merseyside's Political Organisations, 1890-1920* (Liverpool: Liverpool University Press, 2004); Karen Hunt, 'Making Politics in Local Communities: Labour Women in Interwar Manchester', in Matthew Worley (ed.), *Labour's Grass Roots: Essays on the Activities and Experiences of Local Labour Parties and Members, 1918-1945* (Aldershot: Ashgate, 2005). Local studies of the suffrage movement have changed our understanding of that campaign. For an overview of some publications see June Hannam, '"I had not been to London". Women's Suffrage – A View from the Regions', in June Purvis and Sandra Stanley Holton (eds), *Votes for Women* (London: Routledge, 2000). See also Douglas Catterall and Jodi Campbell (eds), *Women in Port: Gendering Communities, Economies and Social Networks in Atlantic Port Cities, 1500-1800* (Leiden and Boston: Brill, 2012) and Deborah Simonton and Ann Montenach (eds), *Female Agency in the Urban Economy: Gender in European Towns, 1640-1830* (New York: Routledge, 2013).

7 Of the 39 figures Board painted only three are women: Carpenter, More and Mary Robinson.

8 Helen Meller, *Leisure and the Changing City 1870-1914* (London: Routledge and Kegan Paul, 1976); Elizabeth Baigent, 'Bristol Society in the Later Eighteenth Century with Special Reference

to the Handling by Computer of Fragmentary Historical Sources' (DPhil. Dissertation, University of Oxford, 1985); Jonathan Barry, 'The Cultural Life of Bristol, 1640-1775' (D.Phil. thesis Oxford University, 1985); Ellen Malos, 'Bristol Women in Action 1839-1919,' in Ian Bild (ed.), *Bristol's Other History* (Bristol, 1983), pp.97-128.

9 For example see, Brian S. Smith, *A History of Bristol and Gloucestershire* (Chichester: Phillimore, 1996); Kenneth Morgan, *Bristol and the Atlantic Trade in the Eighteenth Century* (Cambridge: Cambridge University Press, 1993); David Harris Sacks, *The Widening Gate: Bristol and the Atlantic Trade 1450-1700* (Berkeley: University of California Press, 1993) does briefly allude to women in his discussions of trade. Martin Boddy, John Lovering, Keith Bassett (eds), *Sunbelt City? A Study of Economic Change in Britain's M4 Growth Corridor* (Oxford: Clarendon Press, 1986) contains some information on female employment but does not provide a sustained gender analysis; Brian S. Smith and Elizabeth Ralph, *A History of Bristol and Gloucestershire* (Chichester: Phillimore, 1996).

10 Mary E. Fissell, *Patients, Power, and the Poor in Eighteenth-Century Bristol* (Cambridge: Cambridge University Press, 1991).

11 Martin Gorsky, *Patterns of Philanthropy* (Woodbridge, Suffolk: Boydell and Brewer for the Royal Historical Society, 1999); Moira Martin, '"Managing the Poor": The Administration of Poor Relief in Bristol in the Nineteenth and Twentieth Centuries,' in Madge Dresser and Philip Ollerenshaw (eds), *The Making of Modern Bristol* (Bristol: Redcliffe Press, 1996), pp.156-183.

12 Mary Waldron, *Lactilla, Milkwoman of Clifton: The Life and Writings of Ann Yearsley, 1753-1806* (Athens and London: The University of Georgia Press, 1996); Marie Mulvey-Roberts (ed.), *Literary Bristol: Writers and the City* (Bristol: Redcliffe Press/The Regional History Centre, University of the West of England, Bristol, 2015); Anne Stott, *Hannah More: The First Victorian* (Oxford: Oxford University Press, 2003); Paula Byrne, *Perdita, the Life of Mary Robinson* (London: Harper-Collins, 2004); Kerri A. Andrews, *Ann Yearsley and Hannah More, Patronage and Poetry: The Story of a Literary Relationship* (London: Pickering & Chatto, 2013).

13 Shirley Brown with Dawn Dyer, *100+ Women of Bristol* (Bristol: Bristol City Council, 2002); Lorna Brierley and Helen Reid, *Go Home and Do the Washing! Three Centuries of Pioneering Bristol Women* (Bristol: Broadcast Books, 2000).

14 June Hannam, '"An Enlarged Sphere of Usefulness": The Bristol Women's Movement, c. 1860-1914,' in Dresser and Ollerenshaw (eds), *The Making of Modern Bristol*, pp.184-209; Madge Dresser, 'Sisters and Brethren: Power Propriety and Gender amongst the Bristol Moravians 1755-1833', *Social History*, 21 (1996), pp.72-87; Peter Fleming, *Women in Late Medieval Bristol* (Bristol: BBHA, Local History Pamphlet 103, 2001).

15 Jill Liddington, *Vanishing for the Vote: Suffrage, Citizenship and the Battle for the Census* (Manchester: Manchester University Press, 2014), chap.14; Lucienne Boyce, *The Bristol Suffragettes* (Bristol: the author by Silverwood Books, 2013).

16 Eugene Byrne and Clive Burlton, *Bravo Bristol! The City at War 1914-1918* (Bristol: Redcliffe Press, 2014); Jacqueline Wadsworth, *Bristol in the Great War* (Barnsley: Pen & Sword Books, 2014).

17 Judith Bennett, *History Matters: Patriarchy and the Challenge of Feminism* (Manchester University Press, 2006) in Gleadle, 'The Imagined Communities of Women's History,' *Women's History Review*, 2, 4 (2013), p.526.

Chapter One Women in Bristol 1373-1660

1 Caroline Barron, 'The "Golden Age" of Women in Medieval London', *Reading Medieval Studies*, 15 (1990), pp.35-58. For a useful overview, see Philip J. Goldberg, *Women, Work and Life Cycle in a Medieval Economy: Women in York and Yorkshire, c.1300-1520* (Oxford: Clarendon Press, Oxford University Press, 1992), pp.3-20.

2 For good introductions to the topic, see Mavis Mate, *Women in Medieval English Society* (Cambridge: Cambridge University Press, 1999); Lindsey Charles and Lorna Duffin (eds), *Women and Work in Pre-Industrial England* (London: Oxford Women's Press, 1985); Martha C. Howell, *Women, Production and Patriarchy in Late Medieval Cities* (Chicago: University of Chicago

Press, 1986); Goldberg, *Women, Work and Life-Cycle in a Medieval Economy*; Caroline Barron and Anne Sutton (eds), *Medieval London Widows, 1300-1500* (London: Hambledon, 1994); Barbara Hanawalt, *The Wealth of Wives: Women, Law and Economy in Late Medieval London* (Oxford: Oxford University Press, 2007); Jennifer Ward, *Women in England in the Middle Ages* (London: Continuum, 2006).

3 John Lynch, *For King and Parliament: Bristol and the Civil War* (Stroud: Sutton, 1991), passim.

4 General accounts of Bristol in this period include Peter Fleming, *Time, Space and Power in Fifteenth-Century Bristol* (Forthcoming. Leiden: Brill, 2016), and David H. Sacks, *The Widening Gate: Bristol and the Atlantic Economy, 1450-1700* (Berkeley & London: University of California Press, 1991). An illustrated overview of later medieval Bristol is Peter Fleming and Kieran Costello, *Discovering Cabot's Bristol: Life in the Medieval and Tudor Town* (Tiverton: Redcliffe Press, 1997). Bristol's experience of the Reformation is discussed in Martha Skeeters, *Community and Clergy: Bristol and the Reformation, c.1530-c.1570* (Oxford: Oxford University Press, 1992). The best introductions to Bristol and the seventeenth-century civil wars are Lynch, *For King and Parliament*, and Patrick McGrath, *Bristol and the Civil War* (BBHA 1981). For accounts of the port of Bristol in this period, see: James W. Sherborne, *The Port of Bristol in the Middle Ages* (BBHA, 1965), and Jean Vanes, *The Port of Bristol in the Sixteenth Century* (BBHA, 1977). For the merchants and later medieval trade, still unsurpassed is Eleanora M. Carus-Wilson, *Medieval Merchant Venturers: Collected Studies* (1st edn., 1954, 2nd edn., London: Methuen, 1967). For Bristol's wine trade, see Anne Crawford, *Bristol and the Wine Trade* (BBHA, 1984).

5 A useful overview of historians' approaches to women in this period, if now somewhat dated, is Amanda Vickory, 'Golden Age to Separate Spheres? A Review of the Categories and Chronology of English Women's History', *The Historical Journal,* 36 (1993), pp.383-414.

6 These returns are printed and discussed in Michael Faraday (ed.), *The Bristol and Gloucestershire Lay Subsidy of 1523-1527* (Bristol: Bristol and Gloucestershire Archaeological Society, 2009). For taxation records in this period, see Maureen Jurkowski, C. L. Smith and David Crook, *Lay Taxes in England and Wales, 1188-1688*, Public Record Office Handbook no. 31 (Kew: PRO Publications, 1998).

7 For Tudor domestic servants, see Alison Sim, *Masters and Servants in Tudor England* (Stroud: Sutton, 2006), and Roger C. Richardson, *Household Servants in Early Modern England* (Manchester University Press, 2010).

8 Barron and Sutton (eds), *Medieval London Widows,* provides valuable insights into the comparable experiences of London widows.

9 TNA, PROB 11/10/35. Similarly, Maud Esterfeld's will of 1491 assures us that it was written with the consent of her husband: Thomas Proctor Wadley, *Notes or Abstracts of the Wills Contained in the Volume Entitled the Great Orphan Book and Book of Wills, in the Council House at Bristol (1381-1605)* (Bristol: Bristol and Gloucestershire Archaeological Society, 1886), p.177. In 1407 Margaret Yonge made a will in which she left some clothes and money to her servants, and the residue to her husband, Thomas: TNA, PROB 11/2A/229.

10 Sheila Lang and Margaret McGregor (eds), *Tudor Wills Proved in Bristol, 1546-1603* (Bristol Record Society (hereafter, BRS), vol.44, 1993), no.155.

11 E.g. BRO 04026, p.155: a butcher's wife paying 6s 8d on being made sole merchant (1532-3).

12 TNA C1/9/181; Anita L. Beethan-Fisher, 'The Merchants of Medieval Bristol, 1350-1500' (Ph.D. thesis, University of Oregan, 3 vols, 1987), vol. 2, p.330.

13 Ilana K. Ben-Amos, 'Women Apprentices in the Trades and Crafts of Early-Modern Bristol', *Continuity and Change*, 6 (1991), pp.227-83, pp.237-8 & n.30.

14 Peter Fleming, *Women in Late Medieval Bristol* (BBHA, 2001), pp.4, 6.

15 Francis B. Bickley (ed.), *The Little Red Book of Bristol* (2 vols, Bristol: Arrowsmith, 1900), vol.2, pp.127-8; Edward W. W. Veale (ed.), *The Great Red Book of Bristol* (5 vols, BRS, 1931-53), *Text,* vol. 2, pp.68-9.

16 Veale (ed.), *Great Red Book of Bristol, Text,* vol. 3, p.87; Bickley (ed.), *Little Red Book of Bristol*, vol. 2, p.171.

17 Wadley, *Notes or Abstracts,* pp.88-9, 94, 98-9; Lang and McGregor (eds), *Tudor Wills Proved in*

Bristol, no. 10 (see also nos 45, 177).

18 Ben-Amos, 'Women Apprentices in the Trades and Crafts of Early-Modern Bristol', pp.242-4.

19 Wadley, *Notes or Abstracts,* pp.97, 112, 168; TNA, PROB 11/2B/32.

20 Wadley, *Notes or Abstracts,* p.127.

21 Wadley, *Notes or Abstracts,* pp.155-6.

22 TNA, PROB 11/2A/163.

23 TNA, PROB 11/2b/374.

24 TNA, PROB 11/11/552.

25 Lang and McGregor (eds), *Tudor Wills Proved in Bristol,* no. 67.

26 Wadley, *Notes or Abstracts,* p.168.

27 TNA, PROB 11/2a/113; Lang and McGregor (eds), *Tudor Wills Proved in Bristol,* no. 168. Noncupative wills are given orally by the testator, rather than written down, typically very soon before death.

28 TNA, PROB 11/7/316. All quotations from contemporary documents given in this chapter have been translated into modern English.

29 For Icelanders in fifteenth-century Bristol see Madge Dresser and Peter Fleming, *Bristol: Ethnic Minorities and the City, 1000-2001* (Chichester: England's Past for Everyone, University of London/Phillimore, 2007), pp.30-1.

30 I am very grateful to Dawn Dyer of the Bristol Central Library for supplying this information.

31 The following discussion of women and apprenticeship is based on Fleming, *Women in Later Medieval Bristol,* pp.9-11; Anne Yarborough, 'Apprentices as Adolescents in Sixteenth-Century Bristol', *Journal of Social History,* 13 (1979), pp.67-82; Jean Vanes, *Education and Apprenticeship in Sixteenth-Century Bristol* (BBHA, 1982); Ben-Amos, 'Women Apprentices in the Trades and Crafts of Early-Modern Bristol', and Ilana K. Ben-Amos, *Adolescence and Youth in Early Modern England* (New Haven and London: Yale University Press, 1994); Michael Roberts, '"Words they are Women, and Deeds they are Men": Images of Work and Gender in Early Modern England', in Charles and Duffin (eds), *Women and Work in Pre-Industrial England,* pp.142-3. For the apprentice books see Denzil Hollis (ed.), *Calendar of the Bristol Apprentice Book, 1532-1565, Part I, 1532-42* (BRS, 14, 1949); Elizabeth Ralph and N. M. Hardwick (eds), *Calendar of the Bristol Apprentice Book, 1532-1565, Part II, 1542-1552* (BRS, 33, 1980); Elizabeth Ralph (ed.), *Calendar of the Bristol Apprentice Book, 1532-1565, Part III, 1552-1565* (BRS, 43, 1992).

32 Ben-Amos, 'Women Apprentices in the Trades and Crafts of Early-Modern Bristol', pp.238-42.

33 Ralph and Hardwick (eds), *Calendar of the Bristol Apprentice Book,* vol. 2, p.x.

34 I owe this reference to the generosity of Dawn Dyer.

35 Wadley, *Notes or Abstracts,* pp.84, 104; Beethan-Fisher, 'The Merchants of Medieval Bristol', vol. 2, pp.325-6.

36 Wadley, *Notes or Abstracts,* p.84.

37 TNA, PROB 11/2b/374.

38 TNA, C1/72/73.

39 Beethan-Fisher, 'The Merchants of Medieval Bristol', vol. 2, pp.318, 327-8; Carus-Wilson, *Medieval Merchant Venturers,* pp.76, 93-4.

40 Eleanora M. Carus-Wilson, *The Overseas Trade of Bristol in the Later Middle Ages* (BRS, 7, 1937), pp.225-7, 233-4, 240, 258, 263, 276.Wadley, *Notes or Abstracts,* pp.161-3; TNA, PROB 11/6/479.

40 Lang and McGregor (eds), *Tudor Wills Proved in Bristol,* no. 121.

41 Ibid., no. 119.

42 TNA, C1/538/11.

43 TNA, C1/530/12-14.

44 Lang and McGregor (eds), *Tudor Wills Proved in Bristol,* nos 159, 145.

45 Peter Fleming, 'Women and Property in Early Tudor Bristol', in Peter Wardley (ed.), *Bristol Historical Resource,* CDROM (University of the West of England Regional History Centre, 2000).

46 Lang and McGregor (eds), *Tudor Wills Proved in Bristol,* no. 98.

47 Ibid., no. 8.

48 Ibid., nos 52, 163.

49 H.E. Nott (ed.), *The Deposition Books of Bristol, Volume I, 1643-1647* (BRS, 6, 1935), pp.105-6.

50 Ibid., pp.105-6.

51 Ibid., p.67.

52 Lang and McGregor (eds), *Tudor Wills Proved in Bristol,* no. 53.

53 Ibid., no. 93.

54 Ibid., nos 35, 64, 71, 76.

55 Dora Mary Livock (ed.), *City Chamberlains' Accounts in the Sixteenth and Seventeenth Centuries* (BRS, 24, 1966), p.40; John Latimer, *The Annals of Bristol in the Seventeenth Century* (Bristol: William George, 1900), pp.79, 91.

56 Latimer, *Annals of Bristol in the Seventeenth Century,* p.254.

57 Hilary Beckles, *A History of Barbados: From Amerindian Settlement to Caribbean Single Market* (Cambridge: Cambridge University Press, 2007), pp.1-7.

58 [Miss] H. E. Nott and Elizabeth Ralph (eds), *The Deposition Books of Bristol, Volume II, 1650-1654* (BRS, vol. 13, 1948), pp.153-5, 31.

59 Toby C. Barnard, *Cromwellian Ireland: English Government and Reform in Ireland, 1649-1660* (London: Oxford University Press, 1975), pp.34-46, 54; Nott and Ralph (eds), *The Deposition Books of Bristol, Volume II*, pp.117-18.

60 *The Deposition Books of Bristol, Volume II, 1650-1654*, pp.49-50.

61 TNA, KB9/191, f. 17-19, KB27/562, rex, mm. 1, 3d, 22, KB29/45 mm. 11-12, JUST 1/1549; HMSO, *Calendar of Patent Rolls, 1399-1401* (London, 1903), pp.272, 313, 315, 521; HMSO, *Calendar of Close Rolls, 1399-1402* (London, 1927), pp.143, 195; Bickley (ed.), *Little Red Book of Bristol*, vol. 2, pp.74-5; Chris Given-Wilson (ed.), *The Parliament Rolls of Medieval England* (CD Version: TNA, History of Parliament Trust, Scholarly Digital Editions, London, 2005), pp.3, 457, m. 14; James H. Wylie, *History of England under Henry the Fourth* (4 vols, London: Longmans, Green, 1884), vol. 1 p.120; Edward M. Thompson (ed), *Chronicon Adæde Usk, A.D. 1377-1421*(London: H. Frowde, 1904), pp.6/255.

62 For Christina More, see: Norman Tanner, 'Lollard Women (*act.c.*1390-*c.*1520)', *ODNR*, Oxford University Press, 2004 http://www.oxforddnb.com/view/article/ 50538 [accessed18 January 2014]. For Bristol and Lollardy, see: John A. F. Thomson, *The Later Lollards, 1414-1520* (Oxford: Oxford University Press, 1965), pp.20-51; Kenneth B. McFarlane, *John Wycliffe and the Beginnings of English Nonconformity* (London: English Universities Press, 1952), pp.127, 154-5, 176; Joseph Bettey, *Morning Stars of the Reformation: Early Religious Reformers in the Bristol Region*, ALHA Books, no. 8 (Bristol: Avon Local History and Archaeology , 2011); but see also Clive Burgess, 'A Hotbed of Heresy? Fifteenth-Century Bristol and Lollardy Reconsidered', in Linda Clark (ed.), *The Fifteenth Century III: Authority and Subversion* (Woodbridge: Boydell, 2003), pp.43-62 for an alternative view. For the 1414 rebellion see: Paul Strohm, *England's Empty Throne: Usurpation and the Language of Legitimation, 1399-1422* (New Haven and London: Yale UP, 1998), pp.65-86. Those prosecuted for participating in the rebellion have been discussed by Edward Powell, *Kingship, Law and Society: Criminal Justice in the Reign of Henry V* (Oxford: Clarendon Press, 1989), pp.141-67.

63 This paragraph is based on: Roger Hayden, 'Hazzard, Dorothy (d. 1674)', *Oxford Dictionary of National Biography*, Oxford University Press, 2004, http://www.oxforddnb.com/view/article/ 72736 [accessed 28 Sept 2013]; Laura Clark, 'Dorothy Hazzard', http://www.broadmeadbaptist. org.uk/historypage.php?content=history/hazzard.htm [accessed 5 Aug 2015]; David H. Sacks, 'Bristol's "Wars of Religion"', in Roger C. Richardson (ed.), *Town and Countryside in the English Revolution* (Manchester and New York: Manchester University Press, 1992), particularly pp.117, 120; Edward B. Underhill (ed.), *The Records of a Church of Christ, Meeting in Broadmead, Bristol. 1640-1687* (London: The Hanserd Knollys Society, 1847), pp.10-236, 518-9, and passim; Barry Reay, *The Quakers and the English Revolution* (London: Temple Smith, 1985). While the Quaker James Nayler's 'blasphemous' entry into the city in 1656 was a national *cause célèbre*, and his following included many women, none of these seem to have had strong Bristol links: Christine Trevett, *Women and Quakerism in the Seventeenth Century* (York: Sessions Book Trust, Eborard

Press,1991), pp.29-40. For early Bristol Quakers see Russell S. Mortimer, *Early Bristol Quakerism: The Society of Friends in the City, 1654-1700* (BBHA, 17, 1967), which draws on its author's unpublished 1946 University of Bristol MA Thesis, 'Quakerism in Seventeenth-Century Bristol'.

64 William Page (ed.), 'Hospitals: Bristol', in *A History of the County of Gloucester: Volume 2* (London: Victoria County History, 1907), pp.118-119, p.118.

Women and Funerary Commemoration c.1373-1660

1 Nigel Saul, *English Church Monuments in the Middle Ages: History and Representation* (Oxford: Oxford University Press, 2009), pp.58, 110.

2 In John Mylton's will of 1436 (TNA PROB 11/3/354), he names his daughter Joan as the wife of William Canynges, merchant of Bristol. For William Canynges, see James W. Sherborne, *William Canynges* (BBHA, 59, 1985).

3 Clive Burgess, 'Canynges, William (1402-1474), ODNB, http://www.oxforddnb.com/view/article/4581 [accessed 24 October 2012].

4 Saul, *English Church Monuments*, p.110.

5 Robert Kitchin's will is TNA, PROB 11/85/14.

Chapter Two Bristol Women in the Long Eighteenth Century, c.1660-1835

1 In 1696, when tax records first give us a reliable estimate of the city's population (of 20,000), there were 83.4 men for every 100 women, see David Souden, 'Migrants and Population Structure of Later 17th-Century Provincial Cities and Market Towns', in Peter Clark (ed.), *The Transformation of English Provincial Towns, 1600-1800* (London: Hutchinson, 1980), p.150; according to the Census for 1841, the exact figures were 112,296 total population – 55,392 males and 66,904 females. The gender role disparity was even more marked for Clifton, which was not counted as part of Bristol at this time – see 1841 Census, *Abstract of the Answers and Returns…, Age Abstract* (London: W. Clowes and Son, 1843), p.197.

2 Hannah Barker, 'Women and Work', in Hannah Barker and Elaine Chalus (eds), *Women's History: Britain, 1700-1850* (London: Routledge, 2005), pp.137-142 ; Sheryllynne Haggerty, *The British-Atlantic Trading Community, 1760-1810: Men, Women and the Distribution of Goods (The Atlantic World)* (Leiden and Boston: Brill, 2006), pp.68ff., 248-53; Deborah Simonton and Anne Montenach (eds), *Female Agency in the Urban Economy: Gender in European Towns, 1640-1830* (New York: Routledge, 2013), pp.93-116; Douglas Catterall and Jodi Campbell (eds), *Women in Port: Gendering Communities, Economies, and Social Networks in Atlantic Port Cities, 1500-1800* (Leiden and Boston: Brill, 2012); Rosemary Sweet and Penelope Lane (eds), *Women and Urban Life in 18th-Century England* (Aldershot, Hants: Ashgate, 2003), Leonore Davidoff and Catherine Hall, *Family Fortunes: Men and Women of the English Middle Class, 1780-1850* (London: Hutchinson Education, 1987); Elizabeth C. Sanderson, *Women and Work in Eighteenth-Century Edinburgh* (Basingstoke: Macmillan, 1996); Penelope Corfield, 'Business Leaders and Town Gentry in Early Industrial Britain, *Urban History*, 39 (2012), pp.20-50, at p.176.

3 Simonton, 'Widows and Wenches', pp.95-6.

4 Elizabeth Baigent, 'Bristol Society in the Later Eighteenth Century with Special Reference to the Handling by Computer of Fragmentary Historical Sources' (DPhil. thesis, University of Oxford, 1985), p.240; Simonton, 'Widows and Wenches, pp.96-7; Douglas Catterall and Jodi Campbell, 'Introduction' pp.1-38, p.3-4; in Catterall and Campbell (eds), *Women in Port*, pp.1-40, p.3-4, and Catterall and Campbell, 'Section One: Metropolitan Frameworks', in ibid., p.38 and Noble David Cook, 'Conclusion', in ibid., p.400; Haggerty, *The British-Atlantic Trading Community*, pp.3-7.

5 David Richardson, 'Slavery and Bristol's Golden Age', *Slavery and Abolition*, 26 (2005), p.49.

6 Daniel Defoe, *A Description of England and Wales: Containing a Particular Account of Each County…*, vol. VIII (London: Printed for Newbery and Carnan, 1769), p.130, at http://books.google.co.uk/books Defoe's *Tour Thro' the Whole Island of Great Britain* (1738, 2nd ed.), II, p.86, at http://books.google.co.uk/books.

7 Baigent, 'Bristol Society', p.138.

8 Ibid., p.240.

9 Peter Clark, 'Introduction', in Clark (ed.), *The Transformation of English Provincial Towns,* p.14.

10 Peter Borsay, *The English Urban Renaissance: Culture and Society in the Provincial Town, 1660-1770* (Oxford: Clarendon Press, 1989); Madge Dresser, *Slavery Obscured: The Social History of the Slave Trade in Bristol* (London: Continuum Books, 2001 [as *Slavery Obscured: The Social History of the Slave Trade in an English Provincial Port*], Bristol: Redcliffe Press, 2007), pp.117-118; *Felix Farley's Bristol Journal* (hereafter FFBJ), 25 February 1764.

11 Baigent, 'Bristol Society', p.396.

12 Elizabeth Baigent, 'Economy and Society in Eighteenth-Century English Towns: Bristol in the 1770s', in Dietrich Deneck and Gareth Shaw (eds), *Urban Historical Geography: Recent Progress in Britain and Germany* (Cambridge: Cambridge University Press, 1988), pp.109-24, at p.117.

13 Martin Gorksy, 'The Growth and Distribution of English Friendly Societies in the Early Nineteenth Century', *The Economic History Review*, 2nd Series, 51 (1998), pp.489-511, at p.499.

14 The Moravians were a Continental Protestant sect who were established in Britain by the mid-eighteenth century. Madge Dresser, 'Sisters and Brethren: Power, Propriety and Gender among the Bristol Moravians, 1746-1833', *Social History*, 21 (1996), pp.304-29, at pp.304-6. For more on Tambour works see *FFBJ,* 8 February 1783.

15 Baigent, 'Bristol Society', p.315.

16 Carl Estabrook, *Urbane and Rustic England* (Manchester: Manchester University Press, 1998), p.72.

17 See Madge Dresser, 'Middling Women and Work in Eighteenth-century Bristol,' Working Paper. University of the West of England (2013), at http://eprints.uwe.ac.uk/22127/ for an earlier and more detailed version of this section. [Hereafter, Dresser, 'Middling Women']

18 Elizabeth Ralph and Mary Williams (eds), *The Inhabitants of Bristol, 1696* (Bristol: Bristol Record Society, 1968), XXV, p.xxiv, at http://books.google.co.uk/books.

19 According to the 1851 census (the first time an occupational census for the city is available). Out of a total population of just under 157,000 (a figure including the city of Bristol and Clifton but excluding Bedminster, St Philips and St George's), female servants count as the largest single occupational group for females, with 7,226 general servants listed for the city and the census by then containing separate categories for charwomen and laundresses: over 2,200 laundresses, washerwomen and laundry housekeepers over the age of 20 were listed for Bristol and its wealthy suburb, Clifton, not all of whom could be classed as servants. This ignores the substantial number of girls under 20 working in domestic service who were listed separately. John Latimer, *The Annals of Bristol in the Nineteenth Century* (Bristol: W.F. Morgan, 1887), p.324. Bristol Reference Library (hereafter BRL), 'Population Tables II', in *Census of Great Britain, 1851* (London: George Edward Eyre and Wm Spottiswoode, printers to the Queen's Most Excellent Majesty, 1854), p.446.

20 BRL, Braikenridge Collections for Bristol, vol. XXIX, Clifton, p.206.

21 See for example Bristol Museum and Art Gallery (hereafter BMAG), 25TFA, Rolinda Sharples, *The Bristol Fair.*

22 John Cary, *An Account of the Proceedings of the Corporation of Bristol in Execution of the Act of Parliament for the Better Employing and Maintaining the Poor of that City* (London: F. Collins, 1700), pp.14-15; Bristol Record Office (hereafter BRO), 28048M/1/1 'Letter to Miss Woodhall,' 4 December 1794; John Latimer, *The Annals of Bristol in the Eighteenth Century* (Bristol: John Latimer, 1893; reprinted Bath: Kingsmead Press, 1970), p.515. (All subsequent reference to this source are from this reprinted edition.)

23 Ivy Pinchbeck, *Women Workers in the Industrial Revolution* (London: Cass, [1930], 1969), p.277; for earthenware industry see Joseph Mathews, *The Bristol Guide: Being a Complete Ancient and Modern History of the City of Bristol...Fifth Edition, Revised, Etc.* [1825], p.96; for coal hauliers see 'Report by ELIJAH WARING, Esq., on the Employment of Children and Young Persons in the Collieries of South Gloucestershire and on the State, Condition, and Treatment of Such Children and Young Persons' (Wigan: Ian Winstanley and Picks Publishing, 1998), the Coal Mining History Resource Centre, at http://www.cmhrc.co.uk/cms/document/1842_Gloucester.pdf; for staymakers see *Bristol Mercury*, 9 June 1823; Frederic Morton Eden, *The State of the Poor* (London: J Davis, 1797,

reprinted London: Frank Cass, 1966), vol. 2, pp.184-187.

24 Baigent, 'Bristol Society', p.240; Margaret R. Hunt, *The Middling Sort: Commerce, Gender, and the Family in England, 1680-1780* (London: University of California Press, 1996), p.15.

25 Joanne Bailey, 'Favoured or Oppressed? Married Women, Property and "Coverture" in England, 1660-1800', *Continuity and Change*, 17 (2002), pp.351-372, at pp.351-3, 367-8; Amy Erickson, *Women and Property in Early Modern England* (London: Routledge, 1993), pp.26, 100-1, 150; Margot Finn, 'Women, Consumption and Coverture in England', *Historical Journal*, 39 (1996), pp.703-22; Nicola Phillips, *Women in Business, 1700-1850* (Woodbridge, Suffolk: The Boydell Press, 2006), pp.46-7.

26 See Chapter 1 of this volume for a fuller explanation of this regulation.

27 For Cicell [aka Cicel] Carue, see Bristol Record Office (hereafter BRO), 043594, p.186, entry 2, Burgess Book 1699 [/1700] 13 March; for Mary Herring, see 04359/14, p.48, entry 454. Thanks to Margaret McGregor for corroborating this reference.

28 W.J. Pountney, *Old Bristol Potteries* (Bristol: J.W. Arrowsmith, 1920; Wakefield: E.P. Publishing, 1972), pp.240-43; BRO, Bristol and Avon Family History Society, 'Bristol Apprenticeship Books' (transcribed registers available online at BRO).

29 I am indebted to Alyson Marsden for this information in an email of 24 February 2014.

30 A preliminary consideration of the apprenticeship index for 1754-60 reveals that out of 1,068 masters only 11 were widows: BRO Index to Bristol Apprenticeship Books for 1 March 1754-60. This list, compiled by volunteers of the Bath and Avon Family History Society, lists only the names of male masters and does not indicate if wives were also named.

31 BRO, M/BCC/CCP (1745-9), 24 February 1749, pp.115, 120.

32 BRO, 43193/L/1, Orders for prosecution for selling goods in the borough or city of Bristol if not a freeman in contravention of the order of 14 December 1726.

33 BRO, M/BCC/CCP/1/12 (1745–54), 29 September 1754, p.160.

34 Gerald Lorentz, 'Bristol Fashion: the Maritime Culture of Bristol' (Ph.D. thesis, University of Toronto, 1997), pp.304-5. See chapter 1 for the discussion of 'portwomen' who were allowed along with 'portmen' to engage in the ale and bakery trades without burgess status.

35 Society of Friends, Men's Meeting Minutes, 14 May 1690, vol. 2, p.90 cited in Russell Mortimer, 'Quakerism in Seventeenth Century Bristol' (Ph.D. thesis, University of Bristol, 1946), p.515 n 5.

36 Lorentz, 'Bristol Fashion', pp.304-5; David Harris Sacks, *The Widening Gate: Bristol and the Atlantic Trade 1450-1700* (Berkeley: University of California Press, 1993), p.322.

37 Hannah Barker, 'Women and Work', in Barker and Chalus (eds), *Women's History*, p.137; Alice Clark, *Working Life of Women in the Seventeenth Century* ([1919] 3rd edn, London: Routledge, 1992).

38 Penelope Corfield, 'Business Leaders and Town Gentry in Early Industrial Britain, *Urban History*, 39 (2012), pp.20-49, at pp.2, 19, 256; Baigent, 'Bristol Society', p.133; Haggerty, *The British-Atlantic Trading Community*, pp.68ff., 248-53; Sheryllynne Haggerty, '"Ports, Petticoats and Power?" Women and Work in Early-National Philadelphia', in Catterall and Campbell (eds), *Women in Port*, pp.103-126, at pp.107-8; Hannah Barker and Karen Harvey, 'Women Entrepreneurs and Urban Expansion: Manchester, 1760-1820', in Sweet and Lane (eds), *Women and Urban Life*, pp.111-30, at pp.114-15; Christine Wiskin, 'Urban Businesswomen in 18th-Century England', in Sweet and Lane (eds), *Women and Urban Life*, pp.92-93.

39 Of the 754 women included, only 288 have specified occupations, the rest being women of 'gentle' status. Baigent, 'Bristol Society', pp.133, 258; Corfield, 'Business Leaders and Town Gentry', p.35; James Sketchley, *Sketchley's Bristol Directory* (Bristol: James Sketchley, 1775).

40 An Elizabeth Skuse is listed as a member of the Bristol Baptist Society at the Pithay in 1699. Bristol Baptist College Library, G96, Box G, 14738, and 'Book Belonging to the Baptist Society Meeting in the Pithay'; Insurance Policy Holders 1714-1731. Bristol, Somerset and Wiltshire, CD-ROM compiled from policy registers at the Guildhall Library, London by the Bristol and Avon Family History Society, n.d. [hereafter 'Bristol Insurance Policy Holders']. Of the 240 registered policyholders in Bristol, fully 33 were women, but only 7 had a stated occupation.

41 BRO, 451676/1, Becher Papers, 14 August 1743.

42 Dresser, 'Middling Women,' pp.13-14.

43 Amy Erickson, 'Clockmakers, Milliners and Mistresses: Women Trading in the City of London Companies, 1700-1750' (University of Cambridge, Dept of Geography, research projects, 2011), pp.1-41, at p.34.

44 Ralph and Williams (eds), *The Inhabitants of Bristol, 1696*, XXV; Souden, 'Migrants and Population Structure', p.159; another female vintner, May Winpenny, was listed as a bankrupt in 1726, *Taunton Journal*, 14 November 1726.

45 'Bristol Insurance Policy Holders'; Dresser 'Middling Women,' p.8 and n. 35 and 36.

46 *FFBJ*, 4 June 1768.

47 *FFBJ*, 26 March 1763; Henry K. Plomer, *A Dictionary of the Printers and Booksellers Who Were at Work in England, Scotland and Ireland from 1668 to 1725* (Oxford: Oxford University Press, 1922), p.249; William West, *Fifty Years Recollection of an Old Bookseller…* (London: Printed by and for the author, 1837), p.132, at http://books.google.co.uk/books [accessed 30 July 2013]; Latimer, *The Annals of Bristol in the Eighteenth Century*, p.282; Jonathan Barry, 'The Press and the Politics of Culture in Bristol, 1660-1775', in Jeremy Black and Jeremy Gregory (eds), *Culture, Politics and Society in Britain, 1660-1800* (Manchester: Manchester University Press, 1991), pp.49-81, at p.53.

48 *FFBJ*, 26 March 1763.

49 BRL, B1079/BL 7E, 'The Mad Wife tame'd by a Jolly Butcher', in 'Scrap Book of Broadsides' (n.d. but c.early/mid-1700s); See Daniel Defoe, *The Complete English Tradesman*, ECCO [1745] p.279.

50 'Mary Sarjeant,' at http://www.cems.uwe.ac.uk/~rstephen/livingeaston/local_history/womens_history.html; Nancy Cox, 'Darby, Abraham (1678-1717)', *Oxford Dictionary of National Biography*, Oxford University Press, 2004; online edn, Jan 2008, at http://www.oxforddnb.com/view/article/7137 [accessed 3 Aug 2015]

51 BMAG, TC2746. 'Fry Genuine patent Cocoa...made by Anna Fry & Son the patentees, ...' Printed by Henry Fry No.8 Middle Moorfields, London.; Madge Dresser, (ed.), *The Diary of Sarah Champion Fox* (Bristol: Bristol Record Society, 2012), vol. 55, p.10.

52 BRO, Pamphlet 261, 'Transcriptions of Quarter Session Lists for 1760', in *Notes on Bristol History No. 9, Compiled under the Guidance of E. Ralph and p.McGrath, 1971* (University of Bristol Extra-Mural Department) and Green file; Nicholas Rogers, *Manning the Royal Navy in Bristol*, (Bristol: Bristol Record Society 2014), vol. LXVI pp.17-18; *The Oracle Country Advertiser*, 9 May 1767.

53 Edwin and Stella George (eds), *Bristol Probate Inventories, 1657-1689* (Bristol: Bristol Record Society, 2005), vol. 57, p.156.

54 'Insurance Policy Holders.'

55 TNA, Estwick v. Evans, 25 January 1712, C6/406/18.

56 Re Mrs Ledbetter, Roger Leech, *The Topography of Medieval and Early Modern Bristol: Part 1* (Bristol: Bristol Record Society, 1997), vol. XLVIII, p.3; for Mrs Read, see Samuel Johnson, *The Works of Richard Savage Esq…with an Account of the Life and Writings of the Author* (London: T. Evans, 1767), pp.v.i, cii., and Freya Johnston, 'Savage, Richard (1697/8-1743)', *Oxford Dictionary of National Biography*, Oxford University Press, 2004, online edn, January 2008, at http://www.oxforddnb.com/view/article/24724 [accessed 5 March 2014]. For Mrs Barry, see BRO, 1628/1, Ancient Lease, Corporation of Bristol to Ann Barry, 1743, 2 August; P.K. Stembridge, *The Goldney Family: A Bristol Merchant Dynasty* (Bristol: Bristol Record Society, 1998), vol. XLIX, p.156; *Bristol Oracle*, 12 March 1742, in Pountney, *Old Bristol Potteries*, p.241; for Whealen, see *FFBJ*, 9 July 1768; for Sarah Perry, see *FFBJ*, 12 March 1768.

57 *FFBJ*, 23 June 1759; Rees is mentioned in *FFBJ*, 19 March 1768.

58 Wiskin, 'Urban Businesswomen', p.109.

59 Dresser, *Slavery Obscured*, p.18.

60 Patrick McGrath (ed.), *Merchants and Merchandise in Seventeenth Bristol* (Bristol: Bristol Record Society, 1955, reprinted 1968), vol. XIX, p.253.

61 Ibid.; TNA, PROB 11/300/322, will of Cicily [aka Cecily] Hooke TNA PROB 11/300/322, 17 October 1660.

62 TNA, E190/1201/2, 20 July 1728, 31 July 1728, 11 September 1728 and E 190/1201/34 September 1728.

63 N.C.P. Tyack, 'The Trade Relations of Bristol with Virginia during the seventeenth century' (M.A. thesis, Dept. of History, University of Bristol, 1930), p.22.

64 TNA, E190/1156/2.

65 Edwin and Stella George (eds), *Bristol Probate Inventories: Part III: 1690-1804* (Bristol: Bristol Record Society, 2008),vol. 60, pp.57-60. TNA, RG4/3765, Register of Births, Marriages and Deaths, Priscilla Fry, d.11 June 1706, RG4, Bristol, Broadmead, Baptist, 1679-1746, http://www.ancestry.co.uk [accessed 21 November 2013]; it is not known if Fry, Bradley & Co., tobacconists & snuff-maker listed in Mary le Port Street in *Sketchley's Bristol Directory*, is descended from the same Fry family.

66 BRO, 33647/37890/4, marriage settlement, 6 February 1753, mentions Mary Staines, tobacconist of Princess Street, St Stephens; *The Bristol Weekly Intelligencer* (hereafter *BWI*) 30 May 1752 advertises the Bond Street shop of Elizabeth Noblett and James Wade who sold *inter alia* 'snuffs of all kinds'; Elizabeth Johnson in Baldwin Street is named in *Sketchley's Bristol Directory* (1775); Grace Maggs is named in 1779 in lease, BRO, P/St.T/D/141; Ann Esterbrook took over her husband's business in Old Market, *FFBJ*, 15 November 1783.

67 Wives were named with their husbands, 'Clay Pipe Apprentices and Employees', at www.kalendar.demon.co.uk/pottapp.3htm [accessed 21 November 2013, the site compiled by the independent researcher Rod Dowling is no longer active]; *Bristol Observer*, 10 December 1921; BRL, B22946; Roger Price, Reg Jackson and Philomena Jackson (eds), 'Bristol Clay Pipe Makers: A Revised and Expanded Version' (unpublished typescript, 1979).

68 *FFBJ*, 7 July 1770; Price *et al.*, 'Bristol Clay Pipe Makers'(rev. edn, 1979); Reg G. Jackson and Roger H. Price, *Bristol Clay Pipes: A Study of Makers and their Marks* (Bristol: Bristol City Museum: Research Monograph No. 1, 1974), p.76; BRO, 17126, Tobacco Pipe-Makers' Book.

69 BRO, 451676/1, Becher Papers; TNA, C107/12, Bundle A, James Rogers Papers.

70 *FFBJ*, 31 December 1768; like Alice Sloper she seems connected to the Duddlestone family. For Stroud see Anne Laurence, *Women in England, 1500-1760* (London: Weidenfeld and Nicolson, 1994), p.132, and Voyage ID no. 17542 aboard *Cape Coast* (1764), at http://www.slavevoyages.org/tast/database/index.faces [accessed 13 November 2013].

71 BCL, B9845, 'Mother Nagrom, a Poem', 27 March 1793; Braikenridge Collections for Bristol, vol. XXIX, Clifton, p.439; BMAG, K763, Samuel Tovey, Bristol High Cross.

72 Haggerty, 'Ports, Petticoats and Power', pp.112-113.

73 *FFBJ*, 16 January 1768, *FFBJ* 10 or 16 Jan 1768, 24 Dec 1768.

74 Estabrook, *Urbane and Rustic England*, p.79.

75 William Goldwin, *A Description of the Antient and Famous City of Bristol. A Poem* (Bristol: Printed for Joseph Penn bookseller against the Cornmarket in Wine-Street Bristol, 1712).

76 R.T.W. Denning (abridged and ed. by), *The Diary of William Thomas of Michaelston-Super-Ely, near St. Fagans Glamorgan, 1762-1795*, 9 April 1767 [from transcripts by J.B. Davies and G.H. Thys] (Cardiff: South Wales Record Society and South Glamorgan County Council Libraries and Arts Department, 1995), p.184.

77 BRO, F/M/We/ 1776-1807.

78 BRO, P.St M/OP/4/6, 2 October 1692.

79 BRO, VC/AB.1(k) 17.

80 Mary E. Fissell, *Patients, Power, and the Poor in Eighteenth-Century Bristol* (Cambridge: Cambridge University Press: 1991), p.65.

81 Ibid., p.64.

82 *FFBJ*, 25 Feb 1764; 19 March 1768. By 1768 she had moved to 'the Pestle and Mortar' opposite the Greyhound in Broadmead where clients could enter through a discreet back entrance, Fissell, pp.64-65.

83 *BJ*, 14 January 1775; Fissell, *Patients, Power and the Poor*, p.64.

84 George Munro Smith, *A History of the Bristol Royal Infirmary* (Bristol: Arrowsmiths and London: Simking, Marshall, Hamilton, Kent & Co. 1917), p.21.

85 BRO, 35893//d_i, section on Elizabeth Preece, 'Biographical Sketches of the Founders, Officers

and Students of the Bristol Infirmary' compiled by Richard Smith Jun., Biographical Memoirs' vol. 4 1780-1784, np. It is not clear if it was Richard Smith Junior (1772-1843) who wrote this account or whether he merely compiled and transcribed an observation by a contemporary of Mrs Preece. The vivid account of her dress and demeanour seems to indicate the latter.

86 Ibid.

87 Simonton, 'Widows and Wenches', pp.103-4; *FFBJ*, 14 July 1787, for mention of marriage of Miss Nichols 'of the Circulating Library at Stokes Croft'.

88 Dresser, 'Middling Women,' pp.14-17.

89 Ibid., p.17ff.

90 Jonathan Barry, 'The Cultural Life of Bristol, 1640-1775' (D.Phil. thesis, Oxford University, 1985), pp.119-20.

91 Historical Texts is a searchable subscription collection of databases including ECCO on which much of this section is based, see http://historicaltexts.jisc.ac.uk/

92 Dresser, 'Middling Women,' p.18.

93 Ibid.

94 Ibid; Jonathan Barry (ed.), *The Diary of William Dyer: Bristol in 1762* (Bristol: Bristol Record Society, 2012), vol. LXIV, p.208. Bands were small groups within a Methodist congregation who came together for prayer and spiritual support.

95 Dresser, 'Middling Women', p18

96 Ibid.

97 Ibid, p.19; John Latimer, *Annals of Bristol in the Eighteenth Century*, p.397.

98 Ibid.

99 Ibid.

100 'A Letter Delivered by Mr. Wood to the Commissioners for Rebuilding the Bridge at Bristol, and Opening the Avenues to It, Etc.'(Bristol: S. Farley, 1760), ECCO database, and 'A Second Letter from Mr Wood, to the Commissioners for Rebuilding the Bridge at Bristol, and Opening the Avenues to It, Etc.' (S. Farley, 1760), ECCO.

101 *Six Sermons on Important Subjects,* by Josiah Tucker (Bristol: Printed by S. Farley; and sold by her; [by] the booksellers in Bristol and Bath; and by S. Bladon, London, 1772).

102 Dresser, 'Middling Women', p.19.

103 Ibid., p.20.

104 Ibid.

105 John Penny, 'Chronological Hand-List of Eighteenth-Century Newspapers Published in Bristol, Gloucestershire and Somerset, Compiled by John Penny' (Fishponds Local History Society, 1995), omits Catherine Roth's name from the list of proprietors but, aside from her own invoice, Beaven confirms she took over the business in 1800 and continued until 1806; *Bristol Lists. Municipal and Miscellaneous,* compiled by the Rev. Alfred B. Beaven (Bristol: T.D. Taylor, Sons & Hawkins, 1899), p.451; 'William Routh', at http://www.myheritage.com.

106 BRO, 12881/4, Tradesmen's bills: Catherine Routh, printer of Sarah Farley's *Bristol Journal*, 18 Bridge Street (1804).

107 Clive Burgess, (Ed), *The Pre-Reformation Records of all Saints' Church, Bristol Part II* (Bristol Record Society 2000) vol.53, pp.13, 58-59. Manymoney seems to have been one of succession of such schoolmistresses employed by the parish and more investigation of other parish records is needed. Thanks to William Evans for this reference.

108 Latimer, *The Annals of Bristol in the Eighteenth Century*, p.12.

109 Dresser, 'Middling Women', p.20; John Frederick Bryant, *Verses...Together with an Account of His Life,* (London: printed for the author, 2nd ed., 1787), p.iv at https://books.google.co.uk/books?id= jd9bAAAAQAAJ &dq=John+Frederick+Bryant&source=gbs_navlinks_s [Accessed 15 July 2015].

110 BRO, M/BCC/CPP/1/10, 'Council Proceedings 1722-1738', 12 December 1723, pp.36, 38; Mills took over from the school run by Hannah More and her sisters which was ultimately located in Park Street.

111 *FFBJ*, 31 March 1743.

112 Dresser, 'Middling Women,' p.21.

113 Ibid.

114 Anne Stott, *Hannah More: the First Victorian* (Oxford: Oxford University Press, 2003), p.9.

115 Ibid.; BRO, 36893 (36), d, I, e and ii, miscellaneous materials regarding the scandal and the school including a contemporary account of 'The Trial of Richard Vining' (Bristol ND, *c*.1784); see also Anne Stott, *Wilberforce* (Oxford: Oxford University Press, 2012), pp.87-102. In 1799, Selina Mills married her fiancé Zachary Macaulay, the evangelical abolitionist, and retired from her professional career.

116 See *Matthew's New Bristol Directory for the Year 1793-4*, which lists, inter alia, Ann Grummant's 'Ladies boarding school' in Queen's Parade; see also pages 64-64 of this book.

117 Frank Prochaska, 'Carpenter, Mary (1807-1877)', *Oxford Dictionary of National Biography*, Oxford University Press, 2004, at http://www.oxforddnb.com/view/article/4733 [accessed 31 March 2014].

118 Barbara Taylor, 'Martin, Emma (1811/12–1851)', *Oxford Dictionary of National Biography*, Oxford University Press, 2004, http://www.oxforddnb.com/view/article/45460 [accessed 31 March 2014]; Marilyn French, *From Eve to Dawn: Infernos and Paradises, the Triumph of Capitalism in the Nineteenth Century* (New York: The Feminist Press at the City University of New York, 2007), p.100. See Chapter 3.

119 *BM*, 2 February 1830.

120 See, for example, advertisement in *FFBJ*, 10 July 1784, for a female-run school supporting several staff which was then sold to two of the teachers employed there.

121 *BM*, 15 October 1819, 14 June 1824 and 27 October 1826.

122 Peter Thomson, 'Cautherley, Samuel (*c*.1747-1805)', *Oxford Dictionary of National Biography*, Oxford University Press, 2004, at http://www.oxforddnb.com/view/article/64326 [accessed 9 March 2014]. See also, BRL, Braikenridge Collections for Bristol, vol. XXIX, Clifton, p.105, for cutting on Jane Hippisley; B25949, 'A Prologue by Miss Pitt at the Theatre at Jacob's Well, 19 August 1761; BUTC, KB/22; BUTC, KB 10/1-2; BUTC, KB/221742; BUTC, Richard Southern, 'English Theatres Eighteenth Century'.

123 The church was demolished in the Blitz but the memorial was recorded in George Rennie Powell, *The Bristol Stage: Its Story* (Ulan Press, 2012), p.16. For more on Hippisley see Mark Batty, 'Hippisley, John (1696-1748)', *Oxford Dictionary of National Biography*, Oxford University Press, 2004, at http://www.oxforddnb.com/view/article/13359 [accessed 5 March 2014]; Richard Jenkins, *Memoirs of the Bristol Stage…with Notes Biographical* (Bristol: Printed for the author by W.H. Somerton, 1826), p.23; National Portrait Gallery, D2803, *Jane Green (née Hippisley) as Mrs Cadwallader* (1803 etching after an unknown artist). Thanks to Dawn Dyer for the point about St Paul's Cathedral.

124 Dresser, 'Middling Women,' p.22. 'Sarah Harrington', in Hermann Hecht, *Pre-Cinema History: An Encyclopaedia and Annotated Bibliography of the Moving Image before 1896* (East Grinstead, West Sussex: Bowker Saur in association with The British Film Institute, 1993); Arthur Mayne, *British Profile Miniaturists* (London: Faber and Faber, 1970), pp.19, 31, 42-3, 53; Joy Ruskin Hanes, 'Shady Ladies: Female Silhouette Artists of the 18th Century', *New England Antiques Journal*, at https://www.antiquesjournal.com/pages09/monthlypages/june09/ladies.html [accessed 4 November 2013] – thanks to Ruth Hecht for this reference. *Bonner and Middleton's Bristol Journal*, 7 January 1775; *Bristol Journal*, 7 January 1775, 4 March 1775, 1 April 1775; see also *Bristol Journal*, 19 July 1775.

125 *FFBJ*, 19 July 1783.

126 *FFBJ*, 27 Jan 1781; 'Catherine Andras', Victoria and Albert Museum website, http://collections.vam.ac.uk/item/O77802/lord-nelson-relief-andras-catherine/', Catherine Andras, British Museum website, http://www.britishmuseum.org/research/search_the_collection_database/term_details.aspx?bioId=91905 'Nelson Displayed', National Maritime Museum website, http://www.rmg.co.uk/sites/default/files/media/pdf/Authentic-Nelson.pdf. Andras's

father appears to have been from a Hungarian family who came to England as Protestant refugees. A Sarah Andras (probably her mother) was listed in *Sketchley's Directory* of 1775 as a perfumer located in St Augustine's Back and the Andrases are mentioned in the records of the Moravian Collection held at UBLSC.

127 Both women exhibited at the Royal Academy in London. Francis Greenacre, 'Sharples, Rolinda (1793-1838)', *Oxford Dictionary of National Biography*, Oxford University Press, 2004; online edn, January 2012, at http://www.oxforddnb.com/view/article/25242 [accessed 6 March, 2014].

128 Kathryn Metz, *Woman's Art Journal*, vol. 16, no. 1 (Spring-Summer 1995), pp.3-11, especially published by: Woman's Art Inc., at http://www.jstor.org/stable/1358624 [stable URL].

129 Ibid.; Greenacre, 'Sharples, Rolinda (1793-1838)'; Susan Waller, *Women Artists in the Modern Era: A Documentary History* (Metuchen, NJ, and London: The Scarecrow Press Inc., 1991), pp.38-41; see Royal West of England Academy website at http://rwa.org.uk/about/history/ for a different account of her financial legacy.

130 The paintings named are all part of the collection at BMAG. *The Trial of Colonel Brereton* is at MShed (the Museum about Bristol) and the others are at the Bristol Museum and Art Gallery, Queens Road, at time of writing.

131 BRL, *Miscellany of poems, compos'd and word'd with a Needle, on the Backs and Seats etc. Of several Chairs and Stools, and Humbly Dedicated to Mrs Elizabeth Freke…by the Lady Norton* (Bristol: Printed by W. Bonny, 1714), p.2. The Freke family were an important merchant family in early-eighteenth-century Bristol.

132 *Bristol Chronicle*, 5 January 1760, cited by Jonathan Barry, 'The Press and the Politics of Culture', p.62.

133 See, for example, Anon., *An Account of Mrs Elizabeth Johnson, Well Known In The City Of Bristol For More Than Half A Century For Her Piety And Benevolence To Which Is Added An Extract From Her Diary* (Bristol: W. Pine and Son, 1799) which, according to one source, was written by a Miss Elizabeth Ritchie.

134 The above discussion is distilled from a range of works including Mary Waldron, *Lactilla, Milkwoman of Clifton: The Life and Writings of Ann Yearsley, 1753-1806* (Athens and London: University of Georgia Press, 1996); Stott, *Hannah More*; Paula Byrne, *Perdita, the Life of Mary Robinson* (London: HarperCollins, 2004); Kerri Andrews, *Ann Yearsley and Hannah More, Patronage and Poetry: The Story of a Literary Relationship* (London: Pickering & Chatto, 2013); Kerri Andrews 'In Her Place: Ann Yearsley or "The Bristol Milkwoman",' in Marie Mulvey-Roberts (ed), *Literary Bristol: Writers and the City* (Bristol: Redcliffe Press, 2015), pp.94-104.

135 Clark Library, (UCLA). Hannah More Letters, Ms. 1997.009, folder HM, to Mrs Kennicott and Mr Pepys, 15 June 1781-25 December 1789, 5, no. 12, HM to Mrs K Bristol, 1 April 1783.

136 Ibid.

137 Frances Adams Hyett and William Bazeley, *The Bibliographer's Manual of Gloucestershire Literature* (Ulan Press, 2012), p.91; Waldon, *Lactilla*, pp.211-217; Andrews, *Ann Yearsley and Hannah More*, p.103, but see pp.140-143.

138 The inscription on Yearsley's gravestone in the upper churchyard was recorded by Mary Campbell member of the Bristol and Gloucestershire Archaeological Society. Joseph Grozer, after Sarah Shiells, *Portrait of Mrs Ann Yearsley, The Bristol Milkwoman,* [bap.1753, d.1806], print, Bristol Museum and Art Gallery, M3108; Joseph Manning, *Portrait of Ann Yearsley*, 1828, BMAG, M4069.

139 BRL, B248/3B1, Anne Powell, *Poems* (1821); for Hoare see BRL B5052/3B. Thanks to Dawn Dyer for these references.

140 Edward Bryan (d. 1814) , was listed as proprietor of the City Printing Office at 52 Corn Street and had a second shop at 15, Clarence Street. He gained prominence in the 'Bristol scene' 'as a printer of broadsheets which recorded the emotional issues of the day,' according to William Tyson, *The Bristol Memorialist* (Bristol: Printed by and for the author, 1823), p.60. Bryan continued his mother's tradition of publishing Baptist works, including a number of the Baptist divine John Ryland's sermons between 1811-1813 which are documented, at the Baptist Heritage

website at http://media2.sbhla.org.s3.amazonaws.com/baptistheritage/Starr/Starr _Volume020. pdf, [accessed 1 August 2015]. The business continued for over a decade after his death under Mary Bryan and the Corn Street premises were depicted in Edward Cashin's watercolour of 1826. For the token scheme which helped lead to E. Bryan's financial woes, see Tyson and also James O'Donald Mays, 'Silver Tokens and Bristol' (Bristol Numismatic Society publication, 1978), at http://www.britnumsoc.org/publications/Digital%20BNJ/pdfs/1978_BNJ_48_11.pdf.

141 Claire Knowles, *Sensibility and Female Poetic Tradition, 1780-1860: The Legacy of Charlotte Smith* (Farnham, Surrey: Ashgate Press, 2009), pp.53 and 78.

142 Anon. *A Sketch of the Life of the Late Richard Reynolds of Bristol, the Great Philanthropist...* (Bristol: Mary Bryan, 51 Corn Street, 1816). This volume, signed by the leading male citizens of the day, seems to have been a high-prestige publication.

143 Sharon A. Ragaz, 'Writing to Sir Walter: The Letters of Mary Bryan Bedingfield', *Cardiff Corvey: Reading the Romantic Text*, no.7 (December 2001), at http://www.cardiff.ac.uk/encap/ journals/corvey/articles/cc07_n02.html [accessed 8 March 2014]; a note on Mary Bryan (1780-1838; née Langdon, later Bedingfield) at http://www.orgs.muohio.edu/ womenpoets/poetess /works/headnotes [accessed 10 March 2014]; Anon., 'Review of *Longhollow*, by Mrs. Bryan Bedingfield', *The Spectator*, 28 March 1829, p.13; Charles Lamb: Works of Charles and Mary Lamb, VI and VII, letters, at http://lordbyron.cath.lib.vt.edu/contents.php?doc = ChLamb.1905.Contents&Persons&selectPerson=MaBedin1829 [accessed 10 March 2014].

144 *Bristol Mirror*, 2 January 1830; 'Lesser Columbus' [pseud.], *Greater Bristol* (London: The Pelham Press, 1893), p.80; Gorksy, p.21.

145 John Cranidge, *A mirror for the burgesses and commonality of the City of Bristol, in which is exhibited to their view a part of the great and many interesting benefactions and endowments, of which the city hath to boast and for which the corporation are responsible, ...* (Bristol: Cranidge, 1818), pp.28-9, at http://books.google.co.uk/books; for Mrs Sarah Ridley's Charity, 1726-1891, BRO, 35684/16.

146 Cranidge, *A mirror for the burgesses*, p.166; Thomas John Manchee (ed), *The Bristol Charities: Being the Report of the Commissioners for Charities in Bristol* (Bristol: Printed for T.J. Manchee, 1831), 2 vols, vol.1, p.200; Anne Stott, 'Britain in the Eighteenth Century', at http://anne-18thcentury. blogspot.co.uk/2006/11/charity-schools.html; Cranidge, *A mirror for the burgesses*.

147 TNA, PROB 11/1318/101, Will of Elizabeth Merlott, 14 January 1799 which names another Elizabeth Merlott as her sister-in-law and it is this Miss Merlott who in 1810 bequeathed an extra £1,000 in her lifetime and more than £3,000 after her death to the charity, according to Thomas John Manchee (ed), *The Bristol Charities: Being the Report of the Commissioners for Charities in Bristol* (Bristol: Printed for T.J. Manchee, 1831), 2 vols, vol.1, pp.105-6; Bristol Charities, 'Description of Grant Giving Charities', at http://www.bristolcharities.org.uk/search /node/blind [accessed 31 October 2013]; see also BRO, F/AC/Box/125/2 'Miss Ludlow's Gift'; for another substantial female donor.

148 Martin Gorsky, *Patterns of Philanthropy* (Woodbridge, Suffolk: Boydell and Brewer for the Royal Historical Society, 1999), p.21; Bristol Charities Website, http://www.bristolcharities.org.uk/ about/history-grant-giving-charities. Another bequest came from Ann Casamajor who was also from a Huguenot background. For Ann Peloquin, see Madge Dresser and Peter Fleming, *Bristol: Ethnic Minorities and the City 1000-2000* (Chichester: Phillimore, 2007 reprinted 2009), pp.57-58.

149 By the late eighteenth century, older Dissenting denominations (such as the Quakers and Baptists) were increasingly affected by the wave of evangelical fervour that had originally inspired the Methodists and many Anglicans. The more rationalist Unitarians also spearheaded a number of charitable endeavours.

150 The Gloucestershire Society was established in 1657 by 'Gloucestershire Gentlemen that inhabit the city of Bristol', The Gloucestershire Society/History, at http://www.gloucestershiresociety.org.uk/History [accessed 1 November 2013]

151 BRL, B7530, Bristol Library Society Subscription, Book 11, January 1773 to 1872, pp.11, 12, 13, 14, 17, 23, 24, Maria Edgeworth to Mr Ruxton, 29 December 1791, in Edward Martin and Bill Pickard (eds), *600 Years of Bristol Poetry* (Bristol: City of Bristol, 1973), p.12; Paul Kaufman,

'The Community Library: A Chapter in English Social History', *Transactions of the American Philosophical Society*, New Series, vol. 57, no. 7 (1967), pp.1-67.

152 BRL, B7891, The Bristol Dispensary for the Relief of the Sick Poor; Barry (ed.), *The Diary of William Dyer*, p.194.

153 Gorsky, *Patterns of Philanthropy*, p.177.

154 Ibid., p.165.

155 Marion Pluskota, *Prostitution and Social Control in Eighteenth-Century Ports* (Abingdon: Routledge, 2015) ; Steve Poole, 'The Way to Hell and the Chamber of Death: Prostitution, Low Culture and Its Discontents in Bristol, 1720-1820' (unpublished paper for the Regional History Centre, University of the West of England, 26 November 2003); BRL, B9183-6, *Reports of the Bristol Penitentiary of Magdalen House*, 181, 1821, 1822.

156 BRO, P.St T/Ch/1/21, 1820, Extract of the Will of Mary Gresley, 10 November 1800.

157 Anon. [Elizabeth Ritchie?], *An Account of Mrs Elizabeth Johnson* (Bristol: W. Pine, 1799); Madge Dresser, 'The Book of Your Own Heart: Moravian Women's Religious Experience in Georgian Bristol', in Joseph Bettey (ed.), *Historic Churches and Church Life in Bristol* (Bristol: Bristol and Gloucestershire Archaeological Society, 2001), pp.134-48; Dresser, *Slavery Obscured*, (2007), pp.84-85; H.J. Foster, 'One of Wesley's Unpublished Abridgements', in *Proceedings of the Wesley History Society*, pp.57ff., http://www.biblicalstudies.org.uk [accessed 11 November 2013].

158 Andrea A. Rusnock and Vivien E. Dietz, 'Defining Women's Sickness and Work: Female Friendly Societies in England, 1780-1830', *Journal of Women's History*, vol. 24, no.1 (Spring 2012), pp.60-85.

159 Gorsky, *Patterns of Philanthropy*, pp.166, 170. Rusnock and Dietz, 'Defining Women's Sickness and Work', pp.60-85, esp.p.4 and p.23, n.13.

160 Thomas Pole, *A History of the Origin and Progress of Adult Schools* (1814 first ed., London: Woburn Press, 1968), pp.87, 21.

161 J. Gregory Dees and Miriam and Peter Haas, 'The Meaning of Social Entrepreneurship' (paper for Graduate School of Business, Stanford University, 31 October 1998), at http://www.partnerships.org.au/library/the_meaning_of_social_entrepreneurship.htm [accessed 8 March 2014].

162 The 'Panopticon', originally proposed by the reformer Jeremy Bentham in 1787, was 'a circular prison with cells arranged around a central well, from which inmates can be observed at all times'. The idea was to prevent abuses by making both prisoners and guards accountable for their actions. Approved in principle by Parliament in 1797, no prison was established along these lines until a year after Morgan published her pamphlet in 1815.

163 Miss Morgan, 'Gaol of the City of Bristol, Compared with What a Gaol Ought to Be', 1815, BRL, B957 ; see William Tyson, *The Bristol Memorialist* (Bristol: W. Tyson, 1823), pp.87, 222.

164 *Gentleman's Magazine*, vol. 86, part 2 (1816), pp.251-2; Latimer, *The Annals of Bristol in the Nineteenth Century*, p.53; BRL, B9181, *State of the Prudent Man's Friend Society for the Year 1814*; *BM*, 3 January 1820.

165 *BM*, 6 April 1830; *BM*, 22 January 1827 – thanks to Margaret McGregor for this reference and to John Stevens for the reference to *BM*, 20 February 1836.

166 *BM*, 22 January 1827.

167 BRO, Town Clerks' Boxes, 1820, Box 201/1, 1821.

168 Michael Neve, 'Natural Philosophy, Medicine and the Culture of Science' (Ph.D. thesis, University of London, 1984), p.415; Manchee (ed.), *The Bristol Charities*.

169 References are taken from a forthcoming piece I am preparing for publication, Madge Dresser, 'Sarah Guppy' (forthcoming 2016), *Oxford Dictionary of National Biography*. Thanks to Peter Revelle and Sheila Hannon who generously shared their own research, references and insights with me. Hannon's play, *An Audience with Sarah Guppy*, was first staged in 2008 by Show of Strength Theatre in Bristol, http://showofstrength.org.uk/productions/an-audience-with-sarah-guppy, [accessed 15 October 2015]. See also *FFBJ*, 23 August 1788, 6 September 1788, 11 April 1789; Baker Perkins Historical Society, at http://www.bphs.net/EarlyHistory/Origins.

170 *The Register of Arts, and Journal of Patent Inventions*, vol.7 Luke Herbert (ed), (London: B. Steill, Paternoster row, 1832), 1.

171 Madge Dresser, 'Sarah Guppy' (forthcoming 2016), *Oxford Dictionary of National Biography*.

172 Anne Stott, 'Patriotism and Providence: The Politics of Hannah More', in Kathryn Gleadle and Sarah Richardson (eds), *Women in British Politics, 1760-1860* (Basingstoke, Hampshire: Macmillan Press, 2000), pp.39-55, at p.40; Frank O'Gorman, 'Campaign Rituals and Ceremonies: The Social Meaning of Elections in England 1780-1860,'*Past & Present* No. 135 (May, 1992), pp.79-115, at p.86.

173 *Letters from a Moor at London to his friend at Tunis. Containing an account of his journey through England, by Moor at London*, ECCO database [1736], p.243; M(anasseh) Dawes, *Observations on the Mode of Electing Representatives in Parliament for the City of Bristol, with a Proposed Reform* (Bristol: J. Lloyd in Wine-Street; London: For H. Goldney, Pater-Noster-Row, 1784), pp.14-15; Elaine Chalus, 'Women, Electoral Privilege and Practice in the Eighteenth Century,' in Gleadle and Richardson (eds), *Women in British Politics*, pp.19-38, at pp.23-4.

174 Nicholas Rogers, *Manning the Royal Navy in Bristol: Liberty, Impressment and the State, 1739-1815* (Bristol: BRS, 2014), vol. 66, pp.58, 178; Latimer, *The Annals of Bristol in the Nineteenth Century*, p.20.

175 Charlotte F. Otten (ed.), *English Women's Voices, 1540-1700* (Miami: Florida International University Press, 1992), p.58.

176 Cathy Hartley, *A Historical Dictionary of British Women* (first published as *The Europa Dictionary of British Women* in 1983, rev. ed. 2003). This edition ebook, Francis and Taylor, 2005, p.160.

177 *BM*, 23 August 1831.

178 Clare Midgley, *Feminism and Empire: Women Activists in Imperial Britain 1790-1865* (London: Routledge, 2007), p.82. M. Dresser, *Slavery Obscured* (2007), pp.204-08

179 BCL 2009525, William Dyer's epitomised Diaries, May 1763; John Oldmixon, *The Bristol Riot. Containing, I. A full and particular account of the riot in general, with several material circumstances preceding II. The…* by Oldmixon, ECCO database [1714].

180 Mark Harrison, 'To Raise and Dare Resentment: The Bristol Bridge Riot of 1793 Re-Examined', *The Historical Journal*, vol. 26, no. 3 (September 1983), pp.557-85, at p.577.

181 Jane Cave Winscom (*c*. 1754-1813) was born in Wales, published her first volume of poems in 1783, married an exciseman shortly thereafter and moved to Bristol in 1792. See Catherine Ingrassia,'"Calmly to Heav'n Submit Your Causes": Jane Cave Winscom and the Bristol Bridge Riot of 1783', *ABO Interactive Journal for Women in the Arts, 1640-1830*, vol.1 (2011), pp.1-28 at http://scholarcommons.usf.edu/cgi/viewcontent.cgi?article=1053&context=abo [accessed 8 March 2014]; Catherine; Norbert Schürer, 'Jane Cave Winscom: Provincial Poetry and the Metropolitan Connection,' *Journal for Eighteenth-Century Studies*, vol. 36, no1. 3 (2013), pp.415-431; For Yearsley see Andrews, *Ann Yearsley and Hannah More*, pp.133-136.

182 Harrison, 'To Raise and Dare Resentment', p.579.

183 BRL, R. Paddock, *The Recontre: A Poetic Tale (Founded on Fact) Descriptive of the Late Violent Proceedings in the City of Bristol…*(Bristol: Printed by J. Penley, June 1801).

184 Ibid.; Latimer, *The Annals of Bristol in the Nineteenth Century*, pp.151, 156, 165;William James Muller and Engelmann & Co., *Queen Square on the Night of 30 October 1831*, M Shed, Bristol, BMAG, M269. Sir John Wetherell who had formerly been Attorney General under Wellington was by 1830 the Recorder of Bristol, which was a senior judicial position.

185 Rolinda Sharples, *The Trial of Colonel Brereton*, 1834, M Shed, Bristol, BMAG, K1074; Greenacre, 'Sharples, Rolinda', states that not all of those painted *actually* attended the meeting.

Gentry Women

1 BRO, AC/WO/16/11, Basilwood, 'Summary of John and Rebecca Elbridge's account with the Spring Plantation, RECEIPT,' 1736; Anton Bantock, *The Later Smyths of Ashton Court: From Their Letters 1741-1802*, (Bishopsworth: Malago Publications, 1984) pp. 155-165.

2 BRO, AC/WO/16/36 (b), 28 July 1752, also cited in Anton Bantock, *The Later Smyths of Ashton Court*, p. 161.

3 BRO, AC/WH/17/22/A-C, *List of letters between Samuel Whitchurch and Jane Whitchurch*, Samuel Whitchurch to Jane Whitchurch, May 1775 and Jane Whitechurch to Samuel Whitchurch, n.d.

4 Ibid.; Bernard, Capp, *When Gossips Meet: Women, Family and Neighbourhood in Early Modern England*. (New York: Oxford University Press, 2003.) pp.268-274. Carl. B, Estabrook, *Urbane and Rustic England: Cultural Ties and Social Spheres in the Provinces, 1660-1780* (Manchester: Manchester University Press, 1998), p.91

5 See also Elaine Chalus. *Elite Women in English Political Life 1754-1790* (Oxford: Oxford University Press, 2005) p.231; (eds) Louise Duckling, Angela Escott and Carolyn D. Williams, *Woman to Woman: Female negotiations during the Long Eighteenth Century*, (Massachusetts: Rosemount Publishing 2010), pp.19-24 and 88-93; Lawrence, Klein, 'Gender and the Public/private Distinction in the Eighteenth Century: Some Questions About Evidence and Analytic Procedure', *Eighteenth Century Studies*, vol. 29, no. 1 (1995), pp.99-105. Joanne, Bailey, *Unquiet Lives: Marriage and Marriage Breakdown in England, 1660-1800* (Cambridge: Cambridge University Press, 2003) p.193. Will, Coster, *Family and Kinship in England 1450-1800* (London: Pearson Education Inc. 2001) pp.1-10.

6 BRO, AC/C/100/1-4, Ann Smyth in 'John Smyth at Oxford from his sisters, personal (Postmarks). 1717-1722'. BRO, AC/F7/27, Smyth, Ann. Last Will and codicil of Ann Smyth, 5 September 1754; BRO.

7 Hannah Barker and Elaine Chalus, *Women's History: Britain, 1700-1850 An Introduction* (London: Routledge, 2005), pp. 1-5; Bernard Capp, *When Gossips Meet: Women, Family and Neighbourhood in Early Modern England*. (New York: Oxford University Press, 2003), pp. 16-18. Rebecca D'Monte and Nicole Pohl (eds.), *Female Communities 1600-1800: Literary Visions and Cultural Realities* (London: MacMillan Press Ltd. 2000), pp. 3-7; Carl, B. Estabrook, *Urbane and Rustic England: Cultural Ties and Social Spheres in the Provinces, 1660-1780* (Manchester: Manchester University Press, 1998).

8 BRO, P/HEN/CH/4/1. James Davis, *Receipt book for annuities (of five pounds half-yearly) paid by vicar and churchwardens of parish of Henbury issuing out of lands called Redcliffe Meads in the parish of Bedminster, Somerset, for teaching girls to read, knit and sew pursuant to will of Mrs. Ann Smith. 1760*; BRO, AC/F7/27, Last Will and codicil of Ann Smyth, 5 September 1754; Judith, Bennett, 'Women's history: A Study of Continuity and Change', *Women's History Review 2*, (1993), pp.173-179.

Chapter Three Women in Bristol 1835-1914

1 Bristol Reference Library (hereafter, BRL), *Nursery Rhymes. Book of the Family Fair and Bazaar,* Victoria Rooms, Clifton, December 1884.

2 William F. Ayres, *The Highbury Story: The First Fifty Years* (London: Independent Press, 1963), pp.66-71; Samson Bryher, *An Account of the Labour and Socialist Movement in Bristol*, Part 2, reprinted and published by *Bristol Labour Weekly,* 1929, pp.16-19.

3 For an overview of women's social position in the period see Katherine Gleadle, *British Women in the Nineteenth Century* (Houndmills, Basingstoke: Palgrave, 2001); Leonore Davidoff, Megan Doolittle, Janet Fink and Katherine Holden, *The Family Story: Blood, Contract and Intimacy, 1830-1960* (London: Longman, 1999), chap.4.

4 Jane Lewis, *Women and Social Action in Victorian and Edwardian England* (Aldershot: Edward Elgar, 1991); Anne Summers, *Female Lives, Moral States: Women, Religion and Public Life in Britain* (Newbury: Threshold Press, 2000).

5 For women's public life in Glasgow see Eleanor Gordon and Gwyneth Nair, *Public Lives: Women, Family and Society in Victorian Britain* (New Haven, CT: Yale University Press, 2003).

6 Charles Harvey and Jon Press, 'Industrial Change and the Economic Life of Bristol since 1800', in Charles Harvey and Jon Press (eds), *Studies in the Business History of Bristol* (Bristol: Bristol Academic Press, 1988), p.2.

7 'Pin Making in East Bristol in the Eighteenth and Nineteenth Centuries', https//www.flickr.com /photos/brizzlebornandbred/2132253513/ [accessed 18 September 2015].

8 'The Great Western Cotton Works', *Work in Bristol: A Series of Sketches of the Chief Manufactures in the City*, 1883, reprinted from *Bristol Times and Mirror,* Bristol Reference Library; S.J. Jones,

'The Cotton Industry in Bristol', *Transactions and Papers* (Institute of Geographers), 13 (1947), pp.61-79.

9 Helen E. Meller, *Leisure and the Changing City* (London: Routledge and Kegan Paul, 1976), pp.36-45.

10 These movements are discussed in Anna Clark, *The Struggle for the Breeches: Gender and the Making of the British Working Class* (Oakland, CA: University of California Press, 1995); Barbara Taylor, *Eve and the New Jerusalem: Socialism and Feminism in the Nineteenth Century* (London: Virago, 1983).

11 Jane Rendall, *The Origins of Modern Feminism* (London: Macmillan 1985), pp.217-18.

12 Trevor Pearce, 'Bristol Socialists, 1837-43' (M.A. dissertation, University of the West of England), p.27.

13 *Bristol Gazette*, 7 January 1841.

14 Barbara Taylor, 'Martin (née Bullock), Emma, 1811/12-1851: Socialist and Freethinker', *Oxford Dictionary of National Biography*, Oxford University Press, at http: //www.oxforddnb.com/view/article/45460?docPos=2 [accessed 29 November 2014].

15 Asa Briggs, *Chartist Studies* (London: Macmillan, 1959); Malcolm Chase, *Chartism: A New History* (Manchester: Manchester University Press, 2007).

16 For example, see John Cannon, *The Chartists in Bristol* (Bristol: Bristol Historical Association, 1964). For women's involvement see Jutta Schwarzkopf, *Women in the Chartist Movement* (Basingstoke: Palgrave Macmillan 1991).

17 *Morning Chronicle*, 28 December 1838.

18 David Jones, 'Women and Chartism', *History*, 68 (1983), pp.1-21, p.9.

19 Jones notes how Dorothy Thompson assumed that female involvement fell away after 1842 and that this was part of a broader withdrawal of working-class women from political life. He argues that women's political associations do survive beyond 1842. Jones, 'Women and Chartism', p.13; Dorothy Thompson, 'Women and Nineteenth-Century Radical Politics: A Lost Dimension', in Juliet Mitchell and Ann Oakley (eds), *The Rights and Wrongs of Women* (London: Virago, 1976).

20 Clare Midgley, *Women Against Slavery: The British Campaigns, 1780-1870* (London: Taylor and Francis, 1995).

21 Bristol and Clifton Ladies Anti-Slavery Society (hereafter, B&CLASS), Minutes, Microfilm of the John Estlin Collection in John Williams Library, BRL.

22 Douglas C. Stange, *British Unitarians Against British Slavery* (Madison, NJ: Farleigh Dickinson University Press, 1984); Joseph Estlin Carpenter, *The Life and Work of Mary Carpenter* (London: Macmillan, 1879); Obituary of Mary Carpenter, *Times*, 18 June 1877; Obituary of Mary Estlin, *Shield*, December 1902.

23 Anne Summers, 'The Estlin papers', Bristol Record Office (hereafter, BRO), REF: 17562 (1-28); Paul Jefferson (ed.), *The Travels of William Wells Brown* (Edinburgh: Edinburgh University Press, 1991), pp.143-7.

24 B&CLASS Minutes, 27 March 1851.

25 Clare Taylor, *British and American Abolitionists: An Episode in Transatlantic Understanding* (Edinburgh: Edinburgh University Press), 1974.

26 This point is made by Caroline Bressey, *Empire, Race and the Politics of Anti-Caste* (London: Bloomsbury, 2013), p.29.

27 'Monarchies and Freedom, Republics and Slavery', An Address Delivered in Bristol, England, April 1 1847, in *Bristol Mercury and Western Counties Advertiser*, 3 April 1947.

28 Summers, 'The Estlin Papers'.

29 Bressey, *Empire, Race*, p.67.

30 'Mary Carpenter's Address on Female Education in India', *Englishwoman's Review*, 5, October (1867), pp.316-18.

31 Sandra Stanley Holton, 'From Anti-Slavery to Suffrage Militancy: The Bright Circle, Elizabeth Cady Stanton and the British Women's Movement', in Caroline Daley and Melanie Nolan (eds), *Suffrage and Beyond: International Feminist Perspectives* (Auckland: University of Auckland Press, 1994).

32 Martin Gorsky, *Patterns of Philanthropy: Charity and Society in Nineteenth-Century Bristol* (Suffolk: Boydell Press, 1999), p.177.

33 This point is also made for Glasgow in Gordon and Nair, *Public Lives,* p.224.

34 Barbara Caine, *Victorian Feminists* (Oxford: Oxford University Press, 1992).

35 Peter E. Hughes, 'Cleanliness and Godliness: A Sociological Study of the Good Shepherd Convent Refuges for the Social Reformation and Christian Conversion of Prostitutes and Convicted Women in Nineteenth century Britain' (Ph.D. thesis, Brunel University, 1985), http://bura.brunelac.uk/handle/2438/4976 contains several references to Bristol and other Good Shepherd Convents; John A. Harding, *The Diocese of Bristol, 1850-2000* (Bristol: Clifton Catholic Diocesan Trustees, 1999), pp.60, 76-7, 241.

36 See also the home for vulnerable women and girls set up by the Sisters of Mercy in 1849. Jean Olwen Maynard, 'Sisters of Mercy, Bristol', Mercy Union Generalate (London: Mercy Union Generalate, undated).

37 'Immorality and the Poor', *Report of the Committee to Inquire into the Condition of the Bristol Poor* (London: P.S. King & Son and W. Lewis & Sons, 1884), pp.88-108; Gill James, 'The Bristol Female Mission Society, 1859-1884: Prevention or Cure' (2003), http://humanities.uwe.ac.uk/swhisnet/03resources/gill%20James/The%20Bristol%20Female%20Mission%20Society.doc [accessed 18 September 2015].

38 Elizabeth Sturge, *Reminiscences of My Life* (Bristol: printed for private circulation, 1928).

39 Frances Power Cobbe, 'The Preventive Branch of the Female Mission', *The English Woman's Journal*, 7, 46, November (1861), pp.145-51; Frances Power Cobbe, *Life of Frances Power Cobbe As Told By Herself* (London: Swan Sonnenschein & Co., 1904); Lori Williamson, *Power and Protest: Frances Power Cobbe and Victorian Society* (London: Rivers Oram Press, 2004).

40 BRL, B12280, *Twenty-third Report of the Preventive Mission,* 1892, p.2.

41 For accounts of Mary Carpenter's life, see Ruby J. Saywell, *Mary Carpenter of Bristol* (Bristol: Bristol Historical Association, 1964); Jo Manton, *Mary Carpenter and the Children of the Streets* (London: Heinemann Educational Books, 1976); Julia Parker, *Women and Welfare: Ten Victorian Women in Public Social Service* (Houndmills, Basingstoke: Macmillan, 1988); Frank Prochaska, 'Carpenter, Mary (1807-1877)', *Oxford Dictionary of National Biography,* Oxford University Press, 2004 at http://www.oxforddnb.com/view/article/4733?docPos=1 [accessed 29 November 2014].

42 RuthWatts, 'Breaking the Boundaries of Victorian Imperialism or Extending a Reformed "Paternalism"? Mary Carpenter and India', *History of Education*, 29, 5 (2000), pp.443-56.

43 'The Ladies Evidence: Poor Relief', *English Woman's Journal*, 7, 42, August (1861), pp.407-8. For a discussion of the NAPPS, see Kathleen McCrone, 'The National Association for the Promotion of Social Science and the Advancement of Victorian Women', *Atlantis*, 8 (1982), pp.44-66.

44 Brian Harrison, *Dictionary of British Temperance Biography* (Sheffield: Society for the Study of Labour History, 1973).

45 Cobbe, *Life*.

46 Ethel E. Metcalfe, *Memoirs of Rosamund Davenport Hill* (London: Longmans, Green& Co., 1904); Margaret Shaen, *Memorials of Two Sisters: Susannah and Catherine Winkworth* (London: Longmans, Green & Co. 1908).

47 'Interview with Mrs Beddoe', *Women's Penny Paper*, 25 January 1890.

48 Lorna Brierley and Helen Reid, *Go Home and Do the Washing: Three Centuries of Pioneering Bristol Women* (Bristol: Broadcast Books, 2000), pp.39-41; 'Some Prominent Local Philanthropists', http://humanities.uwe.ac.uk/bhr/Main/women_routes/6_some.htm

49 Maynard, 'Sisters of Mercy', p.93.

50 Hughes, *Cleanliness and Godliness,* pp.212, 228-3; Harding, *The Diocese,* pp.76-7. For other examples of industrial schools see BRO40556. John Lavars, *Volume of Extracts from the Western Daily Press – regarding 53 Schools, Hospitals and Benevolent Institutions,* Stanhope House Industrial School, XXXVIII; Carlton House Industrial School, XXIX.

51 Ibid., Park Row Asylum, XLVI.

52 For an overview, see Krista Cowman, *Women in British Politics, c. 1689-1979* (Houndmills, Basingstoke: Palgrave Macmillan, 2010), chap.2. For a more detailed account of the women's movement in Bristol, see June Hannam, '"An Enlarged Sphere of Usefulness": The Bristol

Women's Movement c.1860-1914', in Madge Dresser and Philip Ollerenshaw (eds), *The Making of Modern Bristol* (Bristol: Redcliffe Press, 1996); Ellen Malos, 'Bristol Women in Action', in Ian Bild (ed.), *Bristol's Other History* (Bristol: Bristol Broadsides, 1983).

53 *Suffrage Petition of 1866*, Helen Blackburn Collection, Girton College.

54 For biographical details of the Priestman sisters, see 'Obituary of the Misses Priestman', *Shield*, January, 1915; BRL, Sarah A. Tooley, *Ladies of Bristol and Clifton*, 1896; Judith Walkowitz, *Prostitution and Victorian Society: Women, Class and the State* (Cambridge: Cambridge University Press, 1982), chap.6.

55 Sarah J. Tanner, *How the Women's Suffrage Movement Began in Bristol Fifty Years Ago* (Bristol: Carlyle Press, 1918); Helen Blackburn, *Women's Suffrage: A Record of the Women's Suffrage Movement in the British Isles* (London: Williams and Norgate, 1902), pp.66-7; National Union for Women's Suffrage, *Annual Report*, 1872.

56 Blackburn, *Women's Suffrage;* Linda Walker, 'Blackburn, Helen (1842-1903), campaigner for women's rights', *Oxford Dictionary of National Biography,* Oxford University Press, 2004 at http://www.oxforddnb.com/view/printable/31905 [accessed 28 November 2014].

57 Blackburn, *Women's Suffrage*, pp.110, 112. For a detailed account of the suffrage movement in Bristol, see Elizabeth Crawford, *The Women's Suffrage Movement in Britain and Ireland. A Regional Study* (London: Routledge, 2006).

58 Mrs W.H. Wills was also involved.

59 Sturge, *Reminiscences*, pp.16-17; Gwen M. Williams, *Mary Clifford* (Bristol: J.W. Arrowsmith, 1920), pp.90-1.

60 Brierley and Reid, *Go Home*, pp.60-3; Moira Martin, 'Single Women and Philanthropy: A Case Study of Women's Associational Life in Bristol, 1880-1914', *Women's History Review,* 17, 3 (2008), pp.395-417.

61 Walkowitz, *Prostitution*, pp.57-65, chap.4.

62 Josephine Butler to Anna Maria Priestman, 13 October 1872; Henry J. Wilson to Margaret Tanner, 24 May 1875, Josephine Butler Letter Collection, Women's Library, London School of Economics.

63 Walkowitz, *Prostitution*, p.125.

64 Bristol Ladies' National Association (hereafter, LNA), *Annual Report,* 1877, Subscription Lists.

65 Walkowitz, *Prostitution,* p.136*;* Bristol LNA, *Annual Report*, 1877, Subscription Lists.

66 Bristol LNA, *Annual Report*, 1878.

67 Patricia Hollis, *Ladies Elect: Women in English Local Government, 1865-1914* (Oxford: Oxford University Press, 1989), p.240.

68 Anna M. Priestman, 'The Industrial Position of Women as Affected by their Exclusion from the Suffrage', paper delivered to the NAPSS Conference, 1875 and reprinted in *Women's Suffrage Journal*, 1 October 1875.

69 Harold Goldman, *Emma Paterson: Her Life and Times* (London: Lawrence and Wishart, 1974).

70 BRL, *Contemporary Biographies – Medical*, p.268.

71 *Women's Union Journal*, October 1878.

72 Ibid*.,* April 1884. The name is sometimes given as Miss Meyrick.

73 1911, Census, *Occupations of the People, Bristol,* BRL.

74 Harvey and Press, *Studies in the Business History of Bristol;* Bernard Alford, *W.D. & H.O. Wills and the Development of the UK Tobacco Industry, 1786-1965* (London: Methuen 1973).

75 Gerry Holloway, *Women and Work in Britain Since 1840* (London: Taylor and Francis, 2005); Ellen Mappen, *Helping Women At Work: The Women's Industrial Council, 1889-1914* (London: Hutchinson, 1985).

76 Bristol Mercury, *Homes of the Bristol Poor* (Wm Lewis & Sons, 1884), Chapter IV.

77 BRL, Royal Commission on Labour, 'Report of Miss Orme *et al* on the Employment of Women, 1894, Bristol', p.34.

78 Ibid.

79 Alford, *Wills*, pp.287-8.

80 'Messers W. D. & H.O. Wills' Tobacco Factory', in *Work in Bristol* (Bristol: *Bristol Times & Mirror*, 1884), p.84.

81 Alford, *Wills*, p.286.

82 The following statistics have been calculated from the 1911 Census, *Occupations of the People, Bristol.*

83 1911 Census, Household Schedules, Ancestry.com.

84 1911 Census, *Occupations of the People. Bristol.*

85 Peter Groenewegen, *A Soaring Eagle: Alfred Marshall, 1842-1924* (Aldershot: Edward Elgar, 1995), pp.235-6.

86 University of Bristol Library, Special Collections (hereafter UBLSC), DM219, Marian Pease, *Some Reminiscences of University College, Bristol,* Unpublished paper, 1942.

87 Marelene Rayner-Canham and Geoffrey Rayner-Canham, *Chemistry was their Life: Pioneering British Women Chemists, 1880-1949* (London: Imperial College Press, 2008), pp.200-4.

88 Brierley and Reid, *Go Home,* pp.76-82.

89 For example, the purchase of Stanhope House for an Industrial School was facilitated by a number of large donations from women, including £105 from Miss Stephen. *First Report of the Bristol Certified Industrial School for Girls, 1866-67* (Bristol: I. Arrowsmith, 1868), p.21.

90 Maynard, *Sisters of Mercy,* pp.60, 77.

91 See Peter Shapely, 'Charity, Status and Leadership: Charitable Image and the Manchester Men', *Journal of Social History,* Fall (1998), pp.157-177, for the importance of charitable giving.

92 Preventive Mission, *Twenty-third Report,* p.14.

93 Sandra Stanley Holton, *Quaker Women: Personal Life, Memory and Radicalism in the Lives of Women Friends, 1780-1930* (London: Routledge, 2007), pp.37-44.

94 Holton, *Quaker Women,* pp.157-9; Emily Tothill died 1904 and left money to her brother, Waring Tothill, and her nieces, Mabel and Gertrude Tothill. Waring Tothill died 1910 and left over £61,000 to his daughters, Mabel and Gertrude. Probate records. Ancestry.com.

95 BRL, B12360 *Western Daily Press* (hereafter, WDP), 16 June 1883, *Local Notes,* newspaper cuttings.

96 *Annual Reports of Bristol and Clifton Charity Organisation,* 1889-1910 (Bristol: J.W. Arrowsmith), BRL.

97 Sturge, *Reminiscences,* pp.54-5.

98 For details of how such schemes worked see Moira Martin, 'A Future not of Riches but of Comfort: The Emigration of Pauper Children from Bristol to Canada, 1870 to 1915', *Immigrants and Minorities,* 19, 1 (2000), pp.25-52.

99 *Report on the Condition of the Bristol Poor,* 1885, pp.31-50; Shaen, *Memorials of Two Sisters;* Madge Dresser, 'People's Housing in Bristol (1870-1939)', in Bild, *Bristol's Other History,* pp.129-60.

100 Frances M. Unwin, *Ada Vachell of Bristol* (Bristol: J.W. Arrowsmith, 1928), p.42.

101 Linda Wilson, '"Domestic Charm, Business Acumen and Devotion to Christian Work": Sarah Terrett, the Bible Christian Church, the Household and the Public Sphere in Late Victorian Britain', in John Doran, Charlotte Methuen and Alexandra Walsham (eds), *Religion and the Household* (Woodbridge, Suffolk: Boydell & Brewer, 2014).

102 Meller, *Leisure and the Changing City,* chap.7.

103 R.W. Thompson, *The History of the Shaftesbury Crusade, Kingsland Road, St Philips,* (Bristol, Partridge and Love), p.6.

104 Williams, *Clifford,* pp.186-7.

105 Linda Walker, 'Party Political Women: A Comparative Study of Liberal Women and the Primrose League, 1890-1914', in Jane Rendall (ed.), *Equal or Different: Women's Politics, 1800-1914* (Oxford: Blackwell, 1987).

106 *Bristol South Gazette,* 1, 2, November 1893.

107 Ibid.

108 Bristol Women's Liberal Association, *Annual Report,* 1882.

109 Linda Walker, 'Gender, Suffrage and Party: Liberal Women's Organisations', in Myriam Boussahba-Bravard (ed.), *Suffrage Outside Suffragism* (Houndmills, Basingstoke: Palgrave Macmillan, 2007); Claire Hirshfield, 'Fractured Faith: Liberal Party Women and the Suffrage

Issue in Britain', *Gender and History*, 2 (1990), pp.173-97. David Large, *The Municipal Government of Bristol, 1851-1901* (Bristol: Bristol Record Society, 1999), pp.1-3.

110 BRL, B18779, *The Jubilee Book of the Clifton High School, 1897-1927* (Clifton, 1927). By 1895 there were four female governors of Red Maids School.

111 Williams, *Mary Clifford*, p.103.

112 See Martin, 'Single Women'; Moira Martin, 'Managing the Poor: The Administration of Poor Relief in Bristol in the Nineteenth and Twentieth Centuries', in Dresser and Ollerenshaw (eds), *The Making of Modern Bristol*; Moira Martin, 'Guardians of the Poor: A Philanthropic Elite in Bristol', *The Regional Historian*, issue 9 (2002), pp.6-9.

113 *Bristol Mercury,* 9 June 1883.

114 Williams, *Mary Clifford*, pp.125-6.

115 Felix Driver, *Power and Pauperism: The Workhouse System, 1834-84* (Cambridge: Cambridge University Press, 1993), p.68.

116 Mike Richardson, *The Bristol Strike Wave of 1889-90: Socialists, New Unionists and New Women: Part 1, Days of Hope. Part 2, Days of Doubt* (Bristol: Bristol Radical Pamphleteer, 21 & 22, 2012); Roger Ball, *The Origins and An Account of Black Friday December 23 1892* (Bristol: Bristol Radical Pamphleteer, 24, 2013).

117 Workers' Organising Committee Minutes, October 1889-July 1892.

118 June Hannam, 'Stacy, Enid (1868-1903)', *Oxford Dictionary of National Biography,* Oxford University Press, 2004, at http://www.oxforddnb.com/view/article/51602?docPos=1, [accessed 29 November 2014]; Katharine Bruce Glasier, *Enid Stacy*, 1924; Chris Wrigley, 'Glasier, Katharine St John Bruce (1867-1950)', *Oxford Dictionary of National Biography,* Oxford University Press,2004 at http://www.oxforddnb.com/view/article/42338 [accessed 29 November 2014].

119 *WDP*, 19 October 1892.

120 Enid Stacy, 'A Century of Women's Rights' in Edward Carpenter (ed.), *Forecasts of the Coming Century* (Manchester: Labour Press, 1896).

121 NUWW, *Conference Report*, 1892, p.71.

122 Isabella O. Ford, 'Industrial Conditions Affecting Women of the Working Classes', NUWW *Conference Report,* 1892, pp.54-64; June Hannam, *Isabella Ford: 1855-1924* (Oxford: Blackwell, 1889).

123 Sturge, *Reminiscences,* pp.42-4.

124 *Women's Penny Paper*, 8 February 1890.

125 NUWW *Conference Report*, 1892, pp.64-5; Letter to Miss Hicks, August 29, 1895, LSE, in which she notes that 'the Bristol Working Women's Association is an entirely separate organisation with which we have very slight connection, and with the basis of which I do not at all agree'.

126 BRO, 32080/TC4/25, Railway Women's Guild, Bristol Branch Minutes.

127 Gillian Scott, *Feminism and the Politics of Working Women: The Women's Co-operative Guild, 1880s to the Second World War* (London: UCL, 1998).

128 These were at Lawrence Hill, St George's Rd and Bedminster. Edward Jackson, *A Study in Democracy* (Manchester: CWS, 1911), pp.513-17.

129 Ibid., p.514.

130 Ibid., pp.529-32.

131 *WDP*, 21 July 1914.

132 Obituary, *WDP*, 20 November 1944.

133 'A Chat with Miss E.H. Smith', *The Bristolian*, October 1913, pp.283-4.

134 Obituary, *WDP*, 20 November 1944.

135 Anon, *Hilda Cashmore, 1876-1943* (Gloucester: J. Bellows, n.d., c 1950); John B. Thomas, 'Cashmore, Hilda (1876-1943)', *Oxford Dictionary of National Biography,* Oxford University Press, 2004, at http://www.oxforddnb.com/view/article/52725 [accessed 29 November 2014].

136 Hilda Jennings, *University Settlement Bristol: Sixty Years of Change, 1911-1971* (Bristol: University Settlement Bristol Community Association, 1971), p.8.

137 Brenda Bardgett, *Bristol Association of University Women: The Early Years, 1911-28,* Unpublished

paper, Bristol University.

138 Katherine Gleadle, *British Women in the Nineteenth Century* (Houndmills, Basingstoke: Palgrave, 2001), chap.11.

139 Jennings, *University Settlement Bristol*, pp.11-13.

140 Ibid., p.16.

141 June Hannam, '"To Make the World a Better Place": Socialist Women and Women's Suffrage in Bristol', 1910-1920', in Boussahba Bravard (ed.), *Suffrage Outside Suffragism*.

142 Bryher, *An Account*, Part 3, p.3; UBLSC, Bristol Socialist Society Minutes, 1910-12.

143 The East Bristol branch was a separate group and altogether it was claimed there were 900 members in Bristol: W.H. Ayles, 'ILP in the South West', *Labour Leader*, 17 October 1912; UBLSC, ILP Bristol Branch Minutes, 1909-12.

144 Women's Labour League, *Annual Report*, 1911, 1912; Christine Collette, *'For Labour and For Women": The Women's Labour League, 1906-1918* (Manchester: Manchester University Press, 1989).

145 For an overview of the suffrage movement and all the groups involved, see Paula Bartley, *Votes for Women, 1866-1928* (Abingdon: Hodder & Stoughton, 1998).

146 Paper read by Mrs Martin, Bedminster branch, to the Western Sectional Conference, 25 March 1897.

147 Lucienne Boyce, *The Bristol Suffragettes* (Bristol: the author by Silverwood Books, 2013), pp.69, 75-6.

148 K. Seltorp, 'The Women's suffrage movement in Bristol, 1868-1906' (thesis, Kobenharns Universitet, 1982, copy held in Women's Library, LSE), chap.6, fn 71.

149 Boyce, *The Bristol Suffragettes*; Diaries of Mary and Emily Blathwayt, Gloucester Record Office.

150 June Hannam, 'The 1913 Pilgrimage, Electioneering and Women's Politics in Bristol', *Regional Historian*, issue 28 (2014), pp.29-34.

151 1911 Census, Household Schedules, Ancestry.com; Elizabeth Crawford, *The Women's Suffrage Movement: A Reference Guide, 1866-1928* (London: Routledge, 2001), pp.84, 549-63, 645; *Bristol Times & Mirror*, 28 June 1913.

152 *Common Cause*, 25 July 1913.

153 For a full account of the Election Fighting Fund, see Sandra Stanley Holton, *Feminism and Democracy, Women's Suffrage and Reform Politics in Britain, 1900-1918* (Cambridge: Cambridge University Press, 1986).

154 Ibid., p.107.

155 It is difficult to determine when the East Bristol group was formed, although Elizabeth Crawford suggests it was as early as 1909 and that a shop was set up at 195 Black Boy Hill as a joint endeavour by the Bristol East Society and the Women's Reform Union. The latter had been established in the 1890s by the Priestman sisters who had always been interested in encouraging working-class women to take part in the suffrage campaign. Elizabeth Crawford, *The Women's Suffrage Movement in Britain and Ireland*, p.132.

156 Collette, *For Labour and For Women*, pp.84-5; UBLSC, Bristol ILP Branch Minutes, 1912.

157 *Common Cause*, 3 October and 23 May 1913.

158 Quoted in Holton, *Feminism and Democracy*, p.107.

159 John Saville and Bob Whitfield, 'Ayles, Walter Henry (1879-1953): Trade Unionist, Pacifist and Labour MP', in John Saville and Joyce Bellamy (eds), *Dictionary of Labour Biography*, Vol.5 (Houndmills, Basingstoke: Palgrave Macmillan, 1979), pp.10-13; *Labour Leader*, 13 March 1913; He was described as 'an ardent worker for the equality of the sexes, *Bristol and Clifton Social World*, June 1914.

Chapter Four Bristol Women in the Twentieth Century

1 One of the first to use this term was Arthur Marwick, see *Britain in the Century of Total War: War, Peace and Social Change, 1900-1967* (Houndmills, Basingstoke: Macmillan, 1968); *The Deluge* (Houndmills, Basingstoke: Macmillan, 1965).

2 Cheryl Law, *Suffrage and Power: The Women's Movement, 1928-1928* (London: I.B. Tauris, 2000), chap.2.

3 Penny Summerfield, 'Women and War in the Twentieth Century', in June Purvis (ed.), *Women's History: Britain 1850-1945* (London: UCL, 1995); Susan R. Grayzel, *Women and the First World War* (Harlow: Pearson Education, 2002); Deborah Thom, *Nice Girls and Rude Girls. Women Workers in World War 1* (London: I. B. Tauris, 1998); Nicoletta F. Gullace, *'The Blood of Our Sons'. Men, Women and the Renegotiation of British Citizenship during the Great War* (Houndmills, Basingstoke: Palgrave Macmillan, 2002).

4 *Western Daily Press* (hereafter *WDP*), 12 August 1914; 6 January 1915; 10 February 1915.

5 Thom, *Nice Girls and Rude Girls,* chap.3.

6 Eugene Byrne and Clive Burlton, *Bravo Bristol. The City at War 1914-1918* (Bristol: Redcliffe Press, 2014), p.66.

7 Ibid., p.62.

8 *Bristol & The War*, April 1916; February 1917.

9 Charles Wells and George F. Stone (eds), *Bristol and the Great War* (Bristol: Arrowsmith, 1920), chap.3.

10 Byrne and Burlton, *Bravo Bristol*, p.104.

11 *Bristol & the War*, June 1915.

12 Ibid.

13 Byrne and Burlton, *Bravo Bristol*, pp.66, 119.

14 Women members of the Bristol National Federation of Women Workers rose from 400 to 1000, *Woman Worker*, March 1916.

15 Ibid.

16 Ibid., July 1918.

17 Ibid., October 1916.

18 *Bristol & the War*, February 1916.

19 *WDP*, 20 April 1915. For an account of the Women's Peace Congress and of feminist attitudes towards peace, see Anne Wiltsher, *Most Dangerous Women: Feminist Peace Campaigners of the Great War* (London: Pandora, 1985); Leila J. Rupp, *Worlds of Women: The Making of an International Women's Movement* (Princeton, NJ: Princeton University Press, 1997); Jo Vellacott, *Pacifists, Patriots and the Vote: The Erosion of Democratic Suffragism in Britain during the First World War* (Houndmills, Basingstoke: Palgrave, 2007).

20 Women's International League, *Annual Report*, 1916 and 1917. In large cities in the North of England membership averaged 100-200 and Manchester had over 500 members.

21 For an account of the ILP and its views, see Keith Laybourn, *The Rise of Socialism in Britain c. 1881-1951* (Stroud: Sutton Publishing, 1997); June Hannam, *Bristol Independent Labour Party: Men, Women and the Opposition to War* (Bristol: Bristol Radical Pamphleteer, 31, 2014); for a detailed local account, focussing on Huddersfield, see Cyril Pearce, *Comrades in Conscience. The Story of an English Community's Opposition to the Great War* (London: Francis Boutle, revised ed. 2014).

22 *Bristol Times and Mirror* (hereafter *BTM),* 30 August, 1 & 4 September 1915.

23 *WDP*, 2 October 1915.

24 For examples of her writings, see *Toleration or Persecution* (Manchester: National Labour Press, n.d.); *Conscientious Objectors at Horfield* (Manchester: National Labour Press, n.d.); *What Every Bristol Man Should Know* (Manchester: National Labour Press, 1916); M.C.T. 'It's a way they have in the Army', *The Bristol Forward*, July 1916. For an account of her activities, see Hannam, *Bristol Independent Labour Party.*

25 Tothill, *Toleration or Persecution.*

26 Lucy Cox was a young schoolteacher from Keynsham who, as Lucy Middleton, was elected Labour MP for Plymouth Sutton in 1945. She claimed that it was poverty and war that persuaded her to join the ILP. Interview for *The News*, 21 July 1978. For women's growing importance in the ILP see Bristol ILP Branch Minutes, 22 November 1916; Annual General Meeting, 22 April 1917, Bristol University, Special Collections.

27 Wells & Stone, *Bristol and the Great War*, chap.3.

28 *WDP,* 18 May 1915.

29 Ibid., 3 May 1916.

30 *The Bristol Forward,* 16 June 1916.

31 See, for example, the role of welfare supervisors in factories. Thom, *Nice Girls and Rude Girls*, pp.73-4, 152, 179.

32 WDP, 19 February 1915; The Bristol Training School for Women Patrols and Police, *Annual Report*, 1916.

33 Bristol Training School for Women Patrols and Police, *Annual Report* 1917. R.M. Douglas, 'Peto, Dorothy Olivia Georgiana (1886-1974)', *Dictionary of National Biography,* Oxford University Press, 2004, online edn., January 2008 at http://www.oxforddnb.com /view/article/76095 [accessed 17 July 2015].

34 The Bristol Training School for Women Patrols and Police, *Annual Report*, 1917, p.10.

35 Ibid., 1920. For more information on women in the police force, see Louise Jackson, *Women Police: Gender, Welfare and Surveillance in the Twentieth Century* (Manchester: Manchester University Press, 2006); Philippa Levine, '"Walking the Streets in a Way No Decent Woman Should": Women Police in World War One', *Journal of Modern History,* 66, 1 (1994), pp.34-78.

36 *WDP,* 16 October 1915.

37 *BTM,* 23 February 1916.

38 Ibid.

39 Cheryl Law, *Suffrage and Power*, chap.5.

40 Cathy Hunt, *The National Federation of Women Workers* (Houndmills, Basingstoke: Palgrave Macmillan, 2014), p.95; The Bristol Tramways Company claimed that all its employees were single women or widows.

41 *WDP,* 27 April, 29 April, 12 May 1920.

42 *WDP,* 6 February 1919; see letter of complaint from local women's trade union organisers and Labour Party organiser Annie Townley, 21 July 1920.

43 *Wills' Magazine,* February 1923, p.131; *Fry's Work Magazine,* January 1923, p.85.

44 1921 Occupation Census, Bristol Reference Library.

45 Don Carleton, *A University for Bristol* (Bristol: University of Bristol Press, 1984), p.40.

46 Lorna Brierley and Helen Reid, *Go Home and Do The Washing: Three Centuries of Pioneering Bristol Women* (Bristol: Broadcast Books, 2000), chap.3; Obituary of Elizabeth Casson at www.otlegacy.ca/past/documents/22.1_HPLeV-Casson.pdf

47 Mrs Senington, a Labour Party member and a magistrate, was responsible for the quotation about Emily Webb, *WDP,* 8 July 1935.

48 See Smith's obituary, *WDP,* 20 November 1944; Bristol Kyrle Society, *Annual Report*, 1927; 'Bristol's Public Men and Women no.38. Councillor Emily H. Smith J.P.', *BTM,* 6 September 1921. The Kyrle Society was first established by Octavia Hill in 1875. Mary Clifford founded the Bristol branch in 1905 and it survived into the 1930s. It aimed to promote civic pride by preserving natural beauty and historical buildings in the environment.

49 *WDP,* 1 February 1919.

50 Spencer Jordan, Keith Ramsay and Matthew Woollard, *Abstract of Bristol Historical Statistics. Part 3.Political Representation and Bristol's Election, 1700-1997* (Bristol: University West of England, 1997), p.xvii.

51 Twelve were married.

52 Corrina Haskins, 'Elected Women in Local Government in Bristol during the Inter-War Years' (M.A. dissertation, University of the West of England, 1981), Appendices 1, 2.

53 'Bristol's Public Men and Women. Councillor Mrs Pheysey', *BTM,* 30 August 1921.

54 Haskins, 'Elected Women', pp.63-4.

55 Ibid.

56 Ibid., p.36.

57 *WDP,* 14 September 1921.

58 Ibid., 9 March 1921.

59 Ibid., 5 February 1926.

60 Ibid.

61 There were 69 Guardians in total. BRL 35510, City and County of Bristol, Guardians of the Poor, Report of Proceedings, 1929-1930.

62 Bristol Record Office (hereafter BRO), 35510/BCC/7/2/1, Bristol City Council Year Book 1927-1928.

63 *BTM,* 28 October 1922; *WDP,* 1 May 1926.

64 BRL 35510, City and County of Bristol PAC, Report of Proceedings, 1.4.31 – 31.3.33; BRL 14620, Bristol Corporation Departmental Reports, PAC Report to 31.3.38.

65 For example, see Martin Pugh, *Women and the Women's Movement in Britain* (Houndmills, Basingstoke: Macmillan, 2nd Revised edn. 2000); Deirdre Beddoe, *Back to Home and Duty: Women between the Wars, 1918-1939* (London: Pandora, 1989).

66 Caitriona Beaumont, *Housewives and Citizens: Domesticity and the Women's Movement in England, 1928-64* (Manchester: Manchester University Press, 2013), p.1.

67 Beaumont suggests they should be seen as a women's, rather than feminist, movement, Ibid., Introduction.

68 'Parliament of Youth. An Interesting Experiment in the West Bristol WLA', by a member, *The Liberal Woman's News,* November 1927, p.151; Mrs Annie Townley, '"Let's Pretend": A Mock City Council', *Labour Woman,* February 1937. *Bristol North Forward,* February 1922.

69 *West Bristol Labour Weekly,* 24 September 1926.

70 BRO 40488/M/3/2, Bristol East Divisional Labour Party, General Council Minutes, 23.1.1935.

71 *WDP,* 15 April 1937. In East Bristol, the Labour Party Women's Sections had fewer than 1,000 members. BRO, 39035/54, Bristol East Divisional Labour Party Annual Reports, 1921-1939.

72 Suzanne Worden, 'Powerful Women: Electricity and Home' in Judy Attfield and Pat Kirkham (eds), *A View from The Interior: Feminism, Women and Design* (London: Women's Press, 1989).

73 *WDP,* 8 July 1920.

74 Brierly and Reid, *Go Home,* p.85.

75 BRO, 31642 (21) d. Soroptomist Club of Bristol, Projects 1934-1939.

76 Hilda Jennings, *University Settlement, Bristol: 60 Years of Change, 1911-1971* (Bristol: University Settlement Bristol Community Association, 1971), p.19; Madge Dresser, 'Housing Policy in Bristol, 1919-39', in Martin Daunton (ed.), *Councillors and Tenants: Local Authority Housing in English Cities, 1919-39* (Leicester: Leicester University Press, 1984).

77 Rosie McGregor, *Angel Remembered: The Life of Angela Gradwell, Tuckett* (Urchfont: WaterMarx, 2015); For Angela and Joan Tuckett, see Graham Stevenson, 'Compendium of Communist Biographies,' http://www.grahamstevenson.me.uk/ [accessed 9 July 2015]; 'Angela and Joan Tuckett', at Bristol Law Society website http://www.bristollawsociety.com/angela-and-joan-tuckett/ [accessed 9 July 2015]; The Bristol Unity Theatre, Warwick University Library website, TUC Archives,http://www2.warwick.ac.uk/services/library/mrc/explorefurther/digital/scw/browse/ [accessed 11 July 2015]; Bernard Barry, 'Angela Tuckett', Working- Class Movement Library website http://www.wcml.org.uk/our-collections/activists/angela-tuckett/ [accessed 11 July 2015]; emails Erynne Baynes to Madge Dresser, 7, 22, 23 August 2015.

78 Brierley and Reid, *Go Home,* p.89.

79 Sue Bruley, *Women in Britain since 1900* (Houndmills, Basingstoke: Palgrave Macmillan, 1999), p.92.

80 Penny Summerfield, *Women Workers in the Second World War* (London: Croom Helm, 1984).

81 Bruley, *Women in Britain,* p.92.

82 Ethel Thomas, *War Story* (Bristol: Self Published, 1989); Joyce Storey, *Joyce's War, 1939-1945* (London: Virago, 1992); V.A.M., *The Diary of a Bristol Woman, 1938-1945* (Ilfracombe: Arthur H. Stockwell, 1950).

83 Thomas, *War Story,* p.188; *WDP,* 14 November 1945.

84 *WDP,* 27 November and 24 December 1942.

85 Thomas, *War Story,* p.89.

86 *Bristol Evening Post* (hereafter *BEP*), 10 September, 1979.

87 Ibid., 22 October 1942.

88 Ibid., 7 February 1942.

89 Storey, *Joyce's War*, pp.85-6.

90 V.A.M., *Diary*, 23 May 1940, p.74.

91 Ibid., 1 March 1943, p.167.

92 Beaumont, *Housewives and Mothers*, p.143.

93 Hannah Tinkler, *The Story of WVS Bristol, 1939-1945* (WRVS Archive and Heritage Collection, 2012), p.4.

94 'V.E. Day', *BEP*, 8 May 2015; John Penny, *Bristol at War* (Breedon Books, 2002).

95 Tinkler, *The Story of WVS Bristol,* pp.6, 9.

96 Thomas, *War Story*, p.120.

97 *WDP*, 29 January 1943.

98 Ibid., 31 May 1941.

99 Bruley, *Women in Britain*, p.108.

100 Krista Cowman, *Women in British Politics, c 1689-1979* (Houndmills, Basingstoke: Palgrave Macmillan, 2010), pp.160-1.VAM, *Diary*, pp.222-3.

101 V.A.M. *Diary*, 12 September 1944; BRO 31642 (21)e, Standing Conference of Women's Organisations of Bristol, committee meeting, 25 January, 1945; 25 November, 1948.

102 Jane Lewis, *Women in Britain Since 1945* (Oxford: Blackwell, 1992), pp.2, 78.

103 Martin Boddy, John Lovering, Keith Bassett (eds), *Sunbelt City?: A Study of Economic Change in Britain's M4 Growth Corridor* (Oxford: Clarendon Press, 1986), p.9.

104 BRO, 38605a/54 Reports of the Council of the Bristol Chamber of Commerce and Shipping, of Commerce Minutes for 1945-1946 p.23; Lady Apsley on Demobilisation, House of Commons Hansard, 943-1104, Fifth Series, Volume 395, 1092-1093 (1943-44) http://gateway.proquest.com/openurl?url_ver=Z39.88-2004&res_dat=xri:hcpp&rft_dat= xri:hcpp:hansard:CDS5CV0395P0-0008 [accessed 22 June 2015].

105 John Britton, *Regional Analysis and Economic Geography: A Case Study of Manufacturing in the Bristol Region* (London: Bell, 1967), p.90, but see pp.88-89 documenting that female employment in manufacturing (insured workers) in 1962 was 28% in Bristol compared with the national average of 32% which he attributes to 'the low level of desire or lack of opportunity to work in that sector.'

106 Ibid., p.89, Table 16; Helen Thomas, Rosie Tomlinson, Mavis Zutshi, *Bedminster's Tobacco Women* (Bristol: Fiducia Press, 2015), pp.17-19 and p.26; Boddy et al (eds)., *Sunbelt City?*, pp.148-9; Frank Walker*, The Bristol Region* (London: Thomas Nelson and Son , 1972), p.10; *Setting out for a New Life: Memories of Coming to England by the Golden Agers* (Bristol: Golden Agers and Marie Tyrwhitt Publications, 2004), p.34; 'Brislington: an Historical View', Brislington Community Partnership website, http://www.brislington.org/history.html [accessed 4 March 2015].

107 Hilda Jennings, *Societies in the Making* (London: Routledge,1962, reprinted 1998, 2000, 2001), pp.38-9.

108 Walker, *The Bristol Region*, pp.281, 322; Boddy et al. (eds), *Sunbelt City?*, pp.15-17. Re shortages, see BRO, 38605a/54/ Reports of the Council [of the Chamber of Commerce], for 1945-1946, p.31; BRO, M/BCC/BC/1/65, Proceedings of the Council, 1946, p.336.

109 Anna Pollert, *Girls Wives Factory Lives* (London: Macmillan 1981), p.15.

110 Bristol Reference Library (hereafter BRL)*, Illustrated Bristol News,* Vol. 6 No. 48, April 1963, p.77; 'I Ended Up Spending 11 Happy Years as a Secretary,' *This is Bristol, Bristol Post* http://www.bristolpost.co.uk/ended-spending-11-happy-years-secretary/story-11268788-detail/story.html [accessed 17 July 2015].

111 Edson Burton, 'African-Caribbeans, 1948-1990,' in Madge Dresser and Peter Fleming, *Bristol: Ethnic Minorities and the City: Bristol 1000-2000* (Chichester: Phillimore, 2007), pp.163-165. For various accounts of such discrimination see *Setting out for a New Life: Memories of Coming to England by the Golden Agers* (Bristol: Golden Agers and Marie Tyrwhitt Publications, 2004).

112 BRL, 'Employment in the Bristol Area', *Bristol Medical Officer of Health Annual Report 1961-1964*, p.8; Boddy et al. (eds), *Sunbelt City?*, pp.148-9; Walker, *The Bristol Region*, pp.11-14. See *BEP*, 12 January 1966; email correspondence 6 and 8 January 2015 and interview with Duncan Greenman by Madge Dresser, 5 December 2014.

113 BRL, MM 942, Folder on the Bristol Commercial Rooms, Corn St., press cutting *Evening Post*, n.d. March 1987. Thanks to Dawn Dyer for this reference; Constitutional Club 43266/1, p.14.

114 Re the Bristol Ladies Business Group see *BEP*, 25 May 1998 and 27 May 1998; Re Vera Hughes see 'Bristol', http://brisray.com/bristol/bemmy4.htm [accessed 4 March 2015]; '61 lose jobs as mailing firm lay off staff', *This is Bristol*. Posted: December 23, 2009 http://www.bristolpost.co.uk/61-lose-jobs-mailing-firm-lay-staff/story-11236601-detail/story.html#ixzz3YjLKB69D [accessed 4 March 2015].

115 'Dr Beryl Corner in interview with Sir Gordon Wolstenholme Oxford, 27 January 1993, 'Oxford Brookes Medical Sciences Video Archive', https://www.brookes.ac.uk/library/speccoll/medical/synopses/corner.html [accessed 4 May 2015,]; Dr. Beryl Corner, South West Paediatric Club http://www.swpc.org.uk/ beryl_corner.pdf [accessed 4 May 2015]; Brierley and Reid, *Go Home*, pp.96-7; David Stevens, 'Corner, Beryl Dorothy (1910–2007)', *Oxford Dictionary of National Biography*, Oxford University Press, 2004, January 2011 at http://www.oxforddnb.com/view/article/98638 [accessed June 16, 2015].

116 Brian Smith, 'The Society's Chronicles: Obituaries: Elizabeth Ralph', *Journal of the Society of Archivists*, Vol. 21, No.2 (2000), pp.227-28; Gerard Leighton, 'Elizabeth Ralph MA, FSA, DLitt 1911-2000: An Appreciation,' in Joseph Bettey (ed.), *Historic Churches and Church Life in Bristol: Essays in Memory of Elizabeth Ralph 1911-2000* (Bristol: J.W. Arrowsmith for Bristol & Gloucestershire Archaeological Society, 2001). Elizabeth Shepherd, *Archives and Archivists in 20th Century England* (London: Ashgate, 2009), p.146; UBLSC, *University of Bristol Newsletter*, Vol. 23 (16 September 1993); emails from Dr. Martin Crossley-Evans, 5 August 2015.

117 BRL, 2E3, *Bristol Medical Office of Health Report 1969-1973*, p.29.

118 Burton in Dresser and Fleming, *Bristol: Ethnic Minorities and the City: Bristol 1000-2000*, pp.168-9.

119 Hodgkin, a Fellow of the Royal Society and the only British woman scientist to hold a Nobel Prize, was a political radical who took an unexpectedly activist role as chancellor, promoting the interests of international students and opposing government cuts which led to the closing of the school of architecture at Bristol University in 1981. http://www.bristol.ac.uk/university/timeline/#/248-dorothy-crowfoot-hodgkin-wins-the-nobel-prize-for-chemistry; Georgina Ferry, 'Hodgkin, Dorothy Mary Crowfoot (1910–1994)', *Oxford Dictionary of National Biography*, Oxford University Press, 2004, online ed. May 2009 at http://www.oxforddnb.com/view/article/55028 [accessed April 7, 2015].

120 Calculated from the Calendar lists of full-time academic staff listed as Professors, Senior Lecturers and Lecturers and excluding other categories. *Calendars of the University of Bristol, 1944-1970*, University of Bristol Special Collections, Serial 4F62.3.

121 Helen Taylor, 'Finding the Female Reality', *Poly News*, May 1974.

122 Margaret Graham succeeded Elsa Nunn as principal of St. Matthias College from 1955-1971.

123 Harold L. Smith, 'The Women's Movement, Politics and Citizenship, 1960s-2000', in Ina Zweiniger-Bargielowska (ed.), *Women in Twentieth-Century Britain* (Harlow, Essex: Pearson Education , 2001), p.278.

124 *WDP*, 12 February 1948.

125 Ibid., 1 April 1950.

126 *BEP*, 4 January 1950.

127 Ibid., 10 January 1950.

128 BCRL, 'Women's Rights Folder' 1457, *Bristol Evening World*, 1 January 1947.

129 *BEP*, 1 February 1950 and Dorothy V. Hall, *Making Things Happen* (London: History of the National Federation of Business and Professional Women's Clubs of Great Britain and Northern Ireland, 1963), pp.142-3; Bristol Women's Club' (2009). https://bristolwc.wordpress.com/about/ [accessed 12 May 2015]; *Illustrated Bristol News* vol. 6

no. 48m June 1963.

130 Roger V. Clements, *Local Notables and the City Council* (London: Macmillan, 1969), pp.31-50. The study excluded local Councillors as they were by then regarded as less influential than others outside local government.

131 *BEP*, 5 April 1974. I am indebted to Mrs Constance Ware, daughter of Lady Janet Inskip for allowing me access to her personal collection of press cuttings and memorabilia relating to her parents. Family records show that Hon. Janet Maclay, daughter of Sir Joseph Paton Maclay, 1st Baron Maclay married at the bride's home, Duchal, Kailmacolm, Renfrewshire on 18th April 1923. Interview with Mrs Constance Ware by Madge Dresser, 23 January 2015; *The Gospel Magazine*, June 1960 www.gospelmagazine.org.uk/pdf [accessed 23 January 2015].

132 *BEP*, 2 December 1957.

133 This college later merged with Queen Mary College and the University of London, institutions known for their progressive attitudes to women's education and social reform, WFD/26/4/24, 'Catalogue of the Archives of Westfield College (1882-1989)', by Toni Hardy, Assistant Archivist. Reminiscences of Janet Inskip http://www.library.qmul.ac.uk/sites/ www.library.qmul.ac.uk/files/users/user22/WFD%20catalogue_0.pdf [accessed 16 June 2015].

134 Obituary, *BEP*, 4 May 1974; *The Friends of Bristol Cathedral, 1971-1972* (Bristol, c.1972), p.5; *BBC Annual Year Book for 1950* http://www.americanradiohistory.com/Archive-BBC-Annual/ BBC-Year-Book-1950.pdf.

135 Helen Reed in *Muddling Through: Bristol in the Fifties as Remembered by James Belsey, Michael Jenner, Roger Bennett, Helen Reed, Michael Cocks, Derek Robinson, et al* (Bristol: Redcliffe Press, 1988), pp.35-8; 'Marian Leibmann', http://feministarchivesouth.org.uk/wp-content/uploads/ 2013/02/Personal-Histories-of-the-Second-Wave-of-Feminism.pdf [accessed 16 June 2015]; Anna Pollert, *Girls, Wives, Factory Lives*, p.97.

136 Kieran Kelly and Mike Richardson, 'The Shaping of the Bristol Labour Movement 1885-1985,' in Madge Dresser and Phillip Ollerenshaw (eds), *The Making of Modern Bristol* (Bristol: Redcliffe Press, 1996), p.224.

137 Marilyn Porter, *Home, Work and Class Consciousness* (Manchester: Manchester University Press, 1983), pp.21-2; see Avner Offer, 'British Manual Workers: From Producers to Consumers c.1950-2000', *Contemporary British History*, vol. 224 (2008) pp.538-71; Kelly and Richardson, 'The Shaping of the Bristol Labour Movement', p.227.

138 BRO, M/BCC/BC/1/81, p.36.

139 The post of Lord Mayor as opposed to Mayor was not instituted until 1889 but the post of Mayor went back to 1216, Bristol City Council website, 'Lord Mayor of Bristol- History', http://www.bristol.gov.uk/page/council-and-democracy/lord-mayor-bristol-history#jump-link-3 [accessed 16 June 2015].

140 BRO, 44303/2/M/1, Minute Book of the North West Westbury on Trym Women's Section of the Labour Party, 27 September, 1967, 15 January 1969; 19 March 1975.

141 Derived from Table iii of Jordan, Ramsay and Woollard, *Abstract of Bristol Historical Statistics Part 3: Political Representations and Bristol's Elections 1700-1997,* 1997 http://humanities.uwe.ac.uk/bhr/Main/abstract_politics/Politics%202.htm;

142 Audrey Canning, 'Stephen, Jessie (1893–1979)', *Oxford Dictionary of National Biography*, Oxford University Press, 2004, http://www.oxforddnb.com/view/article/54411 [accessed April 22, 2015]; *BEP*,19 January 1966; *The Times*, 11 October 1955, pp.3, 17 March 1961 p.23; Sheila Rowbotham, 'Review of Pamela M. Graves, 'Women in British Working-Class Politics 1918-1939', *Feminist Review,* 56 (Summer, 1997), pp.117-19. Stephen also came to speak at Bristol Polytechnic at an (unaccredited) women's studies seminar in the 1970s. For plaque see http://www.bristol.gov.uk/page/leisure-and-culture/list-blue-plaques-bristol#jump-link-46.

143 Canning, 'Stephen, Jessie'.

144 Ibid.; *BEP*,19 January 1966; *The Times*, 11 October 1955, p.3 and 17 March 1961, p.23.

145 BRO, 40097, Memorabilia of Florence M. Brown, first lady Lord Mayor; *BEP*, 11 March 1981; BCRL, B12059, *Magazine*, 1963-1965; *Illustrated Bristol News*, vol. 6, no. 48, October 1963, cover

page; BCRL, B12058, *Wills' Magazine*, 1963-1965 pp.13 and 16; *WDP*, 3 October 1950; 'Childrens' Homes', http://www.childrenshomes.org.uk/BristolBC/ [accessed 5 July 2015], thanks to Chris Williams for this reference; Recollections of Marge Evans in 'Marge Evans' TV documentary by Forum Television, Bristol c. 1990, courtesy of David Parker; Alderman Charlotte Keel (Alderman from 1935-1955) had a health centre named after her in 1956.

146 Constance Ware Collection, untitled press cutting *BEP*, 13 July 1965.

147 *BCRL, B24431,* Cllr. Mrs. Mercia Eveleyn Castle, 'Biography Mayors and Lord Mayors' (typescript May 1969); *Illustrated Bristol News*, March 1968, vol.195, July 1968, vol.14 no.19; BCRL, B12058, *Wills' Magazine*,1963-1965, pp.13,16.

148 It could be said that Bloom was the second Jew to hold mayoral office in Bristol as Joseph Abraham was the first Jew to become mayor in 1865 before the creation of the post of Lord Mayor in 1889.

149 She appears in the records of Bristol's Hebrew Congregation which include programmes of the debating society which is exhibited at the MShed, Bristol.

150 Census Enumerator's Report, 1911 http://interactive.ancestry.co.uk/2352/rg14_15023_0347_03/55822345 [accessed 16 June 2015].

151 See chap.3.

152 BRO, M/BCC/BC/1/81, *WDP,* 21 February 1949, p.36.

153 BRO, 44303/2.M.1, Labour Women's Meeting Stoke Lodge, 19 March 1975. Main information compiled from BRO, Info Box 16/64, Biographical Information on Ald. Mrs. H. Bloom; Info Box 27/114, Biographical Information on Mrs. Helen Bloom Lord Mayor; BRO, 44303,Personal papers of Helen Bloom: *Records relating to the Bristol Fabian Society and the Bristol Labour Party*; *WDP*, 19 March 1947, 2 April1947, 7 May 1947, 11 May 1949, 3 January 1950; *WDP*, 8 May 1964;Judith Samuel, *The Jews in Bristol* (Bristol: Redcliffe Press, 1977), pp.188-9; personal research on Park Row synagogue for MShed in 2005.

154 Pollert, *Girls Wives Factory Lives,* p.15 and Boddy et al. (eds), *Sunbelt City?*, p.12.

155 Boddy et al. (eds), *Sunbelt City?*, pp.67, 79; Pollert, *Girls Wives Factory Lives,* p.16.

156 St Paul's in this instance refers to a concentrated area within the St Paul's ward (renamed the Ashley ward in 1982) bounded by Newfoundland Road (M32), Ashley Road and Stokes Croft; Roger Ball, 'Violent Urban Disturbances in England,1980-81' (Ph.d. thesis, University of the West of England, 2011), pp.194, 176; Boddy et al, (eds), *Sunbelt City?*, pp.12-13 and p.46.

157 Boddy et al. (eds), *Sunbelt City?*, pp.19, 36.

158 The school leaving age was increased from 15 in 1944 to 16 in 1972 and even more girls than boys gained their O levels by 1970. Women did not achieve first degrees in equal numbers to men until 2000 when they exceed male degree holders. Paul Bolton, 'Briefing Paper SN/SG/4252, Education: Historical Statistics' (2012), pp.11, 20 [accessed 5 July 2015]. The proportion of girls gaining A levels or their equivalent nearly doubled from 17% to 31% over the 60s and 70s in the country as a whole and Bristol was noted to have a higher than national rate of such qualifications. This compares with 20% and 34% of men with similar qualifications over the same period, George Smith, 'Schools,' in Albert H. Halsey with Josephine Webb (eds), *Twentieth Century British Social Trends* (Houndmills, Basingstoke: Macmillan 2000), p.209; Albert H. Halsey, 'Further and Higher Education,' in Halsey and Webb (eds), *Twentieth-Century British Social Trends*, p.232.

159 Only just under 7% of men and just over 6% of women were in full- time higher education, though most of the women were in teacher training colleges rather than universities. Only 2.5% of women were full time university students. Between 1962 and 1980 there was a nearly threefold increase in the number of women in further and higher education from 68,000 to 214,000; Halsey, 'Further and Higher Education, p.232; Carol Dyhouse, 'Education,' in Zweiniger-Bargielowska (ed.), *Women in Twentieth-Century Britain*, pp.126-9; Andrew Rosen, *The Transformation of British Life 1950-2000: A Social History* (Manchester: Manchester University Press, 2003), p.83.

160 Selina Todd, *The People: The Rise and Fall of the Working Class 1910-2010* (London: John Murray,

2014), pp.216-34.

161 http://www.debretts.com/people-of-today/profile/24182/Mary-Lesley-PERKINS; Gaynor Pengelly, 'Specsavers boss who is Britain's richest self-made woman shuns jet set lifestyle,' 5 June 2011 http://www.dailymail.co.uk/femail/article-1394342/Specsavers-boss-Mary-Perkins-Britains-richest-self-woman-shuns-jet-set-lifestyle.html#ixzz3XfQQeAlC [accessed 16 June 2015]; 'Bristol-founded Specsavers celebrates 30 years in business...', Southwest Business website, http://www.southwestbusiness.co.uk/news/21012014092753-bristol-founded-specsavers-celebrates-30-years-in-business-with-new-store-at-cribbs-causeway/ [accessed 17 July 2015].

162 'Women in Aviation and Aerospace', Royal Aeronautical Society webpage, http://aerosociety.com/About-Us/specgroups/Women/Committee [accessed 5 July 2015]; Telephone interview with Jenny Body, 30 July 2015; thanks to Duncan Greenman.

163 Smith., 'The Women's Movement', pp.286-7; Pollert, *Girls, Wives, Factory Lives*, p.278 ff. 123-5.

164 '[Report of] ...the first meeting of the consciousness raising group held on the 11th October 1971', Bristol Special Collections, Feminist Archive, DM2123/Per 1; June Hannam, *Feminism* (London: Pearson, 2007), pp.139-44.

165 Feminist Archive North website, Chronology of Women's Liberation Movement in Britain, http://www.feministarchivenorth.org.uk/chronology/1970.htm [accessed 29 May 2015] and UBLSC, Feminist Archive, DM2121/2/pp1, Elizabeth Arledge Ross and Miriam L. Bearce, 'A Chronology of the Women's Liberation Movement in Britain 1969-1979' (Unpublished draft of Research Paper no. 1 Feminist Archive Bradford, November 1996), Appendices 1 and 3.

166 Frankie Rickford, 'The Development of the Women's Movement,' *Marxism Today*, July (1978), pp.229-34.

167 UBLSC, Feminist Archive, DM2123/Per1, '[Report of] ...the first meeting of the consciousness raising group held on the 11th October 1971'.

168 Ros Hopkinson, 'Obituary: Angela Rodaway,' *The Guardian*, 15 November 2012.

169 Feminist Archive Oral history Project, Ilona Singer and Viv Honeybourne (eds), pp.2-3, 7, 23, 64, 129 at www.feministarchivesouth.org.uk/wp-content/uploads/2013/02/Personal-Histories-of-the-Second-Wave-of-Feminism.pdf [accessed 17 June 2015]; The National Joint Action Campaign for Women's Equal Rights had been founded by a group of trade unionists in 1969; interview with Ellen Malos by Grace Evans November 2012 in Grace Evans, 'An Assessment of the Women's Liberation Movement in Britain with particular reference to Bristol (c.1970-1980)' (Undergraduate History Dissertation, University of the West of England, 2013), Appendix 1; The Housewives Register was founded in 1961 after a letter to the *Guardian* 'pointed out the social and intellectual isolation of so many 'housebound housewives with liberal interests and a desire to remain individuals', Lena Jeger, Obituary for Mary Stott, *The Guardian*, 18 September 2002 http://www.theguardian.com/news/2002/sep/18/guardian obituaries.gender [accessed 22 April 2015].

170 Ibid., p.85; UBLSC, Feminist Archive, DM2123/2/pp1, 'List of Members January 1970'; Suzie Fleming co-founded Falling Wall Press in Bristol which published some influential texts advocating wages for housework including Wendy Edmond and Suzie Fleming (eds), *All Work and No Pay* (Bristol: Falling Wall Press, 1975).

171 UBLSC, Feminist Archive, DM21;23/Per1,'Bristol Women's Liberation Newsletter', February 1971. The parting shot from one organizer of the Portways Ladies Club who had invited the WLM in Bristol to speak to an audience of 60 in 1971, and see, DM21;23/Per1, Newsletter, March 1971; telephone interview with Sarah Braun, 16 June 2015 confirms the hostility they sometimes encountered when speaking to groups.

172 Ibid., and see UBLSC, Feminist Archive, DM21;23/Per1, Newsletter, March 1971; telephone interview with Sarah Braun, 16 June 2015 confirms the hostility they sometimes encountered when speaking to groups.

173 UBLSC, Feminist Archive, DM 2123/2/SR5, Press cutting *Bristol Voice*, n.d. but 1973; Deborah Withers and Red Chedgey, 'Complicated Inheritance: Sistershow (Bristol 1973-1974)

and the queering of feminism,' *Women: A Cultural Review*, 21, 3 (2010), pp.309-22; Ellen Malos, 'Sistershow', British Library website, Learning, Sisterhood and After: an Oral History of the Women's Liberation Movement http://www.bl.uk/learning/histcitizen/sisterhood/clips/culture-and-the-arts/visual-arts/ 143131.html [accessed 17 June 2015].

174 UBLSC, Feminist Archive, DM2123/Per1, Bristol Women's Liberation Newsletter, December 1972.

175 UBLSC, Feminist Archive, DM2123/2/SR5, A report for Bristol Women's House Project, The Women's Centre and WLM in Bristol [mimeograph] c.1973.

176 UBLSC, Feminist Archive, DM 2123/Per 1, Bristol Women's Liberation Newsletters, April 1971/March 1973.

177 Sheila Rowbotham, *The Past is Before Us: Feminism in Action since the 1960s* (London: Penguin, 1989), p.151; Interview with Ellen Malos by Grace Evans, 26 November 2012 in Grace Evans, 'An Assessment of the Women's Liberation Movement in Britain', Appendix.

178 *Bristol Voice*, November 1975; May 1977.

179 Ibid., July 1977.

180 UBLSC, Feminist Archive, Arch/48, Bristol Women's Aid. By the late 70s a Select Committee report called 'Violence in Marriage' formed the basis for three important pieces of legislation (The Divorce and Matrimonial Proceedings Act (1976), the Housing Homeless Persons Act (1977) and the Domestic Proceedings and Magistrates Act (1978); UBLSC, Feminist Archive, DM2123/2/SR5, A report for Bristol Women's House Project, 'The Women's Centre and WLM in Bristol' [mimeograph] c.1973; Interview with Ellen Malos by Grace Evans, 26 November 2012; Grace Evans, 'An Assessment of the Women's Liberation Movement in Britain', pp.13, 21.

181 Telephone interviews with Nicola Harwin, 22 June and 25 June 2015.

182 Bristol Women's Studies Group, *Half the Sky: An Introduction to Women's Studies* (London: Virago, 1979), co-authored by Sarah Braun, Elizabeth Bird, Miriam David, Helen Haste, Ellen Malos, Marilyn Porter, Suzanne Skevington, Helen Taylor, Linda Ward and Jackie West. The artist and former graphic designer Sarah Braun whose grandmother had been a suffragette, illustrated the book. Six of the contributors (David, Haste, Porter, Skevington, Taylor and Ward) later achieved professorial posts. Other early feminist academics at the University of Bristol included Sandra Acker, Avtar Brah, Mary Fuller, Hilary Land, Annie Phizacklea, Anna Pollert, Marilyn Porter, Pam Trevithick, Bencie Woll; at Bristol Polytechnic (by 1992 the University of the West of England): Carol Britton, Lesley Doyal, Carol Dyhouse, Madge Dresser, Clara Greed, Annie Guest and June Hannam. Jackie Barron from Cardiff University was also associated with the Bristol feminists.

183 Pollert, *Girls, Wives, Factory Lives*; Marilyn Porter, *Home, Work and Class Consciousness* (Manchester: Manchester University Press, 1983).

184 'Tribute to domestic violence services pioneer. Ellen Malos receiving her Honorary Degree in February 2006'. Ellen Malos receiving her Honorary Degree in February, 30 March 2007, http://www.bristol.ac.uk/news/2007/5382.html and 'School for Policy Studies', http://www.bristol.ac.uk/sps/research/centres/genderviolence/aboutus/ [accessed 18 June 2015].

185 A temporary centre was situated in a hut in Grove Road aka 'The Grove' and later at a bookshop until the nineties.

186 Interview with Anne Hicks by Madge Dresser, 12 February 2015; *BEP*, 3 October 1972 and 21 June 1976; 'Meet the People who Saved Bristol's Harbour,' *The Bristol Post*, September 24 2013, http://www.bristolpost.co.uk/Meet-people-saved-Bristol-s-harbour/story-19836988-detail/story.html#ixzz3dGoEIJFM [accessed 15 June 2015].

187 Kate Pollard, *Totterdown Rising* (Bath: Tangent Books, 2006), p.47; Dorothy Brown, *Bristol and How It Grew* (Bristol: Bristol Visual and Environmental Group, 1975); and *Bristol Castle and the Old Market Area* (Bristol: Bristol Visual and Environmental Group, 1977); *WDP*, 19 October 2013; Dorothy Brown Obituary, *The Guardian*, 4 November 2013 in http://www.theguardian.com/uk-news/2013/nov/04/dorothy-brown-obituary. [accessed 7

July 2015]; Edson Burton and Michael Manson, *Vice and Virtue: Discovering the Story of Old Market Bristol* (Bristol: Bristol Books, 2015), p.67.

188 Melissa R. Gilbert, 'Place, Politics, and the Production of Urban Space,' in Andrew E.G. Jonas and David Wilson (eds), *The Urban Growth Machine: Critical Perspectives Two Decades* (Albany: State University of New York Press, 1999), p.100; Kelly and Richardson 'The Shaping of the Bristol Labour Movement', p.229.

189 KWADS, 'Knowle West Against Drugs'; M. Dresser knew Pat Dallimore during the 1980s through the publishing cooperative Bristol Broadsides and interviewed her for a non-broadcast documentary she made on the Women's Committee, 'The Women's Room,' in 1987. By the 1980s Dallimore was a regular guest broadcaster on Radio Bristol.

190 Madge Dresser, 'Oration for Olive Osborne' (January 1993), M. Dresser, personal papers. Osborne received an honorary degree from the University of the West of England, January 1993. Her group attracted government support only after the St. Paul's disturbances of 1980.

191 Burton in Dresser and Fleming, *Ethnic Minorities*, p.164. Much of Princess's Campbell's activism with regard to better housing and transport facilities and an end to racial discrimination gained public notice after 2000.

192 'Rundown Bristol', *BEP*, 16 December 1987.

193 'Rundown Bristol', *BEP*, 16 December 1987; St Paul's in this instance refers to a concentrated area within the St Paul's (renamed the Ashley ward in 1982) ward bounded by Newfoundland Road (M32), Ashley Road and Stokes Croft), see Roger Ball, 'Violent Urban Disturbances in England,1980-81' (Phd. Dissertation, University of the West of England, September 2011), pp.176 and 194 ; Boddy et al, *Sunbelt City?*, pp.12-13.

194 Ibid.; BCRL pr90p616, 'Avon Equal Opportunities Newsletter', December 1988.

195 Keith Bassett, 'Growth Coalition in Britain's Waning Sunbelt: Some Reflections,' in Jonas and Wilson (eds), *The Urban Growth Machine,* pp.179-80; Smith, 'The Women's Movement', pp.286-7; Interview with Dawn Primarolo, by Madge Dresser, 18 June 2014 and email correspondence.

196 'Bristol politician nominated for centenary degree' in *This is Bristol* Posted: February 06, 2009 http://www.bristolpost.co.uk/Bristol-politician-nominated-centenary-degree/story-11282131-detail/story.html#ixzz3XghidME7 [accessed 16 June 2015]; Madge Dresser, telephone interviews and email correspondence with Jenny Smith, February-April 2015.

197 'Pat Robert's Interview' http://feministarchivesouth.org.uk/wp-content/uploads/2013/02/Personal-Histories-of-the-Second-Wave-of-Feminism.pdf, p.134 [accessed 16 June 2015].

198 *WDP*, 5 June 1987 and 11 June 1987; BRO, Info Box 27/113, G.M. Hebblethwaite. Ironically Hebblewaite's childhood home was 11 Waverly Road in Redland where Ellen Malos later lived and where the first Bristol women's refuge was located, email from Ellen Malos to Madge Dresser 15 July 2015.

199 BRO, 35510/Com/2/1, Women in Bristol issue September/October 1987; Madge Dresser, 'The Women's Room', Film made 1987 on 'Women's Committee,' personal collection; see Bristol Women's Liberation Newsletters for 1984, UBLSC, Feminist Archive, DM 2123/Series5/81.

200 Ibid.

201 Interview with Diane Bunyan by Madge Dresser, 5 May 2015.

202 Tim Bullimore, 'Obituary Penny Brohn', *The Independent*, 12 February 1999; Ann Pilkington had married into the Pilkington Glass dynasty.

203 'People of Today', Debrett's webpage http://www.debretts.com/people-of-today/profile/35146/Bhupinder-Kaur-SANDHU [accessed 4 May 2015].

204 BRL 'Women's folder', 1540, *Bristol Observer*, 7 Feb 2012.

205 Barrie Clement, 'Bitter Anniversary for Print Pickets: The 'Dignity of Labour' Holiday Rings Hollow in Bristol, *The Independent,* 1 May 1994.

206 Personal conversation with Victoria Arrowsmith-Brown, and emails from Victoria Arrowsmith-Brown to Madge Dresser, 12/4/2014, 6 March 2015.

207 House of Commons Hansard Debates for 15 Jun 1993

http://www.parliament.the-stationery-office.co.uk/pa/cm199293/cmhansrd/1993-06-15/
Debate-5.html, cols. 740,742,782-785, [accessed 1 May 2015]; interview with Dawn Primarolo,
18 July 2014.

208 Interview with Gill Loats, 9 May 2015; Gill Loats, *Bristol Boys Make More Noise! The Bristol Music
Scene 1974-1981* (Bristol: Tangent Press, 2014). Loats worked part-time at the Dugout a leading
alternative club in Bristol in the early 1970s.

209 Email from Pam Beddard to Madge Dresser, 2 May 2015; Craig McLean, 'Portishead: Back on
the Beat,' *Daily Telegraph,* 12 Apr 2008, http://www.telegraph.co.uk/culture/music/3672545/
Portishead-back-on-the-beat.html [accessed 16 June 2015].

210 Email from Pam Beddard to Madge Dresser, 2 May 2015; FemFMArchive,
http://www.bristol.gov.uk/page/leisure-and-culture/fem-fm-archive [accessed 16 June 2015].

211 See for example, Marie Mulvey-Roberts, 'Introduction', in Marie Mulvey-Roberts (ed.), *Literary
Bristol: Writers and the City* (Bristol: Redcliffe Press and Regional History Centre University of
the West of England, 2015), pp.7-28.

212 *Victoria Hughes, The Ladies Mile* (London: Abson Books, 1977); Shirley Brown and Dawn Dyer,
'Hughes (née Rogers), Victoria (1897-1978)', in *Oxford Dictionary of National Biography*, Oxford
University Press, 2004, online ed. 2006 http://www.oxforddnb.com/view/article/92322
[accessed May 1, 2015]; Joyce Storey, *Our Joyce* (Bristol: Bristol Broadsides, 1987); http://
spartacus-educational.com/2WWstoreyJ.htm; Pat Dallimore, Joy Phillips, Maureen Burge *et al
Shush Mum's Writing* (Bristol: Bristol Broadsides 1977, and *Up Knowle West* (Bristol: Bristol
Broadsides, 1977); 'In Plain Sight: Knowle West Women Activating Communities' – Dr. Sharon
Irish, May 7, 2014 at https://iaswun.blogs.ilrt.org/2014/05/07/in-plain-sight-knowle-west-
women-activating-communities-dr-sharon-irish/ [accessed 17 June 2015].

213 Angela Tuckett, *The People's Theatre in Bristol 1930-1945, Our History*, Pamphlet 72 (London:
history Group of the Communist Party, 1979).

214 Shirley Brown, 'Obituary: Peggy Ann Wood', *The Independent,* 26 June 1998; Rosie McGregor,
Angela Remembered: The Life of Angela Gradwell Tuckett (Urchfont: WaterMarx, 2015); Graham
Stevenson, 'JoanTuckett', Compendium of 'Communist Biographies,' http://www.graham-
stevenson.me.uk/ [accessed 9 July 2015]; 'Angela and Joan Tuckett', at Bristol Law Society
website, http://www.bristollawsociety.com/angela-and-joan-tuckett/ [accessed 9 July 2015]; The
Bristol Unity Theatre, Warwick University Library website, Trade Union Congress Archives
http://www2.warwick.ac.uk/services/library/mrc/explorefurther/digital/scw/browse/
[accessed 11 July 2015]; Bernard Barry, 'Angela Tuckett', Working-Class Movement Library
website http://www.wcml.org.uk/our-collections/activists/angela-tuckett/ [accessed 11 July
2015].

215 Email from Sheila Hannon to Madge Dresser 18 May 2015.

216 BRO, Info Box 27.88, Daphne Hubbard; Quita Morgan, 'She was Feisty Ahead of Her Time,'
Obituary of Barbara Buchanan, http://www.pressgazette.co.uk/content/she-was-feisty-ahead-
her-time-journalist-who-threw-beer-over-obnoxious-dylan-thomas-dies

217 For Murray, see 'Jenni Murray'.
http://www.bbc.co.uk/programmes/profiles/17dynSh8ZdhxqcljQ99TPqP/jenni-murray
[accessed 18 July 2015]; For Adie, see Seán Street, *Historical Dictionary of British Radio* (Lanham,
Maryland: Rowman and Littlefield, 2015), p.27; for Leeming see BRL, *Bristol and West Country
Illustrated,* April 1980, Vol.4, no.35, p.2; For Susan Osman see https://en.wikipedia.org/wiki/
Susan_Osman [accessed 7 July 2015] and 'Susan Osman Departs Points West,'
http://www.bbc.co.uk/pressoffice/pressreleases/stories/2005/02_february/10/osman.shtml
[accessed 7 July 2015].

218 Madge Dresser telephone interview and email correspondence with Sherrie Eugene-Hart, 11
May 2015, 10 and 12 June 2015.

219 Sheriden Nye, Nicola Godwin and Belinda Hollows, 'Twisting the Dials: Lesbians in British
Radio,' in Caroline Mitchel, (ed.), *Women and Radio: Airing Differences* (London: Routledge,
2014), p.81; Email from Pam Beddard to Madge Dresser, 2 May 2015; FemFM Archive,

http://www.bristol.gov.uk/page/leisure-and-culture/fem-fm-archive [accessed 16 June 2015].

220 'Laura and Harry Marshall', Public and Ceremonial Events Office, University of Bristol website http://www.bristol.ac.uk/pace/graduation/honorary-degrees/2015.html/marshall.html [accessed 19 July 2015].

221 'Phyllida Christian Lloyd', Public and Ceremonial Events Office, University of Bristol website http://www.bristol.ac.uk/pace/graduation/honorary-degrees/hondeg06/lloyd.html [accessed 18 July 2015]; Gillian Thomas is profiled in the Website of the Society of Merchant Venturers, email from Pam Beddard to Madge Dresser, 2 May 2015.

222 McVicar who began as a musician in the alternative music scene, and by the 1980s worked in Bristol's community television and BBC's Drama Department, had become an internationally recognised authority on organic gardening and 'Jekka's Farm' near Bristol became Britain's largest culinary herb farm.

223 Roland Adburgham, *Bristol: Partnership in Governance: 10 years of The Bristol Initiative* (Bristol: Redcliffe Press for Bristol Chamber of Commerce and Initiative, 1998), pp.90-93. Thanks to Andrew Kelly for this source.

224 UBLSC, *Minutes of Senate, 1999-2000*, see pp.108-10. Comparative statistics are unavailable for the University of the West of England.

225 Women were not admitted to the Society until 2003, see Society of Merchant Venturers, http://merchantventurers.com/about-us/key-dates/ [accessed 4 May 2015].

226 See, for example, Alderman Charlotte Keel (1885-1955) member of Bristol City Council, 1935-1955. A Member of the Health Committee and Chairwoman of the Nursing Services Sub-Committee. 'The memory of Charlotte Keel's high idealism, devotion to duty and her humanity will inspire those who serve this district and work within this Clinic,' Cited in Living Easton, Proposed Women's Living History Trail http://www.cems.uwe.ac.uk/~rstephen/livingeaston/local_history/womens_history.html [accessed 29 September 2015]; a plaque at her residence in 15 Hereford Road, St Werburghs attests to her work as a 'health pioneer' http://www.bristol.gov.uk/page/leisure-and-culture/list-blue-plaques-bristol [accessed 29 September 2015].

The Authors

Madge Dresser is Associate Professor of History at the University of the West of England and a Fellow of the Royal Historical Society. Her previous publications include *Slavery Obscured: a Social History of Slavery in Bristol* (2001, 2007 and 2016), *Ethnic Minorities and the City: Bristol 1000-2000* (2007) (co-authored with Peter Fleming) and *Slavery and the British Country House* (which she co-edited with Andrew Hahn in 2013). Her research interests centre on slavery, race, gender and national identity in eighteenth-century Britain and increasingly on the legacy of slavery and immigration in modern Britain and the USA.

Peter Fleming is Professor of History at the University of the West of England. He specialises in later Medieval English history, with a particular focus on Bristol. He has collaborated with Madge Dresser on a project that led to the publication of Ethnic Minorities and the City: Bristol 1000-20000 (2007). He is the author of a number of books, including *Gloucestershire's Forgotten Battle: Nibley Green, 1470* (2003), and, forthcoming for 2016, *Time, Space and Power: Later Medieval Bristol*.

June Hannam is emeritus professor in Modern History, University of the West of England. Her research interests have focused on socialism and feminist politics in the late-nineteenth and early-twentieth centuries, both at a national level and in Bristol. Publications include *Isabella Ford, 1855-1924* (1989) with Karen Hunt, *Socialist Women. Britain, 1880s to 1920s* (2002), *Feminism* (2012) and *Bristol Independent Labour Party: Men, Women and Opposition to War* (2014). Convenor of the Women's History Network Book prize panel and co-chair of the West of England and South Wales WHN. She is a member of the editorial board of *Women's History Review, Labour History Review and LLafur*.

Moira Martin was a Senior Lecturer in History at the University of the West of England until 2011, when she left to pursue a career as a psychoanalytic psychotherapist. Her research focus has been on the history of health and welfare provision in Britain in the nineteenth and twentieth centuries and she is particularly interested in women's social activism at the local level. Her publications include: 'A Future not of Riches but of Comfort: The Emigration of Pauper Children from Bristol to Canada, 1870 to 1915', *Immigrants and Minorities,* 2000 and 'Single Women and Philanthropy: A Case Study of Women's Associational Life in Bristol, 1880-1914', *Women's History Review*, 2008.

Victoria Barnes has an honours degree in History from the University of the West of England, Bristol and completed her PhD in the School of Law, University of Reading in 2015 where she held an ESRC (Economic and Social Research Council) studentship in socio-legal studies. She is currently a Law Fellow at Georgetown University Law Center in Washington D.C.

Marion Pluskota graduated in 2012 at the University of Leicester after completing her PhD on 'Prostitution in Nantes and Bristol 1750-1815' and has recently published *Prosti-*

tution and Social Control in Eighteenth-Century Ports (Abingdon: Taylor and Francis Ltd, 2015). She is now a post-doctoral researcher at Leiden University, The Netherlands, working on Crime and Gender inWestern Europe, 1815-1913. Her interests lie in the relations between gender and co-offending structures and changing prosecution policies in penal codes.

Mike Richardson is a Visiting Fellow at the University of the West of England. He has recently co-edited with D. Backwith, R. Ball and S.E. Hunt, *Strikers, Hobblers, Conchies and Reds: A Radical History of Bristol 1880-1939* (Breviary Stuff Publications, 2014); and with P. Nicholls, *A Business and Labour History of Britain: Case Studies of Britain in the Nineteenth and Twentieth Centuries* (Palgrave Macmillan 2011).

Sheila Rowbotham helped to start the Women's Liberation Movement in the early 1970s and has written many books on women's and labour history, including *Dreamers of a New Day: Women who Invented the Twentieth Century* (2010). She is currently writing *Rebel Crossings: New Women, Free Lovers and Radicals in Britain and the United States* which includes the life stories of Helena Born and Miriam Daniell.

Lily Thornton received her B.A. (Hons) in History from the University of West England, Bristol in 2013. She wrote her dissertation on eighteenth-century Bristol women, with particular reference to the Smyth women of Ashton Court. She is currently working in South Korea as an English teacher after completing a teaching internship in China and plans to pursue a career in education.

Index

Redcliffe Press and the Regional History Centre

Women in the City, Bristol 1373-2000 is the third of a series of studies in local history published by Redcliffe Press in partnership with the Regional History Centre at the University of the West of England, Bristol.

This is a collaborative series of books addressing the history of the city of Bristol and its connections with the surrounding region. The Regional History Centre was established in 1997 to promote research into the history of Britain's south-western counties and to further an understanding of regionalism as a dynamic force in the shaping of domestic and international history.

Taking the ancient city and county of Bristol as its hub, the Centre's area of interest includes Gloucestershire, Wiltshire, Somerset, Devon and Dorset in England, as well as those parts of South Wales with which Bristol and Gloucester have enjoyed historic social and economic links.

University of the
West of England

A City Built upon the Water
Maritime Bristol 1750-1900
Editor: Steve Poole

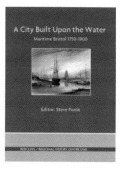

'The Spanish crew of the Rosario had been drinking at the Hole in the Wall for several weeks without incident, but the arrival of the Highlander, with a mixed crew of Englishmen, Scots and Americans, created competition over Bristol girls.'

In *A City Built upon the Water* Steve Poole and contributors define the river and its harbour less as a place of 'trade' and commerce, and rather more as a social and cultural environment – a thoroughfare for the rich and poor, the chancers and the merchants for whom the water was essential. Bristol's waterfront, stretched along the rivers Avon and Frome from Hotwells to St Philips, trisected the city at its core and physically divided its people. Bristolians from the north and south plied the water, bridged it, sailed up and down it, climbed in and out of its tidal mud, and relaxed or scratched a living along its embankments. In the eighteenth and nineteenth centuries, the tension between the social forces of urbanity and industry along the river's edge was instantly discernible to visitor and traveller alike. Indeed, anyone walking the waterfront between the centre and the resort of Hotwells spa in the 1840s, for instance, would find that twenty of the buildings along the main road were beer shops and another six sold gin. Most of the rest, packed into 'narrow courts and blind alleys' were cheap lodging houses, crowded with poor dock workers; 'unemployed servants, sailors, tradesmen and labourers... squalid, filthy from the neglect of ablution and sordid from the miserable garments they are covered with'.

224 pages, illustrated throughout including 8 pages of colour

ISBN 978-1-908326-10-2
£15.00

www.redcliffepress.co.uk
info@redcliffepress.co.uk

Literary Bristol
Writers and the City
Editor: Marie Mulvey-Roberts

'They drew up in a black, deserted street where the lamps made lonely puddles of light on cracked paving stones and walked some distance to a crazy square that stank of rubbish thrown into abandoned areas. Cats, lean and predatory, lurked in overturned dustbins...'

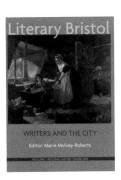

224 pages, illustrated throughout including 8 pages of colour

ISBN 978-1-908326-73-7
£15.00

www.redcliffepress.co.uk
info@redcliffepress.co.uk

As catalyst, progenitor and muse, the streets of Bristol, its factories and wharves, Avon Gorge and bucolic views have influenced some of our greatest authors, poets and playwrights. From Romantic and Gothic to New Wave – in the much-loved adventurers of *Treasure Island* and the dark horrors of *Dracula* and *Frankenstein*, the city is inspiration and muse.

Now, in *Literary Bristol: Writers and the City* we are introduced to its characters – rich and impoverished, weird and wonderful – and escorted by experts in the city's literary tradition: our virtual tour guides across the ages, from Chatterton's ingenious hoaxing and Robert Southey's morbid interest in vampires, to Charles Wood's *Dingo*, a play that shook the foundations of post-war theatre.